America's Germany: National Self and Cultural Other After World War II

Georg Schmundt-Thomas

ISBN 978-1-7336099-1-3 (paperback)
ISBN 978-1-7336099-0-6 (ebook)

For my grandfather Herbert Kirchner (1904-1979)

Contents

Preface to the 2019 edition.

Why re-issue what was written as a doctoral dissertation almost three decades ago? After it was published on microfilm and a few hand-bound copies, it was unpractical, unaffordable, as well as unnecessary career-wise to put it into print. Today the practical constraints are gone, but is there a need and an audience? To my own surprise, I found that over the years my work continued to be referenced in scholarly publications, both for its key arguments as well as its source material. "America's Germany" has staid relevant in a wholly unplanned as well as unforeseen way.[1] I had deliberately published stand-alone parts of the study in journals addressing different academic audiences.[2] This made it more visible initially, but cannot explain why it has endured.

What became "America's Germany" started as a study of contemporary American literature. Tracing sources for Thomas Pynchon's rich and eclectic period backdrop in "Gravity's Rainbow", my research focus soon broadened beyond literature and fiction to include other storytelling formats. And while I did not set out to rediscover marginalized voices, I soon stumbled across African-American and gendered descriptions of the German occupation experience which I found different, interesting and worth recovering. It seems that others saw some value as well in what I brought back. The only reason, then, for this edition is to make more readily accessible the source material and pointers to the historical material and to encourage further exploration of the cultural record.

Erlangen, Germany, January 2019

---

[1] See appendix for a list of citations.

[2] See appendix for list of publications.

"The Germany in one's head is frequently more valuable [...] than the Germany one may visit."

American novelist Walter Abish, 1980

"Hell, these people have sitdown toilets. That practically makes them our allies."

American GI on Germans, 1946

Acknowledgements

In thinking about America's Germany, I have acquired debts to many people and institutions which I wish to acknowledge. I am especially grateful to the members of my dissertation committee, whose perceptive and challenging comments helped me refine my ideas. Gerald Graff read innumerable drafts, asked the right questions at the right time, and never tired of trying to approximate a universal and normative audience. Peter Hayes provided a historian's perspective and saved me from falling into critical jargon too often. Susan Manning could more than once suggest possible solutions to methodological issues.

The members of our dissertation reading group helped me gain critical distance on my own ideas and writing, and let me approach it from outside, as it were. In addition, Petra Gödde and Drew Isenberg let me share their historical knowledge. David Cowart at the University of South Carolina helped me sharpen my ideas about Pynchon and commented on a chapter. Peter Freese at Paderborn University first called my attention to imagology. In a more general way, Heide Ziegler at Stuttgart University offered encouragement and gave my endeavors perspective over the years. Although I benefitted enormously from these friendly critics, none of them should be held accountable for the text's deficiencies.

There are also institutional debts to acknowledge. Northwestern University's Graduate School and the English Department supported me as a graduate student, gave me a part-time position as lecturer, and provided travel grants to attend conferences. The Studienstiftung des deutschen Volkes granted a scholarship in the early phases of this project.

In addition, I want to thank my parents, Gudrun and Christof Schmundt, as well as Maria and John Cox for their generous moral and financial support, which greatly contributed to my peace of mind. An informal "BAFöG" grant also came from Dorothea and Dieter Düring. When halfway through the completion of this project my computer was stolen, Karin and Peter Thomas helped defray the costs of a new one. Ina Wenig at Stein Design in Hannover, Germany, helped me with reproducing the illustrations. Last, but definitely not least, I am also deeply grateful to my wife, Kathrin Thomas, who unfailingly supported me in every possible way and periodically snatched me from the jaws of scholarly insanity.

Parts of my material have appeared before in a collection of essays edited by Peter Freese, Germany and German Thought in American Literature and Cultural Criticism, as well as in Notes on Contemporary Literature, the Journal of Popular Film and Television, and Pynchon Notes. It is used here with kind permission of the respective publishers. I also covered different aspects of my topic in papers given at conferences: the May 1989 German-American conference in Paderborn, Germany, a Special Session on Kay Boyle at the 1991 MLA Convention in San Francisco, and the Twentieth Century Literature conference in Louisville, Kentucky in February 1992.

Evanston, Illinois, May 1992

Introduction

On May 14, 1945, the cover of <u>Life</u> magazine commemorated and celebrated the Allied victory over Nazi Germany on May 8 with a photograph entitled "Victorious Yank." The picture shows an American GI, grinning sheepishly, right hand raised for the Nazi salute in front of a huge stone swastika at the Nuremburg stadium, where Hitler used to hold court for the endless masses of marching supporters (Fig. 1). The photo perfectly visualizes the hubris and ignoble end of Hitler's thousand-year Reich, in tatters after only thirteen. By assuming the Hitlerite posture at the symbolical center of Nazi Germany, the GI also implicitly comments on his own country's democratic traditions, which have proven to be superior to German totalitarianism. The editors of <u>Life</u> in turn probably intended to illustrate the democratic values that informed America's involvement in World War II by putting an anonymous common GI into such a symbolically elevated position. As much as the picture illustrates the end of Nazi Germany, it also marks the beginning of "the American

Figure 1 Imagining the Self as Other: Victorious Yank (<u>Life</u>)

century," which was heralded by the onset of the Cold War. While the photograph unintentionally seems to reflect the newly-found global role of Americans as the new master race, as it were, it also seems to presage the role America would assume in conquered Germany, where GIs would find themselves with the perquisites of the erstwhile Nazis. Moreover, during the Cold War, America repeatedly saw its fate and its concerns reflected in Germany, the country at the front lines of the conflict. Very much like the GI on the Life cover, President Kennedy later went native, so to speak, on his visit to Berlin when he declared, "Ich bin ein Berliner." Thus finally, and most importantly, the picture of the "Victorious Yank," as a cross-cultural image fraught with layers of symbolical meaning as sketched above, not only marks the practical creation of an American Germany during the occupation, it also dramatizes the dynamics of imagining the self-as-other, crucial in the process of shaping (cultural) identity.

In this study I approach the American image of Germany not from the standpoint of political history or media-sociology, but rather try to explain it as a discourse negotiating cultural and national self-identity. At the same time, I see my project as a practical contribution to what Raymond Williams has called a "sociology of culture" which examines the relationship between cultural production and social reality. Specifically, I am trying to show how literature, film, the newsmedia as well as politics turned to Germany in order to participate in the formulation of America's new global role in the wake of World War II. My purpose is to explain the underlying dynamics in American depictions of Germany both by reconstructing a neglected American discourse about Germany and by recontextualizing a number of canonized works.

I also aim to go beyond a mere evaluation of the representational accuracy of the American image of Germany. While I will point out how American preoccupations variously influenced representations of Germany, my overarching concern is to account for these distortions and to explain the kind of cultural work they do. Of course, one necessarily passes judgement (even if only implicitly) on the accuracy of a given representation when one examines the function of representational distortions. Yet, as a matter of emphasis, I will focus on the relationship between the image of Germany and American reality and not on that between American image and German reality. The kind of question I am going to ask in this study is <u>not</u>, how successful has America been in encountering the real Germany?, but rather, what can the peculiarities in representations of Germany tell us about America?

Although my critical readings emphasize the self-reflexive element of American representations of Germany, I also believe that accounts of ethnic alterity are not merely <u>projected</u> <u>images</u> of one's own culture, but also <u>descriptions</u> that provide <u>insights</u> into foreign cultures, in spite of the recent theoretical insistence on the constructedness and radical instability of reality. Descriptions of foreign cultures always work in "both directions," telling us something about the foreign culture <u>and</u> about ourselves. In addition, it also seems worthwhile to keep in mind that a cultural self-critique is finally only possible if there is a stable reference point against which that self-critique can be articulated. If there is no difference between inside and outside, self and other, self-discovery and definition are impossible. Without difference, there are no alternatives.

This project originally grew out of my fascination with the different ways in which three American authors considered to be "postmodern" -- John Hawkes, Thomas Pynchon and Walter Abish -- use a German setting and German characters in their texts. It did not take me long to find out that although there was a plethora of studies about the European and more specifically German depictions and imaginings of America, comparatively few scholars had analyzed the reverse view, America looking at Germany. Moreover, I also soon realized that the diplomatic historians who had written about the relationship between the two countries (mainly as allies in NATO) were not interested in the cultural mediation of the political relationship. Conversely, literary critics turned out to be hardly ever interested in either the specific historical contexts of American literary depictions of Germany.

Originally, I thus intended to fill that critical gap by showing how three literary texts comment on America by talking about Germany. However, I soon realized that the dynamic underlying the depiction of Germany in my three novels also informed the American depiction of Germany in a whole range of other genres. I discovered that the popular cinema, as well as the press from illustrated newsmagazines like <u>Life</u> and

The Saturday Evening Post to weeklies like Time, Newsweek and even intellectual periodicals like The Nation looking at Germany in some form or another found America and ways to comment on it. Moreover, delving into the political memoirs of people who administered the military occupation of Germany, I was amazed to discover that many of the policies formulated for the industrial reconstruction of the vanquished country could be fully understood only as part of a practical debate in America over the consequences of industrialization, a debate that reached back to the turn of the century. I increasingly felt that this forgotten American discourse about Germany deserved recovery as much as my original three novels demanded recontextualization. In contrast to my original question, which ran something like, what is the function of America's Germany?, I began to ask questions like, how do specific American representations of Germany address particular national problems?, and, what kinds of reflexive commentaries on America do selected depictions of Germany imply? My study attempts to provide specific answers to these questions.

I bring to the task a critical language shaped by a number of new methodical directions taken in the humanities in the last two decades or so. Feminist and psychoanalytical readings of (sexual) "otherness," deconstructionist reconceptualizations about the creation of meaning and the idea of differance, revaluations of cultural marginality in what might be described as cultural studies (I am thinking of Edward Said here), as well as the New Historicist practice of analyzing the social constructedness of reality all helped me in a general way in thinking about the functioning of American depictions of Germany. More specifically, Benedict Anderson's conceptualization of nationalism as an "imagined community" and the role of cultural narratives in the creation of a national self-image I find particularly helpful as a general way of understanding how depictions of Germany can function as a reference point in the process of American self-definition and self-critique. In addition to these more general influences, my analysis takes its specific methodological cues from George E. Marcus and Michael M. J. Fischer's description of the culturally critical dimension of ethnographic accounts and the heuristic potential of what they call "defamiliarization by cross-cultural juxtaposition" (138) in Anthropology as Cultural Critique.

In the introductory chapter, I first situate my analyses within a theoretical framework, before giving a selective historical overview of Americans looking abroad to Germany in order to comment on their own culture. Finally, in a kind of prologue to the following specific analyses, I also describe the continuities and discontinuities in the depiction of Germany after World War II.

The second chapter provides a detailed analysis of W.G. Smith's African-American novel of education The Last of the Conquerors and a few stories in Kay Boyle's The Smoking Mountain, which conceive of Germany as utopian space and positive counter-image to America. African-Americans in Europe during the war found the kind of racial and cultural acceptance abroad that was denied them at home, and unlike most liberal critics, African-Americans depicted Germany as utopian space but similarly in contrast to American realities. In Germany as the land of evil, they found the promise of a better America.

In the third chapter, moving from literature to film, I argue that the depiction of foreign relations between the U.S. and Germany in terms of sexual relations between GIs and fräuleins constitutes Hollywood's intervention in the contemporary debate over America's future global role, simultaneously rehashing a periodic political conflict between isolationists and interventionists.

The fourth chapter focuses on politics, mapping the approach of New Deal reformers to industrial reorganization of Germany and the similarity of their plans to literary indictments of industrial capitalism (such as those by Howells and Norris). Moreover, comparable to liberal authors who depicted Germany as imaginary counter-image of America, the New Deal reformers attempted to transform Germany into a practical laboratory and model for progressive legislation. Crowded out of the policy-making establishment after the death of FDR, those old New Dealers saw Germany as the last chance to continue and save the trustbusting tradition begun half a century earlier with the fight against the railroads and Standard Oil.

Returning to literature, the fifth chapter lays out how Thomas Pynchon's Gravity's Rainbow draws both on the political analysis of the New Deal reformers as well as general American perceptions in making Germany and German culture the thematic focus in an effort to trace and criticize the origins of the postwar period and the age of the rocket. Pynchon takes the rocket and the rocket cartel as the emblems of the postwar order, and I will read <u>Gravity's Rainbow</u> as a direct commentary on and critique of the American space program.

The epilogue considers Walter Abish's <u>How German Is It</u>, John Hawkes's <u>The Cannibal</u> and some of Joyce Carol Oates's stories as narrative limiting-cases and postmodern explorations of the pattern of cultural self-reflection traced in the earlier chapters.

Readers usually bring their own preoccupations to a text, and especially both the range of my material, moving from literature to film, journalism, and politics, and the approach I take, recovering and recontextualizing parts of a cultural discourse through close interpretive readings, may raise some obvious questions. Firstly, some readers will object that I am too selective in my choice of texts (I am sure everyone has some favorite that I fail to mention). Yet, for the purposes of my study it was necessary to generalize somewhat in order to highlight what I take to be the dominant perceptions of the time. Obviously, the selected texts and films exhaust neither American literature nor American culture, and partly reflect my own predilections as a student of postwar American culture. Secondly, some readers will feel that my material cries out for more analysis of the institutional and generic forces that shaped it. Such an analysis, however interesting and necessary, would constitute a different undertaking from what I attempt to do here. In Raymond Williams' words such an enquiry would be an analysis of cultural institutions (which mediate between artist and public) or the artistic means of production (the materials at the artist's disposal), while I am interested in what he calls forms and identifications (the relation between art and social formation, art and reality, respectively). Thus I describe the particular ways in which American representations of Germany articulate national identity and reformulate America's global role.

Finally, given the nature of my topic, it seems necessary to explain briefly what it means to me personally. Although this project was not so much analogous to Edward Said's <u>Orientalism</u>, "an attempt to inventory the traces upon me, the Oriental subject, of the culture whose domination has been so powerful a factor in the life of all Orientals" (25), the fascination with my subject matter definitely results from and reflects my curious position as German, trained to be an Americanist in an American institution. The position of outsider trying to understand American cultural discourse from within in many ways facilitates a critical stance towards the material, even if only because so much of the self-celebratory national rhetoric rampant, for instance, in classical theories of American literature, automatically excludes "aliens" like myself. At the same time, the position of outsider looking in can also result in the opposite, a kind of uncritical attitude towards the tradition, just because it seems so different, new and exciting to the outsider that it is sometimes hard to work up an authentic disaffection with it.

But more to the point, as German subject I am automatically exposed to the tensions between my own self-image and the image of myself constructed in American discourse. Although I don't believe that my image of Germany is truer or objectively more correct than the American image of Germany analyzed here, I know that "my Germany" is different because it has a different function for me. Quite naturally, Germany for me is the "self" and not the "other"; yet, this realization leaves open the question of the reality behind either my Germany as "self"-conception or the American conception of Germany as the "other." Thus, finally, I see this project not as an act of liberation, not as an attempt to get even, breaking out of the stereotyping I might have been subjected to by American conceptions of Germany and the Germans. Rather, this project has had the quality of self-discovery and seems like another turn to the intercultural screw: it is an attempt to find out what it means to be German by looking at the way Americans have used Germany to define who they are. This, however, is part of a text yet to be finished, and a feature of the intellectual biography that codetermines the text at hand.

Chapter One - "The Germany He Loved": Looking Abroad

"How impossible to find Germany," Ralph Waldo Emerson observed from his study in Concord, Massachusetts, in 1848. "Our young men went to the Rhine to find the genius which had charmed them, and it was not there. They hunted it in Heidelberg, in Göttingen, in Halle, in Berlin; no one knew where it was; from Vienna to the frontier, it was not to be found, and they very slowly and mournfully learned, that in the speaking it had escaped, and as it had charmed them in Boston, they must return and look for it there" (Emerson 30). In best Transcendentalist fashion, Emerson here disparages his contemporaries' predilection for travel. By the impossibility of finding Germany, Emerson of course means that since all places only have meaning through and in the Oversoul, we only deceive ourselves by travelling and by trying to find different and better places.

In addition, Emerson's observation also calls attention to the fact that every description of another culture implicates and comments on one's own culture. The image of a foreign culture is always also created as a kind of alternative cultural space, as an inverted image to one's own or a projection of one's own culture onto another. When Emerson describes how the young Bostonians were disappointed with the Germany they found abroad and thus had better remained in Boston in the first place, he implies that the country and culture they were looking for was as much an American construction as it was a geographical and historical reality. The "genius of Germany" that eluded the young Bostonians in the actual country, Emerson seems to say, was thus as much a reflection of the flowering of German culture, as it was a commentary on the American struggle for cultural and literary self-making. Much later, Henry James at the close of the 19th century, and yet another generation later the "expatriates" in Paris similarly bemoaned the tragical lack of atmosphere and culture in America, and consequently looked abroad for models and inspiration. And the resulting idolization of various European cultures, born of that American need for cultural inspiration, invariably led to distortions in the depiction of and ideas about those foreign cultures. In short, even Emerson already seems to realize that the American depiction of Germany was as much a reflection of American culture as it was a description of Germany.

A half-century after the return of Emerson's disappointed Americans, Henry Adams found that the actual Germany departed significantly from the quaint picture he had painted in his mind. Having come to Germany in 1858 to finish his education, he spent a frustrating three months in Berlin. In a passage reminiscent of the sentiment in Emerson's Journal entry, Adams sums up his feelings about Germany:

> He loved, or thought he loved the people, but the Germany he loved was the eighteenth-century which the Germans were ashamed of, and were destroying as fast as they could. What he liked was the simple character; the good-natured sentiment; the musical and metaphysical abstraction; the blundering incapacity of the German for practical affairs. [...] Until coal-power and railways were created, she was medieval by nature and geography, and this was what Adams, under the teachings of Carlyle and Lowell, liked. (Adams 83; my emphasis)

What appeals to Adams, as before him to Emerson's New England youths, and what in turn inspired Henry James to describe Concord and environs as a kind of "American Weimar,"[3] is the Germany of the Anglo-American literary imagination, the romantically distorted pre-industrial Germany of Carlyle and Lowell, a Germany vanished by the second half of the nineteenth century -- if ever it had existed in reality.

The reality of Germany, as Adams soon realized, was quite different from his expectations. How impossible to find Germany, indeed. Adams later described that he found Berlin, by mid-century, to be "a poor, keen witted, provincial town, simple, dirty, uncivilized, and in most respects disgusting" and that "life was primitive beyond what an

---

[3] I have been unable to trace the quote. It is reported by Leon Edel in Henry D. Thoreau. Minneapolis: University of Minnesota Press. 1970. 15.

American boy could have imagined" (77).[4] In contrast to the American ideals of a healthy life in the open air and an education as introduction to independent thought, Adams' stay in Berlin was dominated by the cheap amusements in beer-cellars and music halls because for a student they provided the only means of escape from a "lecture system in its deadliest form as it flourished in the thirteenth century" (75). Finally, Adams moved on to Dresden and then Italy to pursue his cultural and educational roamings.

In contrast to the disappointment of Germany, Adams rhapsodized that "Rome was actual; it was England; it was going to be America" (91). Adams here obviously gives his version of the course of empire westward, from imperial Rome to the grandeur of England and on to the America of the future. For Adams, what Italy used to be and what England still was provided the image of coming American grandeur. Conversely, Berlin and Germany only reminded him of the squalor and backwardness of his own country's origins: provincial, simple, dirty and uncivilized. Imperial Rome and England were what America had been aspiring to since the Civil War; Germany was what it had hoped to have long left behind. For Adams, then, the imagined Germany is a positive counterspace to America, as much as the real Germany contrasts negatively with his homeland. On the one hand, Adams imaginatively constructs Germany as a kind of pre-industrial fairy-land, and finds it appealing. On the other hand, the German reality only reminds him of America's ignoble past. But in any case, Italy and England, as much as Germany, only become relevant, acquire their meaning with reference to and in comparison with America. The continent Adams toured was thus an allegorical geography telling of the squalid colonial past, reflected in Germany, and the glorious future in store for America, adumbrated by England and Italy.

Finally, in a contemporary rewriting of the 19th century American educational travelogue, Thomas Berger (best known for Little Big Man) sent his American protagonist Carlo Reinhardt on a Adamsian

---

[4] Henry James, roughly at the same time, made the same observation about Bonn on a visit to Europe, telling a friend that compared with life at home, arrangements in Germany were "truly inferior" (Edel 25).

quest for self-identity through post-war Germany in Crazy in Berlin (1958). Of German ancestry, Carlo has been fascinated with the idea of Germany and sets out to find his intellectual as well as familial roots on a stint as occupation soldier in Berlin, where he meets a whole gallery of historically allegorical figures dramatizing the political and ideological contradictions of the age. But in spite of the almost Byzantine plotting and picaresque turns of the novel, Carlo's quest for self-definition is the traditional quest of young Americans abroad described by Emerson. At some point Carlo realizes, like Henry Adams, that he has been chasing a pipe-dream. "He at last understood that the complement to his long self-identification with Germanness had been a resolve never to know the German actuality" (Berger 176). And moreover, directly echoing Adams, Carlo points out the people he had met in Germany only bored him: "All I ever cared about was old medieval Nürnberg, and that is long gone. Italy, I think, is what I like, with sunshine and that melodic language" (Berger 424). Obviously, Carlo had better have looked for his idealized Germany in literature than in postwar Europe.

The three examples of American perceptions of Germany circumscribe a certain pattern of approaching the foreign country and culture and its historical continuity. Emerson's diary entry, Adams' autobiographical reflections and Berger's novel illustrate that the depiction of the cultural other, in this case Germany, is always co-determined by, and comments on, the image of the cultural self, America. The self is always inscribed into depictions of the other. This is not to claim that depictions of the cultural other are only representations of the self or merely solipsistic images of the originating culture. But every description of another culture both communicates truths about foreign lands and people while also engaging in a dialogue with its own cultural context.

Images of Alterity as Cultural Commentary and Critique

In spite of the monumental scholarly efforts to chart the German influences on and sources of classic American literature in H.A. Pochmann's German Culture in America, 1600-1900 (1957) and S. Vogel's German Literary Influences on the American Transcendentalists

(1955), not too much critical and analytical energy has been expended on the shape of the American image of Germany in general. Moreover, scholars in the past and present have tried to describe the elements, changes and continuities of American representations of Germany,[5] yet, in their explanations they have never seriously considered the possibility that the depiction of the cultural other is co-determined by, and comments on, the image of the cultural self. Indeed, existing research of the American image of Germany has been preoccupied either with describing German influences on American thought, or with isolating the elements of American descriptions of Germany. While Pochmann's monograph is the towering example of the source study approach, a sociological study like Hartmut Keil's "The Presentation of Germany in American Television News" is representative of efforts to distill American perceptions about Germany. Both approaches oftentimes fail to probe further into the reasons why an American author utilizes a particular German source or why American observers emphasize particular elements of their German experience. For instance, using statistical methods, Keil ranks reporting about Germany in descending order under the headings "catastrophes and natural disasters," "the Nazi past," "West Germany's

[5] Barbara Dotts Paul's invaluable, even if not quite exhaustive, bibliography, entitled The Germans after World War II (1990) includes 310 entries for the category "English fiction about Germany by non-Germans." A similar number of journal articles and films is listed. Yet, Arthur R. Schultz' bibliography covering German-American relations 1941-1980 comes up with only a total of 39 entries under the heading "American Views of Germany and the Germans." Only a handful of articles specifically address the question of the image of Germany in American literature after 1945. Apart from an isolated earlier article (Norbert Muhlen's "Deutsche, wie sie im Buche stehen"), they come together in two essay collections, Wolfgang Paulsen's Die USA und Deutschland. Wechselseitige Spiegelungen in der Literatur der Gegenwart (Bern/München: Francke. 1976), and Peter Freese's Germany and German Thought in American Literature and Cultural Criticism (1990). -- The bibliography at the end of Frank Krampikowski's Amerikanisches Deutschlandbild und deutsches Amerikabild in Medien und Erziehung (Baltmannsweiler: Pädagogischer Verlag Burgbücherei Schneider. 1990) lists some further articles not covered in Paul's bibliographic study.

role in NATO," yet he only perfunctorily answers the question why American reporting about Germany would take this form.

Scholars have repeatedly shown that in many cases the American image of Germany departs from German realities and is reductive or stereotypical, but they have never tackled the question <u>why</u> it takes a particular form. Even if critics have sometimes tried to account for the specific shape of American representations, they have mostly rested content with general remarks such as noting that it is always easier to deal with cultural alterity by reducing it to the stereotypical. Similarly, although there are many studies of the American image of Germany at different times, in different discursive genres and originating from different cultural backgrounds, none of those studies really accounts for <u>how</u> those images came to acquire a given shape.

Peter Freese's essay "Exercises in Boundary-Making: The German as the 'Other' in American Literature" is one of the more sophisticated recent analyses, yet symptomatically shows the shortcomings of critical engagements with the American image of Germany that claim to be pushing beyond mere description. Freese tries to theorize the characteristics of the American image of Germany and claims that "the analysis of the images we have of 'others' must not be concerned with their degree of factual appropriateness but with the more pertinent question of why they are developed at all and which psychic needs they are meant to serve" (Freese 94f.). Although Freese here seems to advocate an enquiry into the "why" of particular images, his analysis of some American-German "heteroimages," however, leaves the question of historically and culturally particularized psychic needs unanswered and is mainly concerned with tracing the images' imaginative origins. Freese rests content with stating that "the selected examples are all expressions of boundary-making" (131), and with showing their internal contradictions and their historical perpetuation, but leaves evaluation of these images in a "specific biographical and historical context" to "future research" (131). Thus, for instance, to show its stereotypical character, he traces the image of the German as dipsomaniac backwards from Twain and Cooper to Shakespeare and on to the Roman proto-anthropologist Tacitus, who in turn drew on descriptions in Livius and Plutarch. Freese points out that German dipsomania is already fully established as an ethnic stereotype in Shakespeare's Merchant of Venice (ca. 1598) and Portia's German suitor, who, she is sure, will prefer a glass of Rhenish wine to anything else. In spite of his interesting findings, Freese fails ask why successive literary generations took up an established depiction of cultural alterity and what they had to gain by it. In short, Freese's piece is indicative of the degree to which scholarship about the American image of Germany has failed to explain the dynamics underlying the depiction of cultural otherness.

That so far scholarship about the American image of Germany has been hampered by the failure to ask the pertinent questions about the "why" and "how" of its object of study is particularly surprising since it could have been inspired by existing parallel work. Starting with Edward Said's exploration of European depictions and constructions of Arab culture (in Orientalism), cultural historians from various backgrounds have explored in detail the practice of depicting cultural alterity and analyzed different manifestations of the "ethnographic" imagination at work. In addition, the recent attention given to experimental ethnography in anthropology and the resulting theoretical formulations (particularly George C. Marcus and Michael M.J. Fisher's Anthropology as Cultural Critique) maps a similar development and provides a critical vocabulary to describe the "why" and "how" of the American image of Germany in particular and the function and functioning of the image of another culture in general. And finally, studies about the depiction of the respective cultural "other" in French and German literature, undertaken by the "imagologist" school, essentially attempt to answer many of the same methodological questions left unattended by scholars of the American image of Germany. A quick overview of recent advances in cultural studies, experimental ethnography, and imagology will facilitate a basic understanding of the internal dynamics of the American image of Germany and provide a framework for the discussion of specific examples in the following chapters.

In Orientalism (1979), Edward Said analyzes in detail the genesis and transformations of the West's depiction of the Orient. As such, Said's undertaking seems similar to existing studies about the American image of Germany, except for one significant difference: although Said implies that Western representations of Oriental culture have always been stereotypical, he does not attempt to set the record straight but instead tries to analyze "how" and "why" cultural otherness was depicted in a specific way. Said thus circumscribes his project in Orientalism as follows:

> [The] phenomenon of Orientalism as I study it here deals principally, not with a correspondence between Orientalism and Orient, but with the internal consistency of Orientalism and its ideas about the Orient (the East as career) despite or beyond any correspondence, or lack thereof, with a "real" Orient. (Said 5; my emphasis)

Said makes clear that he is not interested in the degree of verisimilitude or lack thereof in the representations of the Orient, but rather in the internal forces that motivate them and determine their shape. I will make an analogous shift from existing scholarship in my analyses of the American image of Germany. The stereotypical character of that image has been pointed out often enough and illustrated in contrast to German realities. By contrast, I will take a closer look at the internal consistency of American depictions of Germany, focusing on the relationship between the image of Germany and American reality and not on that between American image and German reality.

In Deconstructing America (1990), one of the many important studies undertaken in the wake of Said's ground-breaking work, Peter Mason analyzes in detail the origins and genesis of European Renaissance representations of the New World. Quite apart from the interesting early images of America that he unearths, Mason also makes a crucial distinction between two influences determining the representation of cultural alterity:

> On the one hand [the depiction of America] could fall back upon traditional representations in order to accommodate the new. These representations then served as parameters by which to organise the initially refractory material. The self of Europe could thereby reduce and assimilate the other that it encountered

> outside Europe. On the other hand, Europe had its own
> internal other, and this it could project onto the New
> World outside the confines of Europe. The encounter with
> the New World thus served as a point of articulation [...]
> of European fantasies, fears and desires. (Mason 41)

Mason analyzes in detail both how the new was assimilated to familiar terms and how the new strange lands served as a foil for traditional European fantasies. In particular, Mason shows that the description of the American inhabitants had recourse to the element of what he calls the "Plinian races," a kind of bestiary of mythical monsters historically perpetuated at least since the Greek natural historian Pliny. Thus, practically since time immemorial the alien and new had been described in the same monstrous terms. But at the same time, Mason also shows how Europe's internal other articulated itself in the depiction of America, how European utopian hopes as well as apocalyptic fears determined the representation of the newly discovered continent and its inhabitants.

Both the depiction of the cultural other in traditional terms and its function as a point of articulation for the fears and desires of the self can be found in American representations of Germany. Scholarship like Peter Freese's study of the origins of the German as drunkard mentioned earlier has shown very well how the American imagination has had recourse to age-old and traditional depictions of cultural alterity. At the same time, as the introductory examples make clear and the short historical overview of Americans looking for and towards Germany later in this chapter will illustrate further, Germany has repeatedly been the foil for projections of American fears and desires. And it is this aspect of American representations of Germany that I will analyze in detail in the following chapters. Or, to put it in Mason's words, the focus of this study is how Germany served as a point of articulation for the American internal other, how in the depiction of Germany America could become aware of and work through specific problems in the process of its cultural self-formation.

The recent work done in cultural studies has made it possible to talk about <u>representations</u> of the cultural other apart from the admittedly important correspondences between image of otherness and the realities informing them. This development sometimes seems to lead to a radical bracketing of extra-discursive reality, or even a denial of their existence. Mason's approach is symptomatic in this respect, and at some point he goes as far as to claim that the discourses on a country or culture <u>are</u> that country or culture (cf. 174), since "world as a referent [...] is not an object of knowledge [as] it evades any kind of reality control" (15). Yet, I suspect that Mason does not really mean what he says here, mainly because if he really did, he would seriously undermine his own findings about the origins of European representations of America in the tradition of the Plinian races. If indeed a culture is nothing but the discourse about it, how then does Mason know that in the 15th century newly discovered America was indeed <u>not</u> peopled by the Plinian races? The fact that Mason assumes that it was not, shows that he believes there existed an American reality apart from European representations. Nevertheless, my focus here is not to examine the tricky question of the relationship between signifier and signified, the knowability of the "referent," or the problem of a reality apart from discourse, but to explain the function and functioning of specific representational practices. Recent developments in anthropology may help in further elucidating that question.

If one school within cultural studies has tended to view culture as discourse only, anthropological theory has gone the opposite way, as it were, and tried to relate anthropological discourse to specific non-discursive cultural practices. In particular, experimental ethnography has begun to conceive of the representation of cultural alterity as a form of cultural self-critique. In their analysis of the state of anthropology in the late 20th century in <u>Anthropology as Cultural Critique</u> (1986), Marcus and Fischer try to reconceptualize anthropology as a form of cultural self-critique <u>as well</u> as an attempt to study foreign cultures. Looking at the history of anthropology, Marcus and Fischer point out that the Western imagination and discourse have traditionally constructed exotic and foreign lands as a counter-image and cultural "other," necessary for cultural self-definition and self-assurance.

The two classical examples of this process of projection are colonial Africa and the newly discovered North America, the one the dark continent, the horror-pregnant unconscious and dark side of the soul to the West's bright rationality, the other by turns mythical origin and telos, unspoiled Edenic garden to Europe's decadent courts, and New Jerusalem to Europe's Babylonic political chaos and decay. Africa and America were thus by definition "what Europe was not." Yet, the messianic promise of the New World and the millenial horror of the African continent are not absolute, their positive or negative otherness is intimately related to European self-conceptions. The presumed primitive and natural state of African life, with its supposedly unrestrained sexuality, seemingly atavistic rites, and apparently primitive social organization must be taken not as truthful ethnographic description but as inverted pictures of life in Europe. In depictions of Africa, the repressed European unconscious returns, and in horror, the other is recognized as the darker part of the self. Similarly, the presumably Edenic New World is merely an externalized image of what Europe could have been but is not, the incarnation of a Utopian promise. And again, not unlike the horror of Africa, the promise of America must be understood as the recognition of the cultural other as an alternative and idealized European self.

Marcus and Fischer point out that every account of another culture implies the culture of the observer and comments on it; the repressed elements of the cultural self resurface in the description of the cultural other. Although this approach carries the obvious danger of solipsism, it allows the ethnocentric element in depictions of cultural otherness to constitute the potential for cultural critique. Marcus and Fischer put it very well when they claim that "for a long time, the primitive other -- a vision of Eden, where the problems of the West were absent or solved -- was a very powerful image that served cultural criticism (as well as, in some cases, cultural chauvinism)" (134). According to Marcus and Fischer, under the influence of surrealism and the aesthetics of defamiliarization, anthropologists in the 20th century self-consciously began to employ the ethnocentric element in ethnographic accounts in order to comment on their own society and culture. The aesthetics of defamiliarization go back at least to the theoretical formulations of the Russian formalists, who made it the defining characteristic of Literature. Defamiliarization was also the underlying aesthetic principle in the Surrealist movement with its subversions of traditional modes of perception and representation through juxtaposition of incongruous elements. Through the association of Michel Leiris and Georges Bataille with the Paris Institute of Ethnology (and its founder Marcel Mauss), Surrealism and the concept of defamiliarization influenced modern anthropology.[6] Marcus and Fischer see the ethnographic paradigm of the 1920's and 1930's, the study of foreign cultures abroad as well as marginalized cultures at home, as a "submerged, unrelenting critique of Western civilization as capitalism" (129).

Margaret Mead, with her study of patterns of adolescence on Samoa, seems to be "the model of the anthropologist as cultural critic" (Marcus 130). The controversy over and questions about her findings only seem to underscore the status of her study as cultural critique aimed at America rather than as objective ethnographic account. Marcus and Fischer argue that even if the "facts" of Mead's study were only imaginary and/or projections, they facilitated an outside point of view for a reevaluation of growing up in America. In Anthropology as Cultural Critique this process is labeled "defamiliarization by cross-cultural juxtaposition," and described as "a matching of ethnography abroad with ethnography at home. The idea is to use the substantive facts about another culture as a probe into the specific facts about a subject of criticism at home" (Marcus 138). This seems to be a key statement in their account and also a summary of the critical function of American representations of Germany.

Finally, the "imagologist" school has reached similar conclusions about the the depiction of cultural alterity as cultural studies and experimental ethnography and formalized their findings into a matrix of possible relationships between the depicting self and the depicted other. Comparative imagology had its practical beginnings in the tradition of the French littérature comparé and the work of the critic Jean-Marie Carré and his book Les écrivains français et le mirage allemand (1947). The approach constituted itself theoretically in the work of the German comparatist Hugo Dyserinck and the so called "Aachen school" of

---

[6] Cf. Marcus 122ff. for the Surrealist roots of contemporary experimental ethnology.

comparative studies.[7] Comparative imagology is probably mostly remembered, if at all, for the "crisis in comparative literature" it sparked and René Wellek's attack on it for committing at best the sociological heresy, at worst the heresy of paraphrase.[8] Most interestingly, however, imagology attempted to redefine the task of European comparative literature as the historical and systematic study of the images of other countries in a given national literature. In spite of its promising general program, most imagologist studies have tended to concentrate on the genesis and perpetuation of images of the cultural other in literary production only. But the image of another country always interacts extensively with extra-literary contexts. By restricting the scope of enquiry to literature only, imagology in praxis became little more than sophisticated analysis of cross-cultural sources.

      The purpose of this study is neither to resolve the theoretical differences between René Wellek's New Criticism and comparative imagology nor to evaluate either one. Of relevance for our purposes here is that imagology formulated a general schema of self-other relations that can be of further help in understanding the function and functioning of American representations of Germany. In the schematized imagologist matrix, negative self-conceptions face positive and negative descriptions of the "other," allowing for a permutational series of four interrelationships (cf. Bleicher 17). These interrelationships seem almost self-evident, yet no critic has ever analyzed the American image of Germany within that framework. Although I will use the imagologist matrix neither as hermeneutic tool in my analysis nor as structuring principle for my argument, it seems worth a closer look because it will facilitate a general understanding of the interrelation between different American representations of Germany. At the same time, the imagologist systematization also further illustrates the point that the depiction of the cultural other also refers to the self.

      The four possible relative positions of self and other in the

---

[7] Hugo Dyserinck, "Zum Problem der 'images' und 'mirages' und ihrer Untersuchung im Rahmen der Vergleichenden Literaturwissenschaft." Arcadia, 1 (1966). 107-120.

[8] René Wellek, "The Crisis of Comparative Literature." Proceedings of the Second Congress of the ICLA Chapel Hill: Univ. of N. Carolina. 1958

depiction of (cultural) alterity show the direction of this implication of, or commentary on, the (cultural) self. First, a positive self-conception can find its expression in a favorable depiction of the "other"; thus, for instance, when American GIs commented on the modernity and cleanliness of Germany and the industry of its inhabitants, pointing out that the country was "like America," they commented favorably on their own country as well as the cultural other. The alignment along a positive axis between the self and the other, of course, found its most significant expression in the realignment of Germany as junior partner of the U.S. in the Western alliance.

Second, we have a positive self-conception that is contrasted with an unfavorable depiction of the "other"; a good example is the eternal fight of the American land of light against the evil empire, be it imperial England, popish Europe, Nazi Germany, or Soviet Russia. In this scenario, innocent and freedom-loving all-American boys are pitted against decadent, insane and cruel foreigners.

Third, an unfavorable depiction of the "other" correlates with a critical depiction of the self and thus functions as self-critique. The threat of the self to deteriorate and to become like the other is the underlying dynamic of this relationship. Thus, liberal and leftist critics in the post-World War II period have repeatedly argued that in the same way that big business brought Hitler to power, big corporations were assuming actual leadership of America.

Fourth, a favorable depiction of the "other" can function as self-critique; this dynamic is most obviously at work in "primitivist" sentiment that sees more natural and innocent values and cultural achievements embodied in a natural people, in "savages" who are more civilized than their colonizers. Interestingly enough, we find a prime example of this conception of the cultural other in the depiction of Germany as utopian counterspace by Black American GIs. Very much like the Emersonian youths come to Germany to find their Romantic ideal of the country, or like Henry Adams who expected to find a pre-industrial paradise that would contrast favorably with the historical and cultural development in America, Black GIs saw and lived in Germany the possibilities they were denied at home.

In spite of the different forms they can take, American

representations of Germany can all be read as commentary on and indicators of the American state of mind, as a kind of running cultural commentary. In the remainder of the chapter, serving as a kind of prologue to the specific readings that follow, we will first see, by taking American literature as an example, that from the beginning Germany was depicted as that which America was not. Then, we will take a broad view of how American observers in the post-World War II period have described Germany with America in mind, before we move on to specific analyses of American representations of Germany in the following chapters.

America's Germany in Classic American Literature

Even a cursory reading of 19th century American literary depictions of Germany makes clear that Americans have consistently looked toward Germany to find and reevaluate their own culture.[9] German literary culture clearly had a catalytic function in the creation of one of the first real American novels, Charles Brockden Brown's <u>Wieland</u> (1798). As Alan

---

[9] This section summarizes my own observations of American representations of Germany in classic American literature. Any specific sources I relied on are footnoted in the text. - For detailed studies of German influence on classic American literature see H.A. Pochmann, <u>German Culture in America, 1600-1900</u> (Madison: University of Wisconsin Press. 1957); S. Vogel, <u>German Literary Influences on the American Transcendentalists</u> (Yale University Studies Vol. 127. New Haven: Yale University Press.1955); René Wellek, <u>Confrontations</u> (Princeton: Princeton University Press. 1965); Christoph Wecker (ed.), <u>American-German Literary Interrelations in the Nineteenth Century</u> (American Studies Vol. 55. München: Wilhelm Fink. 1983). For a general overview of German-American relations see Frank Trommler and Joseph McVeigh (eds.), <u>America and the Germans. An Assessment of a three-hundred-year history</u>. 2 Vols. (Philadelphia: University of Philadelphia Press. 1985).

Axelrod has shown,[10] the German writer C.M Wieland helped focus the thematic concerns of Brown's novel, and indeed the forebears of his novel's protagonist, Theodore Wieland, were as much rooted in Germany as Brown's gothic tale. Moreover, Brockden Brown also codified what would later be described as the equation of gothicism with Germanness when he defined a certain dramatic style in Wieland: "According to German custom, it was minute and dictated by an adventurous and lawless fancy. It was a chain of audacious acts, and unheard-of disasters. The moated fortress, and the thicket; the ambush and the battle; and the conflict of headlong passions, were portrayed in wild numbers, and with terrific energy" (Brown, Wieland 78). Yet it seems clear that what Brown here makes out to be German literary custom applies equally well as description of his own style and his predilection for the supernatural in his novel. It seems that the imaginative freedom of the (German) gothic only made possible Brown's engagement with the enlightenment and the American revolution in Wieland. His description of the German style as "lawless fancy" is thus also an implicit indictment of American literal-mindedness and commonsense, a mind-set that deprived him of the artistic means to express his critique of modernity and American traditions.

While Brockden Brown found an imaginative atmosphere conducive to his project in German culture, Washington Irving incorporated elements of German literature even more closely into his writings. The first American author to attain international renown, Irving closely translated parts of German folk tales in his classic The Sketchbook of Geoffrey Crayon, Gent. (1819). Influenced by Sir Walter Scott, whom he had met during an eighteen-year sojourn in Britain, Brockden Brown made tales about romanticized English country life the thematic focus of the Sketchbook. But Scott had also called Irving's attention to the unused potential of German folk tales, and the story "Rip van Winkle" is clearly a transposition of the German Bluebeard myth to an American locale and into a colonial American historical setting. Similarly, the second of the two "American" stories in the Sketchbook, "The

---

[10] Alan Axelrod, Charles Brockden Brown. An American Tale. Austin: University of Texas Press. 1983. 63ff.

Legend of Sleepy Hollow," taps the tradition of German romantic gothicism, and also introduces a German-American figure as the ghostly Hessian headless horseman of the tale. About 30,000 German mercenaries, who came to be called "Hessians" since many of them originated in the area between Kassel and Hanau in Germany, had fought on the British side in the colonial war, and the phantom of Irving's story is the restless ghost of one of them. But more important than the historical origins of this figure, German romanticism provided Irving with a poetics and allowed him to establish American colonial history as a worthy literary subject matter in his two American stories in the Sketchbook.

In spite of the early appearances in Brown's and Irving's fiction, it was not until James Fenimore Cooper's The Pioneers (1823) that Germans were really featured as characters in American fiction. Industrious, efficient and, of course, a military man, Judge Temple's friend Major Fritz is also a dipsomaniac and joins his friend's family regularly for a week of "riotous living" (Cooper 98). In spite of his heavy accent and other ethnic traits, Major Fritz is a second generation immigrant, his family having come from the old country early in the 18th century. "Fritz, or Frederick Hartmann, was an epitome of all the vices and virtues, foibles and excellencies, of his race," Cooper's narrator relates. "He was passionate, though silent, obstinate, and a good deal suspicious of strangers; of immovable courage, inflexible honesty, and undeviating in his friendships" (Cooper 98). Major Fritz, as much as Judge Temple's French and English sidekicks, can be read as an allegory of European immigration to America. The Judge's friends are like external reminders of America's ethnic heterogeneity and cultural origins, as much as Judge Temple seems to fulfill the promise of young America. Major Fritz as German-American is described in favorable terms for what he can contribute to the new commonwealth, namely courage, honesty and loyalty; he is equally caricatured for the residues of his national character that don't fit American ideals too well, namely his inflexibility and his love of drink. Cooper's Major Fritz is thus as much an engagement with Germanness, as he is intended as a model for American character.

Echoes of Cooper's Major Fritz can be found, for instance, in Frank Norris' Mc Teague (1899) and the depiction of father Sieppe, who is as absurdly comical and stereotyped as Cooper's good natured grandfatherly figure. Norris describes old man Sieppe as "a little man of a military aspect, full of importance, taking himself very seriously. He was a member of a rifle team. Over his shoulder was slung a Springfield rifle, while his breast was decorated by five bronze medals" (Norris, McTeague 56f.). In McTeague, Cooper's Major Fritz is no longer a kind of vaguely feudal military man, but reduced to the ridiculous self-importance of petty bourgeois rifle teams. Yet, he also exemplifies the civic virtues German immigrants brought to the New World. Norris again underscored that point when he made one of the farmers who take up arms against the railroad in The Octopus (1901) a German who had fought in the Franco-Prussian war and who is described as a fiercely independent spirit in a tradition similar to that of the colonial Minutemen.

While Cooper and later Norris incorporated German characters into their fiction, Nathaniel Hawthorne was more generally influenced by German culture. German romanticism both afforded Hawthorne a way out of what he saw as the American predicament, the lack of cultural atmosphere, and a point of reference to criticize Emerson and Transcendentalism, which he derided as a German import in "The Celestial Railroad" (1843). In that story, Hawthorne ridiculed the German idealist influence on Transcendentalist philosophy as the Giant Transcendentalism, a monster in the habit of shouting after pilgrims and travellers in "strange phraseology" that puzzles them. More generally, as Hawthorne's narrator points out, "as to his form, his features, his substance, and his nature generally, it is the chief peculiarity of this huge miscreant, that neither he himself, nor anybody for him, has ever been able to describe them" (Hawthorne, "Celestial Railroad" 197). German romanticism, depicted as allegorical monster, provides Hawthorne with a readily available reference point for criticizing the philosophical murkiness of American transcendentalism. Interestingly enough, the Giant Transcendentalist, German by birth, in Hawthorne's somewhat heavy-handed allegorical satire inhabits the cave in which Pope and Pagan used to dwell. Hawthorne is in fact saying that Transcendentalism is un-American, both a German invention and little better than the New Jerusalem's arch enemies popery and heathenism. Ariel casts out Caliban. The cultural other is the not-self. Quite clearly, Hawthorne sets up an equation between German and un-American.[11]

Not only in "The Celestial Railroad" but throughout his writing, Hawthorne equates Germany with (oftentimes occult) learning and science. This depiction, while again investing Germany with a kind of romantic aura, also reflects the rising influence of German universities throughout the 19th century and the apparent lack of comparable institutions in America. Roger Chillingworth in The Scarlet Letter (1850) thus is practically a German import, and the narrator of the novel relates how "Heaven had wrought an absolute miracle [with him], by transporting an eminent Doctor of Physic, from a German university, bodily through the air, and setting him down at the door of Mr. Dimmesdale's study" (Hawthorne, Scarlet Letter 121). Germany not only had to offer learning, but also a romance atmosphere conducive to Hawthorne's allegorical intentions as a writer.

Although overall Hawthorne seems to succeed very well in recreating layer upon layer of American cultural history, he was deeply chagrined about and repeatedly complained of a presumed lack of "atmosphere" or absence of romantic aura. Thus, for instance, in The Marble Faun he wrote that Italy provided

> a sort of poetic or fairy precinct, where actualities would not be so terribly insisted upon as they are, and must needs be, in America. No author, without a trial, can conceive of the difficulty of writing a romance about a country where there is no shadow, no antiquity, no mystery, no picturesque and gloomy wrong, nor anything but commonplace prosperity, in broad and simple daylight, as is happily the case with my dear native land. (Hawthorne, Marble Faun 3)

---

[11] In a spirit of irony one could read McCarthyism and the House Un-American Activities Committee as historical sanctification of that equation. Was not Karl Marx after all a German, and Communism thus only the latest version of Hawthorne's ugly and miscreant Giant of German origin? Had not Lenin and friends returned from exile under German protection, "making them appear to be German agents bent on disrupting the Allied war effort"(Hunt 113)? More Germans, more un-American activities.

Germany, as much as Italy, provided Hawthorne with the much sought-after imaginative relief from the harsh actualities of American life. From Young Goodman Brown of the story with the same name, to Aylmer in "The Birthmark" and Professor Rappaccini in "Rapaccini's Daughter," many of Hawthorne's heroes have their imaginative origins in German culture, and many of them actually engage in German-influenced Faustian quests for absolute knowledge and the inquiry into the nature of evil.

That German romanticism profoundly influenced Hawthorne artistically and provided him with a poetics to explore moral questions is most obvious in the story "Ethan Brand." The protagonist of that story may or may not have come to Germany on his quest for the "unpardonable sin," but the narrative's governing image, literalized at its end, the "heart of stone," has its origins in high Romantic German literature and E.T.A. Hoffmann's "Heart of Stone," the metaphysical tale of a poor charcoal burner's pact with the devil that clearly inspired Hawthorne's story. Clearly, Hawthorne found in the romance world of the German folk tale and its sublimation in German Romanticism the imaginative freedom that he missed in American culture and that he described as a "neutral territory [...] where the Actual and the Imaginary may meet" (Hawthorne, Scarlet Letter 36) in the introduction to The Scarlet Letter. Martin Christadler, in a rather fortuitous account of the German influence on the American Renaissance, remarks: "The rapid adoption of 'modern' German writers by the dissenting [American] intellectuals, through Carlyle and Coleridge, during the 1830's, reflects their need for a kind of discourse and language which would help them emancipate themselves from the accepted theological learning and Christianity of the Establishment" (13). Quite clearly, Hawthorne's description and depiction of German culture as romantic was based on historical fact as much as it was rooted in his need to define an imaginative space for himself as American author.

Apparently, the interchangeability of the descriptive terms Germanness with romantic distortion and gothicism was already so firmly established by mid-century that Edgar Allan Poe felt he needed to defend his Tales of the Grotesque and Arabesque (1840) against the charge that they were pervaded with "'Germanism' and gloom" (Poe 129). Poe answered his critics with the priceless line, "I maintain that terror is not of Germany, but of the soul" (129). Melville would probably have agreed, and in his meditation on the white terror of the whale in Moby Dick ("The Whiteness of the Whale") he takes as premier example the "tall pale man of the [German] Harz forests, whose changeless pallor unrustlingly glides through the green of the groves" (293), the Brocken specter Goethe had described at length. Clearly, neither Melville nor Hawthorne were interested in Germany as such, but only used elements of German culture as examples to illustrate the terror that was their main focus. Just as other American writers before him had to look abroad for a certain cultural atmosphere because they thought they could not find it at home, Poe set his stories in gothic locales, peopled them with foreigners, and seemed to write out of the alien tradition of German high Romanticism.

What many American authors before him must have seen as the promise of German Romanticism, Mark Twain savagely attacked in his A Tramp Abroad (1879). Twain's depiction of German mores in the travelogue is most memorable for its description of the hard drinking and constantly dueling corps students. After a brief description of student life and the election of the beer king, Twain spends several chapters on corps etiquette and on the students' bi-weekly fights. "The students fight duels in the room which I have described, two days in every week during seven and a half or eight months in every year," he observed with awe. "This custom has continued in Germany two hundred and fifty years" (Twain 31; author's emphasis). Twain was not only incredulous about the enormous amount of time and energy spent on those fights, but also about their primitive savagery. While fascinated with the senseless brutality of student life, Twain also described, and ridiculed, the Germany of the romantic imagination, full of history- and folklore-laden ruins and mythical places like the Loreley or the castles on the banks of the Rhine. Particularly the completely spurious rafting tour down the Neckar in A Tramp Abroad, with its detours into the sentimental romance of fables, fairy tales and local folklore, and its sudden end in shipwreck, only makes sense as counter image to Huck and Jim's voyage down the Mississippi, with its stopovers and forays into different forms of American society. Yet, the tour on the Neckar also doubles Twain's critique of misguided Southern chivalry in the Shepherdson/Grangerford feud in Huckleberry Finn; just as the excursion into German romance-space on his Neckar rafting-tour necessarily has to end in shipwreck, the romantic imagination is doomed to flounder on the rocks of reality. Twain's satirical journey through German folklore spaces as critique of sentimentality can be fully understood only if complemented by Huck and Jim's utopian pilgrims' progress through American social spaces, whose realism constitutes the ideological and aesthetic alternative to sentimentality.[12] The disgust with sentimental romance that made Twain name a sunken ship "Sir Walter Scott" in Huckleberry Finn and that led to his scathing analysis of Cooper's Deerslayer, also informs his depiction of Germany. In describing Germany, Twain has thus primarily American literary history in mind -- and not the country he visits.

In the Devil's Territories: Going Native in the Land of Evil

Even this cursory overview of 19th century American literary depictions of Germany makes clear that Americans have consistently looked toward Germany to find and reevaluate their own culture. Somewhat surprisingly, given the intensity of wartime propaganda and the battlefield experiences of American soldiers, we find that the same perceptual pattern informed the cultural perceptions of American GIs stationed in occupied Germany after World War II.

American soldiers again and again imagined Germany as an American space, and continued to discover a familiar ethno-geography in the foreign country. An observer thus noted in his account of the occupation, aptly entitled America's Germany (1946), that "most soldiers in Germany like the country for its solidity, its cleanliness, its relative modernity" (Bach 264), in short: its Americanness. What is striking in account after account is the GIs' delight in finding Germany very American, clearly a reversal of Henry Adams' earlier evaluation but still a response structured by the same underlying pattern of conceiving

---

[12] Cf. Heide Ziegler's radio essay "Heidelbeereberg - Huckleberry Mountain. Mark Twains Beziehung zum Südwesten" (Süddeutscher Rundfunk 2, 30 Nov. 1985).

of cultural otherness in terms of the familiar. Thus, for instance, shortly after the end of the war in Europe, Newsweek ran a long feature on the impressions of American GIs in Germany, pointing out that the average soldier "finds the German land and people very like his own" and glossing their opinions at length:

> "If I can't be home, I'd rather be right here in Germany," said a technical sergeant, pensively watching a small speedboat churning down the Rhine. "Reminds me of the Wisconsin River."
> "Look at this road," said the jeep driver as we sped along the four-lane autobahn. "You'd think you were on the Pennsylvania turnpike."
> "Fraternization or no fraternization," said a private in Friedberg, "these people are friendly and easy to get along with. They're the same kind of smalltown people as back home in Kansas. And you should see inside their houses -- modern and clean as a pin." (Newsweek 30 July 45, 42)

As so many Americans before them, these GIs only find abroad what they know from home. Inundated with propaganda, the GIs expected to encounter a primitive and barbarous country and were surprised at the lack of cultural difference. To them, the presumed cultural other turned out to look a lot like the self. As one GI put it: "Hell, these people (the Germans) have sitdown toilets. That practically makes them our allies" (Newsweek 4 Feb. 46, 58).

Generally slightly less profane, but in the same spirit, the media began to describe the postwar cultural conquest and democratization of Germany in the familiar terms, concepts and ideals by then established in the American mind. Time thus noted approvingly the efforts of German anti-Nazis who "took over public gathering [and] denounced the old order and proclaimed a new one with the vigor of a New England town meeting" (Time 25 June 45, 22). Emerging German democratic sentiment and political dissent are thus rewritten as a repetition of the American tradition of religious and political independence.

While firsthand observers in the occupied country were mostly surprised by the "Americanness" of Germany and often tended to comment on the similarities between their own and the foreign country, American authors in the post-World War II have used the heuristic and critical potential of the cross cultural encounter for a more complex commentary on their own country.

In his survey of dominant perceptions in America during World War II, V was for Victory, cultural historian John Morton Blum observes that as a result both of the intensity of the conflict during World War II and German atrocities during the Third Reich period, "the Nazis and ultimately all Germans acquired in the public mind the attributes of unequivocal evil" (49). But while public perceptions of Germany slowly began to change in America as a result of the emerging Cold War (as we shall see in Chapter 4), another cultural critic has noted that "for the contemporary imagination, Nazism [became] one of the supreme metaphors, that of Evil" (Friedländer 119; my emphasis). Indeed, across narrative genres from high literature to B-movies, the evil (Nazi) German has become a staple figure of the American imagination. Moreover, although one may bemoan the stereotypical character of these depictions, it is important to realize that in almost all cases the equation of German with evil serves as negative contrast to a favorable depiction of the American self.[13]

The examples are legion, of course, and I will just pick one to illustrate the point. Irwin Shaw constructs his German characters as metaphors of evil and as negative counter-images to his American

---

[13] Of course, the equation is sometimes also reversed, and either in order to shock or as a contrarian gesture in a decadent (neo-Romantic) aesthetics, Nazism is valorized as alternative to middle American/bourgeois self-complacency (Punk rock and the gay S&M fringe are recent prime examples of this turn towards a Nazi symbology). - For an earlier detailed analysis of the phenomenon see Susan Sontag's essay "Fascinating Fascism."

protagonists in <u>The Young Lions</u> (1948).[14] The novel follows the slowly converging wartime lives of two American GIs, a Jew and a liberal intellectual (incidentally reminiscent of Lieutenant Hearn of Mailer's <u>Naked and the Dead</u>), and two German soldiers, Christian, a ski instructor turned officer, and Hardenburg, his superior and ardent Nazi. Shaw sets up his Germans as counter-image to the American characters in every respect: over against German delusions of grandeur we have the somewhat stolid but nevertheless "sane and reasonable" Americans; over against the German officers we have enlisted men; and finally, over against German self-destructiveness we have the American struggle to transcend social and ideological limitations.

The ubiquity and lack of change of the characterological pattern displayed in <u>The Young Lions</u> may be explained with a kind of sentimental yearning for the simplicity of the good war. The symbolical return to the fight against Nazism thus becomes an exorcism of the seemingly intractable political problems besetting America in a changed world. Paradoxically, the new world order created by the essentially American victory over the Axis powers seemed to bring, on the one hand, the fulfillment of the American prophecy first enunciated by the Pilgrims, who saw their colony as a New Jerusalem, a claim reiterated and politically bolstered by the fathers of the Revolution of 1776. For a time, the United States became a cynosure with no parallel except perhaps for that of the papacy in Medieval Europe" (May 107). But on the other hand, the role of unrivaled global power also seemed to make democratic America extremely vulnerable to the dangers of a hostile world. Once again, it seemed, America found itself in a position similar to that of the Puritans on the new continent, a situation that one of the foremost Puritan zealots, Cotton Mather, had then characterized as "A People of God in the Devil's Territories."

Clearly, in a volatile world, America had every reason to be anxious in its new global role, and nowhere were those anxieties more summed up and focused than in American involvement in Germany. It was

---

[14] Made into a highly successful screen version by Edward Dmytryk in 1958, and starring Maximilian Schell opposite Marlon Brando as German lieutenant, Dean Martin and Montgomery Clift as American GIs.

in and over Germany that American public opinion worked through the implications of the United States' role as dominant world power. Thus, then, in addition to the sentimental hearkening back to the lost simplicity of the "just war" exemplified by Shaw's The Young Lions, writers and film makers also explored the dangers and challenges of America's new global role by tracing their protagonist's descent into the moral and political hell thrown open in the wake of World War II. Not surprisingly, the new heart of darkness, the center of these allegorical infernal regions was Germany, and again and again we follow American heroes abroad to see what might be in store for America as a whole.

Clearly, the outcome of World War II opened up tremendous opportunities for America,[15] and media magnate Henry R. Luce (owner and founder of Life, Time, and Fortune, among others) divined the signs of change early on. Just as John Winthrop had first enunciated American exceptionalism and staked out the status of the American colony as a "New Jerusalem" and a beacon of hope in the "City on the Hill," Luce as another American zealot recast Mather's exceptionalist rhetoric in terms appropriate for the 20th century. In a lengthy Life editorial shortly after the American entry into World War II, he described America as a land of freedom in a world threatened by tyranny and grandiloquently proclaimed the dawning of the "American Century." For Luce, as much as for Winthrop, America held the key to redemption. "It now becomes our time to be the powerhouse from which the [democratic] ideals spread throughout the world and do their mysterious work of lifting the life of mankind from the level of the beasts to what the Psalmist called a little lower than the angels," Luce rhapsodized (65). According to Luce, American hegemony was not to be confused with that of countless empires ranging from the Romans to that of Stalin and Hitler. To be sure, America was going to dominate the world, but as Luce pointed out, it was going to do it in benevolent fashion, not as an imperial power, but as "Good Samaritan, really believing again that it is more blessed to give than to receive" (65).

---

[15] Also cf. McCormick and his description of "world war as diplomacy" (33), American jockeying for position and careful manipulation both of the domestic public and the Allies abroad in order to emerge as unchallenged dominant global power after the war.

Luce in 1941 articulated what was to become the American post-World War II consensus, which, although it began to erode as early as the ill begotten start of the space race and the "Sputnik scare," was only fully dismantled in the national soul-searching after the Vietnam debacle. But long before My Lai and the American public's shocking realization that American GIs had behaved as atrociously and sadistically as Nazi stormtroopers, the limits of American exceptionalism were being probed by liberals in the American culture industry. Even immediately after the war, the newly-confirmed political and moral virtue of the U.S., its presumed difference from the "other," the tyrannical German enemy, became the issue again and again in fictional explorations and accounts of the war and its consequences.

Repeatedly, the breakdown of the distinction between the cultural self and other is dramatized as the process of "going native," as a crossing and eventual obliteration of the historical and cultural differences between America and Germany. To return to the comparison between Puritan conceptions of new world exceptionalism and American self-conception after the war, structurally these fictional explorations in the post-war period are analogous to Nathaniel Hawthorne's questioning of the Puritan universe in a story such as "Young Goodman Brown." One could even go as far as saying that "Young Goodman Brown," with its dramatization of the crossing of ideological boundaries and the exploration and discovery of the moral "other" within the self, anticipates the dominant mode of fictionalized encounters with the war and with the moral stature of America in the mid 20th century. Like young Goodman Brown, many of the postwar American heroes leave their "Faith" behind, their sense of moral and political superiority, and venture into the allegorical "nightly woods" only to discover the complicity in evil of their community and even of themselves, and to cry out in despair with Goodman Brown, "my faith is gone! [...] There is no good on earth; and sin is but a name. Come, devil! for to thee is this world given" (Hawthorne, "Young Goodman Brown" 83). For many American protagonists in the postwar period, the journey into the "dark territories" ends in similar disillusionment when they realize that in spite of all the exceptionalist rhetoric they share many of the traits of the "other," are not all that different from the enemy as they would have liked to believe.

Graham Greene and film maker Carol Reed's The Third Man (1949) retells Hawthorne's story in 20th century terms. Although both Greene and Reed are British, their dramatization of postwar moral quandaries significantly enough revolves around two American characters.[16] It is as if the two English artists found in the figure of the innocent and the ugly American a ready-made symbolic vocabulary for existential questions very much like Hawthorne had earlier found Puritan figures useful as representative characters for his exploration of moral questions. Although Greene may well have been more interested in the moral quandary of his protagonist, The Third Man also foreshadows the larger crisis in America's national self-conception. Just like Hawthorne's Puritans, Greene's Americans display an initial unproblematic sense of moral superiority and righteousness and thus react the more violently when confronted with evil, when realizing the continuities between the self and the "other."

In Greene's film, Rollo Martins, idealistic American innocent, comes to postwar Vienna by invitation of his idol and school-time friend Harry Lime (Orson Welles) to help him in running a charity-like medical unit. On arriving, Rollo learns that Harry has just been buried, having been killed in an auto accident. Rollo gets indications that Harry might have been an operator on the black market, but convinced of Harry's integrity, he suspects foul play and sets out to find a mysterious third man who must have witnessed Harry's presumed accident. As it turns out, there is no third man and the accident was fabricated. Harry is alive and well, but turns out to be a big player in the black market peddling of diluted and thus worthless penicillin. In contrast to perennial American exaltation of the individual, Harry cynically and ruthlessly thinks in terms of faceless masses. Looking down from a cabin on a Ferris wheel he muses about the people below and about his racket: "Would you really feel any pity if one of those dots stopped moving forever? If I said you can have twenty thousand pounds for every dot that stops, would you really, old man, tell

---

[16] Graham Greene continued what could be called his exploration of the American psyche both in The Quiet American, his chilling prediction of American involvement in Southeast Asia, and in Our Man in Havana, his satirical indictment of American anti-communist and anti-Cuban hysteria.

me to keep my money -- or would you calculate how many dots you could afford to spare?" (Greene 111). Obviously, to Rollo's American innocent, Harry is the ugly American, indistinguishable finally from all the "enemies" of freedom and democracy with their scorn for the individual, be they German Nazis or Russian communists. Since Rollo idolizes and identifies with his friend, but in realizing Harry's evil core, Rollo discovers the self as other. Like young Goodman Brown's journey into the woods, Rollo's descent into the shady underworld of the black market in decaying Vienna results in disillusionment, a descent into hell that climaxes in the hunt for Harry in the sewage system, an apt image for postwar Europe and the state of Harry's morals, and another recasting of Cotton Mather's "devil's territories."

Norman Mailer makes a similar point in The Naked and the Dead (1948) in the depiction of General Cummings, who turns out to have strong sympathies for the Nazis' will to social power. Mailer clearly uses the cultural other as a point of articulation for his liberal critique of the American self and compares virulent un-democratic tendencies in American culture after the war with those in totalitarian Germany .

One of the most important thematic concerns in Mailer's Naked and the Dead is the recreation of the (Nietzschean) "will to power" through General Cummings. The general points out to the author's narrative alter ego, the politically liberal Lieutenant Hearns, that "the only morality of the future is a power morality" (Mailer, Naked and Dead 323) and that the army is "a preview of the future" (Mailer, Naked and Dead 324) and the closest we come yet to a realization of Cummings' totalitarian utopia. The "power morality" described by Cummings finds manifold illustration in the conflicts of everyday army-life, the individual GI's struggle for survival in the Pacific war, epitomized in the story of a platoon's long patrol up Mount Anaka. But Cummings also draws a historical parallel in elucidating what he calls the "process of historical energy," and aptly characterizes his army-state as fascist utopia, and as a continuation of the Nazi revolution: "The concept of fascism [...] merely started in the wrong country, in a country which did not have enough intrinsic potential power to develop completely. [...] But the dream, the concept was sound enough. [...] America is going to absorb that dream, it's in the business of doing it now" (Mailer, Naked and Dead

321). Cummings here provides another reconceptualization of American exceptionalism, another World War II version of the Puritans' New Canaan. But while Henry Luce cloaked his aspirations for American global predominance in Samaritan garb, Uncle Sam appears in military drag in General Cummings' version of world conquest, and Mailer delivers an intentional parody of military megalomania. But most importantly, Cummings defines the emerging American utopia as a kind of super-Germany, a Third Reich with unlimited military and industrial resources. Cummings sees and emphasizes the parallels between Nazi Germany and America, and describes the positive identification with the image of the other as the hope for the future.

By contrast, Mailer creates the fictional Cummings to criticize the aims of the rising military-industrial complex by equating American militarism with German fascism. Thus, parallel to learning about Cummings' grandiose designs, readers and Lieutenant Hearn automatically modify their conception of the General from ally to enemy. With the unfolding of Cummings' American fascist utopia, he goes ideologically native, so to speak, crosses the line between American democratic self and the fascist German other, becomes indistinguishable from the enemy.

While Mailer has his General Cummings only fantasize about a fascist America, Philip K. Dick's The Man in the High Castle (1962) enlarges that fantasy and depicts an America carved up by the Axis powers. Set in 1962, Japan controls the Pacific rim, Nazi Germany the Eastern seaboard, with remnants of the former U.S. left in the middle and dominated by the two powers. In an ingenious narrative turn that almost causes readerly ontological vertigo, a book entitled The Grasshopper Lies Heavy, the fictional account of an alternate world in which the Allies have won the war, becomes the much discussed topic in The Man in the High Castle. The characters in Dick's novel thus read about the actual, "historical" contemporary world as if it were fiction. At one point they discuss the course of the postwar way to prosperity and American global economic aid described in The Grasshopper, and one of the characters criticizes the author for merely having recast fascism as the New Deal welfare state:

You know what he's done, don't you? He's taken the best
about Nazism, the socialist part, the Todt Organization
and the economic advances we got through Speer, and
who's he giving the credit to? The New Deal. And he's left
out the bad part, the SS part, the racial extermination and
segregation. It's a utopia! You imagine if the Allies had
won, the New Deal would have been able to revive the
economy and make those socialist welfare improvements,
like he says? Hell, no; he's talking about a form of state
syndicalism, the corporate state, like we developed under
the Duce. (Dick 151)

"Real" history did take the course discounted by the speaker in this
passage, and although the label "New Deal" had long been dropped, the
U.S. embarked on a course of global economic aid, from the Marshall plan
for the reconstruction of Europe to countless programs for third world
nations. Thus, like Mailer in the ideas of his General Cummings (and
Pynchon in Gravity's Rainbow, as we shall see in a later chapter), Dick
breaks down the distinctions between the self and the cultural and
ideological "other" by stressing the structural similarities of the emerging
power of the military industrial complex in postwar America to fascist
Italy and Nazi Germany.

While Mailer's General Cummings provides the most haunting
illustration of the latent fascism in American postwar culture, and Dick's
commentaries through the book within the novel constitute probably the
formally most sophisticated expression of the same criticism, Stanley
Kubrick's absurd comedy and critique of the suicidal and paranoid logic of
the Cold War, Dr. Strangelove (1964), makes the point more bluntly and
visually in the most economic way by casting Peter Sellers as both the
American President and the spiritus rector of his state apparatus, the
mad and ex-Nazi scientist Dr. Strangelove.[17] Dr. Strangelove as the

---

[17] It could be objected that Peter Sellers is also cast as Lionel Mandrake, General
Ripper's British executive officer, and that thus the striking (personal) continuity
between the president and Dr. Strangelove is diluted and undermined. Yet, it seems
that the Mandrake-Ripper relationship mirrors that of the president and Dr.

"Director of Defense Research and Development" dominates the president and his government, just as the defense establishment is dominated by the technology of destruction, be it the Soviet "Doomsday Device" or the by comparison almost pedestrian bombers of the Strategic Air Command, both of which are beyond recall if once set into motion.

It is mainly Dr. Strangelove's eerie presence that accounts for the atmosphere of "Twilight of the Gods" in the Pentagon's war room as resurrected "führer-bunker" on the eve of global nuclear destruction, reminiscent of the final days of the Reich. As if in illustration of the military dystopia sketched by Mailer, the military pre-empt politics in Dr. Strangelove, and, in mad General Ripper's words, "War is too important to be left to the politicians." The military also are the ones most susceptible to fantasies of racial purity. Brigadier Ripper is haunted by paranoid sexual fantasies about the threat of ideological and bodily infection by a communist conspiracy, the sapping of his life essence. Obsessed about the purity of his bodily fluids just like the Nazis were about racial purity, he unleashes a campaign of destruction against the Russians. Similarly, Dr. Strangelove sketches plans for the survival of an American elite, naturally including "our top government and military men," who would be stashed away with harems of playmates in deep mines for a century to emerge as a new super-race after the end of the nuclear winter.

The final irony of Kubrick's movie is not that the American crusade against communism seems like a continuation of the Nazi madness, "our Germans are better than their Germans," but that America as the hope of democracy has finally become the stronghold of (Nazi) totalitarianism, and wheelchair-bound Dr. Strangelove's triumphant cry at the end of the film, "Mein führer, I can walk," implies that the spirit of

---

Strangelove. In both cases the mad and paranoid schemes prevail over the moderate views. Kubrick's charge in Dr. Strangelove is thus not that a General Cummings has become president, but rather that in spite of an articulate and liberal Stevensonian president like Merkin Muffley, cold-war hardliners determine foreign policy. In short, a liberal and enlightened attitude has failed to stop the suicidal self-dynamic of the military machine.

Nazism is on the move again. America is not merely absorbing the Nazi dream of the corporate state, as Mailer's General Cummings adumbrated, but has long since fulfilled it. In <u>Dr. Strangelove,</u> the former enemy, Nazi Germany, the "other," has become the self, and Dr. Strangelove is Mr. Hyde to the President's Dr. Jekyll, the two being only parts of a schizophrenic whole.

Interestingly enough, liberal artists like Kubrick and Mailer were not the only ones to take (Nazi) Germany as the point of reference for their critiques of America, as an episode of the <u>Star Trek</u> TV series shows. In "Patterns of Force," first aired in February 1968, starship <u>Enterprise</u> tries to get in touch with the cultural observer of the Federation on the planet Ekon, Captain Kirk's former history professor at Starfleet Academy, John Gill. Beamed down, Captain Kirk and Mr. Spock find an indistinguishable replica of the Nazi state on Ekon, complete with Nazi uniforms, internecine squabbles between the Party, SS and Gestapo, and an ongoing racial war between the Ekonians and the radically pacifist and more advanced Zeons (a thinly veiled "Zion" and reference to the Jews, which is also played out in names like Davod, Abrom, Isak). They soon find out that the similarity is no coincidence when they learn that the Ekonian <u>führer</u> is John Gill, who must have recreated the Nazi state for reasons of his own.

Captain Kirk and Mr. Spock try to get access to John Gill, but for obvious reasons this climactic meeting has to be put off until the end of the episode. The inevitable trials and tribulations that Kirk and Spock have to endure include imprisonment and torture by the Gestapo, an escape from the prison, a linkup with members of the Zeonian underground (quite literally under ground in the sewer system), delayed communication with the <u>Enterprise</u> because of disassembled communicators, and the eventual infiltration of Party Headquarters, where John Gill is about to give a speech. Kirk and Spock find out that Gill's assistant Melakon has assumed power and that he merely keeps the professor as figurehead of the party. Gill is isolated from everybody else and apparently drugged or psychotic. With the help of Dr. McCoy, beamed down from the <u>Enterprise</u> in the meantime, the group manages to wake John Gill, who then tells his story why he replicated Nazi Germany on Ekon, in spite of definite Star Command orders not to interfere in alien cultures. Apparently, Gill was fascinated by the efficiency of the Nazi state and strove to replicate it on Ekon. When Captain Kirk objects that Nazi Germany was brutal and perverted and had to be fought at terrible cost, Mr. Spock ventures the explanation that perhaps Gill thought that "run benignly -- could accomplish his efficiency without sadism." Apparently, Gill has the same dream as General Cummings in Mailer's The Naked and the Dead, or for that matter, as Plato in the totalitarian utopia outlined in his Republic, and could not resist the promise of efficiency of centralized and absolute authority. As the crew of the Enterprise finds out, Gill's plan initially seemed to work and primitive Ekon society flowered; but then, Melakon began to usurp Gill's power and things took their inevitable course towards a sadistic totalitarianism.

Of course, both Gill and Melakon die in the final showdown, but only after Gill has realized his mistake and in the last moment reverses his earlier call for total war against the Zeonians in another broadcast. Peace reestablished on Ekon and back on the Enterprise, Kirk sums up the moral and lesson of this episode for his lieutenants and the audience:

> Spock: How could a man as brilliant, a mind as logical as
>   John Gill's have made such a fatal error?
> Kirk: He drew the wrong conclusion from history. The
>   problem with the Nazis wasn't simply that their leaders
>   were evil, psychotic men. They were. But the main
>   problem, I think, was the leader principle.
> McCoy: What he's saying, Spock, is that when a man
>   holds that much power, even with the best intentions
>   he simply can't resist to play God.

Obviously, the ill-fated Nazi experiment, both on Ekon and in Germany, provides the perfect contrast to the democratic virtues of the American-led science-fictional Federation in Star Trek, and serves to re-affirm those political values. Thus (Nazi) Germany figures as the absolute other to the American self, the führer state is the negative complement to American federalism and the system of checks and balances.

Yet, like so many other depictions of German-American

interactions, "Patterns of Force" again dramatizes the process of "going native." Highly respected Professor John Gill, who had earlier impressed both Kirk and Spock with his historical analyses, has gone over to the other side, so to speak, has failed to learn his own historical lessons.[18] Thus, Gill stands for a dangerous tendency of the political and cultural "self"; even in their highly evolved cultural and peaceful state -- after all, the socio-cultural microcosm aboard the USS Enterprise implies a human race above and beyond the divisiveness and warmongering of the not so distant past -- people are still prone to fall prey to the seductions of power. In this sense, the recreated Nazi Germany on Ekon becomes a projection of the American internal "other," of a suppressed and denied potential for totalitarianism in the presumably democratic American self.

"Patterns of Force" not only illustrates the convenient availability of (Nazi) Germany as a kind of shorthand for the complete opposite of American democracy, in its projection of the American internal "other" the episode also articulates a kind of republican critique of American overseas-involvement and its adverse effects on the American body-politic. Cold War historian Thomas J. McCormick has pointed out that disaffection with the Vietnam war extended into the (conservative) political American elite. Faced with the potential alienation of a whole generation of middle class youth, corporate leaders as well as other traditionally non-liberal elites "to voice dissent from the Vietnam War effort and, more broadly, to question the proper relationship of means to ends in fulfilling America's hegemonic role" (McCormick 159). At the same time the emergence of a kind of wartime democracy raised troubling questions about the centralization of power and the dangers of what Arthur Schlesinger called the "imperial presidency," questions that would finally explode into prominence with the Watergate scandal. As

---

[18] The depiction of John Gill, both in his idealistic failure to consider the imperfections of human nature in his well-meant experiment and the apparent irrelevance or even danger of the intellectual in practical (political) matters, must be read as an indictment of the (liberal) intellectual and academic establishment. Especially the implicit appeal to prevent eggheads like Gill from influencing directly the fate of the body politic seems ominously urgent considering the context of political and cultural upheaval in the late 1960's.

Michael Hunt has shown, the question "whether domestic liberty could flourish alongside an ambitious and strongly assertive foreign policy" (21) has determined American politics at least since the republican-federalist debate between Jefferson and Hamilton. While Jefferson militated against too much concentrated power and argued for a non-interventionist foreign policy, Hamilton advocated a strong central government in the hands of an elite and aggressive involvement abroad to defend American interests (cf. Hunt 21-28). The same conflict erupted over and over again, and also informed the struggle between isolationist and interventionist forces in American foreign policy in the 20th century before the emergence of the Cold War consensus and global American policing according to the Truman doctrine.

The apparent failure of U.S. foreign policy in Southeast Asia yet again added fuel to the debate over the form of American involvement abroad and its effects on democracy at home. Hunt sums up that the executive branch profited tremendously from the growing importance of foreign affairs, and that as a result of the "cult of national security" (178) both the political clout of Congress and accountability to the public have been on the wane. These developments, according to Hunt, all constitute "serious blows to the workings of a democratic political system" (178). Or, in the words of Captain Kirk, "the main problem, I think, was the leader principle," the emergence of an imperial presidency. "Patterns of Force" thus articulates a kind of republican critique of U.S. foreign policy. Significantly enough, as Hunt also points out, the Vietnam War and later Watergate eroded "support, especially and most critically among well-informed, influential Americans, for the interventionism associated with previous Cold War policy" (Hunt 181).

In a sense, Kirk and Spock's investigation of what has become of John Gill and what is happening on planet Ekon anticipates the fate of Richard Nixon, undone like the history professor by the undue accumulation of power. But more importantly, and in spite of the obvious imperialist undercurrents of Star Trek and the intergalactic roaming and prospecting of new markets of the aptly named (Free) Enterprise, the series also champions a return to a kind of neo-Jeffersonian republicanism and criticizes what could be called the Hamiltonian political elitism, the concentration of centralized power and interventionist foreign policies. In best Jeffersonian fashion the common members of the crew are thus titled "yeoman," the solar system is organized into the Federation, and the Federation's foreign and cultural policy vis à vis new life forms is one of strict non-interference.

Critics of Star Trek like David Buxton in From the Avengers to Miami Vice (1990) have noted "the displacement of what were current ideological tensions on to planets suitably designed for their resolution" (60). And indeed the series' main rivalries between the Federation, the Klingon and the Romulan empires are easily recognized as the 1960's geopolitical distribution of power between America, China and the Russians. Yet, Buxton may be oversimplifying the ideological thrust of the series, or just denying it its due, when he claims that in Star Trek "an optimistic version of a universal human nature (in its puritan American form) can be upheld while the problems of the twentieth century (in the first place, the Vietnam War) can be displaced on to others" (Buxton 60). True, Kirk and Spock only encounter their "Germany within," the totalitarian internal other of their transparently American culture on a strange and distant planet, but then it is one of their venerated teachers who is responsible for the political aberration in that world. Although displaced, the horror and the realization of the fragility of their democratic traditions and their cultural superiority hit close to home, and, with dying John Gill "Patterns of Force" seems to remind its audience that if teachers can err so fatally, how about the pupils? But most importantly, the Star Trek episode shows that for American social and cultural critics left as well as right, Germany provided a metaphoric system, almost a symbolical language and ready-made set of images for a polemic against the deviation from true democracy in America. And thus, at last, the meaning of "going native" is also borne out in the political dimension: to the same degree that America fails to be truly American and thus democratic, it becomes German and totalitarian.

In contrast to works like The Naked and the Dead, The Man in the High Castle, Dr. Strangelove, and even the Star Trek episode, which all emphasize political aspects in their depiction and use of the image of Germany, other fictional accounts of Germany tend to concentrate on moral issues within a more existential framework and regardless of the specificity of the political situation. Kurt Vonnegut's Slaughterhouse-Five

(1969), incidentally also the most widely known postwar American novel about Germany, is representative in this respect. Advertised in its full title rather baroquely as

> Slaughterhouse-Five or The children's crusade. A duty dance with death. Kurt Vonnegut. A fourth-generation German-American now living in easy circumstances on Cape Cod (and smoking too much), who, as an American infantry scout hors de combat, as a prisoner of war, witnessed the fire-bombing of Dresden, Germany, "The Florence of the Elbe," a long time ago, and survived to tell the tale (Vonnegut iii),

the autobiographically inspired novel revolves around the fire-bombing of the city of Dresden, which surpassed any other air-raid in history, including Hiroshima and Nagasaki, killing 135,000 people, mostly civilians. The firebombing of Dresden is infamous mainly because it was of questionable military value, Dresden having been a non-garrison "open" city, deluged by refugees from the East fleeing the approaching Soviet Armies. Yet, Dresden was an important railway hub and thus of strategic importance for disrupting the enemy's supply lines; but even the military were not quite comfortable with their success and the raid remained largely unpublicized and public awareness low even after the war. Vonnegut off-handedly reports this fact in Slaughterhouse-Five, when his protagonist, Billy Pilgrim, shares a room with an official Army historian, who explains why details had been kept secret for a long time: "For fear that a lot of bleeding hearts [...] might not think it was such a wonderful thing to do" (Vonnegut 165).

Although Vonnegut's moving depiction of the sufferings of the POW's and the almost surreal account of the destruction of Dresden make Slaughterhouse-Five a strong anti-war statement, both the fatalistic naturalization of war in the Trafalmagore sections, in which time is spatialized and history thus becomes deterministic, and the evasion of the underlying specifically historical issues finally make the novel into a curiously ahistorical exploration of a historical incident. Talking about the then work-in-progress, Vonnegut characterized the difficulties he had with the material and said that the subject of Dresden was "extremely hard to think about. You know, you have these enormous concentration camps full of corpses, and then you have a city full of corpses, and, you know, is the city full of corpses right or wrong?" (Scholes 117). Taking up the cue, the interviewer reiterates the central issue, the crucial point not only for Vonnegut but most American writers dealing with the war and Germany, a point implied in the dynamics of "going native," namely the existential question, "how do you tell the good guys from the bad guys in a situation like this?" (Scholes 118).

Like Mailer and Dick's novels, Slaughterhouse-Five thus gravitates towards the erasure of the boundaries between the self and the other, because it is precisely impossible to tell who the good guys are and who the bad. And once again something like the descent into hell, the journey into the "devil's territories," in Vonnegut's novel the journey of the POWs into the heart of Germany and their eventual withdrawal into the meat-locker of the Dresden slaughterhouse, which serves as an improvised shelter from the inferno raging above and around them, results in this breakdown of dividing lines. Yet, Vonnegut chooses not to elaborate the critique of American (foreign) policies implied by the Dresden incident, and instead uses its critical potential to argue against war in general. "I think the only thing I have been able to think of doing as a result of seeing the destruction of that city there and knowing at the same time about the great crimes of Germany is to become [...] a pacifist" (Scholes 118). As a result of this pacifism, the fire-bombing of Dresden becomes just another war-time atrocity, however terrible and haunting, and Slaughterhouse-Five as a historical account loses its latent potential for a specific cultural critique. The novel does not examine the pertinent moral issues confronting post-war America, the limits of moral self-righteousness, and transmutes instead into an exploration of a universal, individualistic, and personal response to the realities of war in general.

Like Vonnegut's novel, Mario Puzo's The Dark Arena (1955) does not make a critical commentary on American culture and politics its primary focus. The "dark arena" that Puzo explores in his narrative is of a personal nature, as he makes clear in the prefacing epigraph, an excerpt from Dostoevsky's Brothers Karamasov: "What is hell? I maintain that it is the suffering of being unable to love" (Puzo ii). In its broad outlines somewhat reminiscent of Hemingway's A Farewell to Arms, the novel charts the alienation of its American protagonist, Walter Mosca, from his country as a result of the war, and his affair with a German woman, Hella. Although Mosca loves Hella, he has lost the respect for himself and his culture. Struggling with the contradictions of war -- "they said this is good today and tomorrow they said you're evil, a murderer, a wild animal, and they made you believe it so much you helped hunt yourself down" (Puzo 157) -- and moreover unable and seemingly unwilling to adjust to a civilian life of normalcy with all its necessary pretenses, Mosca soon goes back as occupation official to "the land of the enemy" after his release from the army.

Like Frederick Henry in Hemingway's novel, Walter Mosca tries to make a separate peace with the "enemy," so to speak, tries to disassociate himself from the political and cultural enterprise of his country. Witness to the seemingly arbitrary nature of good and evil in wartime and repulsed by the pretense of justice and a just cause, Mosca finds fault with the hypocrisy of official discourse about the war, the fiction of good guys and bad. "And he wasn't complaining, that was the world, he wasn't indignant. But when they pulled all the other shit with this and tried to make you feel ashamed and tried to say it was right, justice, then it was shit" (Puzo 157). As a result, he feels that "he hated all the mothers and fathers and sisters and brothers, sweethearts and wives that he saw in the newspapers, the newsreels, in brightly colored magazines." And with acerbic irony Mosca concludes, "But you couldn't blame them because our cause was just" (Puzo 159). Disgusted by his country's pretenses, Mosca, like Hemingway's hero, attempts to define a space for personal happiness outside of history. The "dark arena" of Mosca's struggle is of a personal as much as cultural nature, and although one of his friends charges, "you exercise no free will when you fight on your level, in your narrow circle, your little, personal, arena" (Puzo 195), Mosca's anxieties resonate with those of his culture.

Of course, Mosca's as much as Frederick Henry's attempt to define a space for personal happiness finally fails. Parallel to Frederick Henry's escape to Switzerland and his wife Catherine's subsequent death in childbirth, Hella dies from a simple infection that turns into deadly blood-poisoning because of the low quality of black market penicillin (a narrative turn probably inspired by The Third Man), and Mosca hunts down the dealer who sold him the diluted drugs and kills him.

But more importantly, Mosca's story once again dramatizes the process of "going native," which is motivated by a critical appraisal of his culture vis à vis that of the cultural "other." Mosca distances himself from the occupation enterprise and the clear-cut role as conqueror through his involvement with Hella, whom he wants to marry and ultimately take back with him to the States. With his petition for naturalization of Hella, Mosca suddenly finds himself dependent on the American military bureaucracy and thus in a position analogous to that of the Germans under the occupation. Moreover, when two American nurses mistake him, Hella and their baby for a German family and leave them some chocolate, Mosca realizes that he has come a long way, that perhaps he has already crossed the cultural line between conquerors and conquered: "He had been frightened, as if they [he, Hella and the baby] were really Germans, and had to accept charity, humiliation as one of the conquered" (Puzo 235).

Finally, both Mosca's return to Germany after his release from the army and his ever deepening involvement with Hella, result from a disenchantment with the hypocrisies of the dominant American discourse about the war. As a soldier, Mosca realizes the false pretensions of casting the war as a crusade against tyranny and for democracy. The intentional and cold-blooded murder of an escaped German POW by American MPs (foreshadowing the real My Lai debacle a decade later) that Mosca witnesses and does not stop provides the object lesson for him. Like the German in the moments before his death, "a look of horror [on his face], as if he had seen some terrible and shameful thing in which he had never believed" (Puzo 101), Mosca has seen the self as other and loses faith in the Americans, and the moral superiority of his own culture. Told by endless propaganda harangues that it was only the SS barbarians who killed escapees by turning them loose and then shooting them in the back (a depiction later also perpetuated in films like The Great Escape and others of the same genre), to Mosca it must seem as if the American MPs had suddenly been transformed into Nazi stormtroopers, the good guys become the bad, the moral difference collapsed between the enemy and yourself. "He felt no emotion, only a slight physical nausea and internal looseness" (Puzo 102), but eventually he realizes that as accomplice to even if not perpetrator of the war crime, "he had lost everything inside himself" (Puzo 158), his sense of self respect and self worth, because, as he recalls later, "afterward, I was ashamed and surprised, but I never felt pity and I know that's bad" (Puzo 103). Morally and emotionally, Mosca has thus and then become indistinguishable from the enemy, even if he does not yet realize it. But instead of mourning that loss of personal innocence and personal moral superiority, Mosca blames his country and its duplicity in insisting on moral difference from the enemy.

The collapse of (moral) difference exemplified by the murder of the German POW and the resulting disillusionment is precisely what is dramatized again and again in the narrative dynamic of "going native," thematically so conspicuous in American postwar accounts of Germany. Mosca's personal doubts about his culture thus parallel and express his culture's anxieties. The Dark Arena explores these anxieties, questioning the righteousness of the American cause, and like Mailer, Dick, Kubrick, and Vonnegut, Puzo seems to erode the moral dividing line between Americans and Germans and to break down supposedly essential difference. In the climactic scene of the novel, after he has killed the black market dealer and thus become an outlaw, Mosca realizes that he has severed all bonds to his country, that he has gone native for good: "Finally he had become the enemy" (Puzo 307). Like the MPs, he has killed for revenge, in cold blood, and has thus lost his innocence.

Going native as a theme was even exploited as a superficial plot device by William G. Beymer in Middle of Midnight (1947), which the New York Times Book Review characterized as "a martial rigadoon that will keep you amused, if not entirely convinced" (13 Apr. 47, 35). The novel is set in a fictional Bavarian village, on which the increasingly powerful Nazi underground converges. Among the villains the perennial German rocket scientist, ruthless Professor Schweinitz, who, as it turns out, is developing a nuclear device; the leaders of the underground sullen Kurt Essen and the dominating and beautiful "Queen of Poison," Erika Wolf. Unable to break up or even get a clear picture of the activities of the Nazi resistance, the U.S. army coincidentally finds out that Kurt

Essen has an identical twin brother. Separated from his brother at birth, Rod Braun has been living in America for some years and has served in the army. On special request he volunteers to return to duty, and the army succeeds in switching the two brothers and having Rod assume the position of Kurt inside the Nazi underground.

Predictably, Rod weathers the trials and tribulations arising from his infiltration, solves the mystery of the secret weapon, and together with a company of occupation troops accomplishes the eradication of the Nazi underground in a final shootout that climaxes in the nuclear self-destruction of Professor Schweinitz' lab inside a mountain.

Middle of Midnight cannot be but described as a cheap or not very sophisticated thriller, but the device of the lost twin seems to sum up the prevalent attitude towards Germany in the repeated dramatizations of Americans going native. Although Beymer does not even begin to realize its potential, the twin image provides the most striking expression for the (American) cultural self as other (German), encapsulating the trajectory of identification and non-identification, and the eradication of perceptible difference. After all, like Young Goodman Brown, Mailer, Greene, Vonnegut, Kubrick and Puzo's characters all embark on quests for their dark and hidden personal, moral and/or cultural selves. Like the double motif and a Dr. Jekyll's anxieties about a Mr. Hyde, an unknown, "hidden" self, the preoccupation with the process of going native expresses the fear that beneath a thin coating of civilization lurks animal nature, that a perfunctory democratic layer only thinly masks proto-fascist social structures, or that the supposed moral and political superiority of America is empty rhetoric and nothing else.

It becomes clear that in the postwar period, American authors and film makers have consistently utilized representations of Germany in their predominantly negative commentaries on their own country and culture. Among the examples of this practice -- and clearly, I have not attempted to be exhaustive in my choice of them -- two texts stand out and merit even more detailed consideration than the works discussed so far. In a later chapter, I consider in detail the prime example of this practice, Thomas Pynchon's gargantuan novel Gravity's Rainbow, which constructs almost a whole manichean cosmology around the supposed

German sickness of the Western mind. But for now, we will take a closer look at William Gardner Smith's novel of education <u>The Last of the Conquerors,</u> which constructs Germany as imaginary space for an African-American utopia, as a <u>positive</u> alternative to white America. While Smith's novel clearly articulates American concerns with reference to Germany, it also intervenes in a more direct and specific way in a contemporary political debate (over civil rights) than the examples considered so far.

Chapter Two - In the Land of Evil I: Germany as African-American Utopia

American post-World War II literature often depicted Germany as the cultural and political "other," as "that which America is not," as we have seen in the second part of the previous chapter. Moreover, we have also seen that the political and historical example of Nazi Germany was also used as warning, taken as dark endpoint of a threatening development away from American democratic traditions. But at the same time Germany was also described -- perhaps paradoxically -- as a positive alternative to America, as social utopia by African-American GIs who experienced overseas a degree of racial equality and personal liberty not granted them at home.

William Gardner Smith's novel <u>The Last of the Conquerors</u> (1948) grows out of dominant African-American perceptions and experiences of the occupied country at the time, I will argue, but also perpetuates and inverts the customary pattern of American representations of Germany described earlier. Similarly, Kay Boyle looks at America from abroad in "The Lost" and even utilizes the perspective of a Black GI in "Home," both short stories about Germany during the occupation collected in <u>The Smoking Mountain</u>. Just as Smith, Boyle -- a White author with a liberal political agenda -- uses her fictional protagonist's perceptions and evaluations of Germany for a critique of racial segregation in America, as we will see. Smith's novel and Boyle's short stories are almost unique among imaginative encounters between America and Germany, and in constructing Germany as a utopian space the two texts constitute the opposite approach to the more common examples which saw the country as a dystopic point of reference for their critiques of America; at the same time, the pieces also constitute some of the most striking examples of the self-critical function inherent in the process of creating the image of another country.

Before we take a closer look at how Smith constructs occupied Germany as positive counterspace to contemporary America and how

Boyle uses it for a critique of her own country, however, it will be necessary to make some remarks about the situation of African-American soldiers during and after World War II and to reconstruct some of the historical background for this curious construction of Germany as utopian social and cultural space.

"Double V": African-Americans and World War II

The second world war profoundly changed the relations between Black and White in America, and marks the beginning of many developments that came into full fruition during the civil rights struggle in the late 1950's and 1960's. During World War I, W.E.B. DuBois had urged African-Americans to forgo their campaign for equal rights and to align themselves with the dominant mood in the country in the name of national unity. The Black constituency had gained nothing by that tactic and thus, on the eve of World War II Black leaders insisted on civil rights concessions before the Black community would wholeheartedly join in the war effort.

Largely by-passed by New Deal reform, African-American leaders saw the war as a chance for empowerment. Although Eleanor Roosevelt had long taken a keen interest in the Black question, the president himself generally chose to soft-pedal Black issues in order not to alienate Southern democrats whose support he needed for his New Deal reform programs. Revisionist historian Barton J. Bernstein has pointed out that "in general, what the Negroes gained [during the New Deal] -- relief, WPA jobs, equal pay on some federal projects -- was granted them as poor people, not as Negroes" (Bernstein 279). Overall, New Deal relief agencies preserved Jim Crow practices, and industry as well as the unions discriminated against Blacks (Blum, V was for Victory 182).

While the prospering defense industry had largely solved the problem of White unemployment by late 1940, Black workers continued to suffer the woes of economic depression and had yet to profit from the new boom by that time. The leader of the Brotherhood of Sleeping Car Porters, A. Philip Randolph began to organize an African-American march on Washington in 1941, to "exact [Black] rights in National Defense employment and the armed forces" (quoted in Mead 224). Randolph finally called off the march after he was placated by the president, who signed an executive order ensuring Blacks equal opportunity in the burgeoning state-sponsored defense industry, and created a Fair Employment Practices Committee to oversee its implementation. (The march on Washington was to become a reality two decades later under the leadership of Martin Luther King, Jr.). But in spite of the presidential decree, only the realities of wartime production demands eventually effected real change in the economic situation of Blacks. The war increased manpower demand on an extreme scale, and hiring and training practices had to be changed eventually to meet the production demands of the American war machine. Although Black leaders had to fight for broader representation of Blacks in vocational training programs and in positions of skilled labor, and although all too often Blacks were only hired grudgingly because White labor was in short supply, "as the war ended, Negroes proudly noted their contribution to building the huge war machine so important to the eventual victory. Millions of Negroes participated in war work, and many held positions formerly denied to them" (Buchanan 42).

In hindsight, it seems fair to say that America's fight against Nazi Germany and its racist ideology immensely helped the civil right cause, since it exposed the contradictions of the democratic rhetoric of freedom and equality aimed oversees that obviously glossed over the racial realities at home. Both the contradictions in White America's self conceptions and the struggle between the two nations later in the war were foreshadowed in the contributions of Black athletes to U.S. victories over German contenders, most importantly in Jesse Owens' field and track performance at the 1936 Olympics in Berlin and in the two Joe Louis-Max Schmeling boxing bouts in 1936 and 1937.

Adolf Hitler's refusal to meet fourfold gold medalist Jesse Owens at the Berlin Olympics demonstrated to the American public at large, which usually could not care less for the political ideologies of distant lands, the racial theories of the Nazis. While they probably would have objected to the virulence of Hitler's racial ideas, the everyday realities of White America attested to comparable views of racial superiority and the justification of cultural separateness (later to be termed 'apartheid'). The issue, however, was not merely that Hitler had snubbed Owens as the member of a racial minority, but rather that he had insulted the African-American athlete as the representative symbol of a national <u>idea</u> of equality. Consequently, the press made Owens into a figurehead for the values of American democracy and had found perfect occasion for a political indictment of Nazi Germany. Considering that the Nazis had made every effort to play down their political extremism on occasion of the Olympics in order to placate world opinion, Hitler's failure to pay his respects to the premier American athlete was a major public relations snafu.[19] Yet, the symbolic confrontation between a democratic

---

[19] Owens biographer William J. Baker (in a well-researched and thoughtful study) has suggested that Hitler never intentionally slighted Owens and in this one case might have been a victim of his schedule and of the patriotic sensationalism of the American press. Trying to correct the historical record, Baker points out that Hitler had received two German athletes and a Finnish contender on the morning of the first day of the games, but in the afternoon of the same day left the stadium before African-American high-jumper Cornelius Johnson was awarded the gold medal -- either because the Führer had to leave anyway and it started to rain, or because he did not want to meet Johnson. Owens only won his first gold medal the next day, and, according to Baker, by that time Hitler no longer individually congratulated any gold-medalists, after the president of the Olympic committee had insisted, as host of the games, the German Chancellor either had to meet all victors or, none. In a curious dynamic of its own, the American press first reported that Hitler had not received the American athletes, then claimed that he had refused to see Black athletes, until finally arriving at what would become a politically convenient and historically canonized half-truth, namely that the Führer would not meet Jesse Owens. Baker points out that "ignorant of [the Olympic president's] instructions and confident of its ability to read Hitler's motives, the American press shifted the focus of the snub yarn away from Cornelius Johnson onto Jesse Owens. Every new medal won by Owens enhanced his appeal as the target of Hitler's supposed insult" (91). Baker also suggests that Hitler might not have been ill-inclined towards Owens after all, and reports that Owens mentioned at a radio news

America and a racist Germany would prove convenient for polemical purposes before the U.S. formally entered the war, and made good propaganda later. But more importantly, Owens learned that although America had embraced him as a standard-bearer of democracy, it was not going to bend its racial customs for him or for his family, and on his return to New York found out that several hotels had refused to lodge his parents, who had come to the city to welcome him (cf. Baker 123).

For several reasons, boxer Joe Louis rather than Jesse Owens became the foremost symbol of democratic values for Blacks and Whites alike during World War II. "To a country deeply divided along racial lines, yet desperately wanting to believe it was united against a common foe," biographer Chris Mead sums up Louis' broad appeal, the victorious opponent of Nazi sympathizer Max Schmeling "was a symbol of national unity" (214). Unlike Jesse Owens, who faded comparatively fast from the headlines after his Olympic success (mainly because his desperate attempts to translate his athletic success into monetary gain made him into a pathetic figure who would race against horses, automobiles and trains), Louis' moved in the sporting limelight from 1935 to 1949, years that framed and contained the war. Moreover, the one-on-one confrontation between Louis and Max Schmeling, and the Louis' comeback in the second bout after his defeat in their first match (adumbrating, as it were, America's defeat at Pearl Harbor and the country's consequent comeback) struck a more receptive chord in the public imagination than the indirect and coincidental conflict between Hitler and Owens. Although Owens may have been first in standing up to Hitler, Joe Louis became "the first American to kayo [sic!] a Nazi" (quoted in Mead 221).

When war with Germany finally came, Louis proved a knack for knockout punches not only as a boxer but also as a patriot. Although rather apprehensive as speaker before a crowd, he coined one of the most famous lines spawned by the ideological effort to win the war when he exclaimed: "We gon [sic!] do our part, and we will win, because we are on God's side" (quoted in Mead 218). In fights for military charities and

---

conference shortly after his first victory that "on his way up the stadium steps, he thought he saw Hitler smiling and waving to him. Jesse waved back" (94).

later in his voluntary enlistment in the army, Louis both became a powerful means to sell the war to Black America and a kind of ideological alibi for "whites eager to prove that they were more tolerant than their racist enemies" (Mead 236), because it was so easy to identify and love him. Yet, Louis' efforts for the common patriotic cause also highlighted the inequities of a society that would enlist its minority members to fight for ideals and rights it did not grant them themselves. Thus critics of Louis' fights for a navy charity pointed out that African-Americans were restricted to menial service jobs in that branch of the armed forces. Yet, Louis refused to make civil-rights concerns part of his agenda, fearful of antagonizing a White public. Because of the obvious symbolism of his bouts with Schmeling and because he fulfilled African-American dreams of social mobility as well as White expectations about "good" Blacks, Louis was able to inspire a sense of unity in the American public in general. Not surprisingly, "white Americans found it easier to give Joe Louis a medal than to integrate the army, easier to write an editorial praising Joe Louis than to hire a black reporter," his biographer sums up the boxer's symbolic function, and concludes that "perhaps whites needed to accept a Joe Louis before they could begin to think about justice for all blacks" (Mead 236).

Indeed, America as a whole woke up to the realities of racial conflict that since the Civil War had mainly affected the South, when the huge demographic changes in American life precipitated by the war, most importantly the "shift of Negroes from agrarian to urban life" (Buchanan 131) on a large scale, spread those problems across the nation. In addition, the army did its part, and "many northern whites in the military witnessed conditions in the South which previously they had only read about [, and] even larger numbers of southern whites carried their ideas of race relationships to the North and West" (Buchanan 131). As a result, "the question of the Negro's place in society ceased to be mainly a southern concern and became a national issue" (Buchanan 131). A series of race riots woke Middle America to the ongoing demographic changes and to the new importance of race as a national rather than just Southern question. As cultural historian John Morton Blum points out, "racial antagonism infected all cities to which war industries attracted millions of workers, white and black" (Blum, V was for Victory 199).

Sparked by a housing shortage and widespread White working-class discontent vented against Blacks, race riots erupted in Detroit in June 1943, leaving twenty-five Blacks and nine Whites dead. Earlier the same month, Los Angeles saw the "zoot suit" riots, racially motivated clashes between White servicemen and predominantly Black and Hispanic youths (the "zoot suiters"). To many Blacks, the contradictions between the global fight for freedom and democracy and the realities of racism at home could not have been thrown into relief more starkly, and as a letter to the then president of the NAACP made clear, many of them asked themselves: "Why are these race riots going on there in Detroit and in other cities in this land -- supposedly the land of freedom, equality and brotherhood?" (White 125).

However, it was not only African-American leaders who were concerned about the racial situation. Sensitive to the free world's need for credibility in the global struggle against totalitarianism, the author of a Harper's article charged that "morally speaking, nothing that is being done in the United States to-day gives the Axi [sic!] powers a better opportunity to condemn democracy than the treatment of our colored citizens" (Brown, "American Negroes" 552). And indeed, the Axis powers soon began to capitalize on such unresolved Allied contradictions as the British colonial empire's alleged fight for freedom. Especially "in Asia the Japanese claimed to be fighting against the domination of White, European colonialism, not least as it weighed upon the corrupt government of China" (Blum, V was for Victory 183). Moreover, many American Blacks also began to ask themselves, "what the hell do we want to fight the Japs for anyhow? They couldn't possibly treat us any worse than these 'crackers' right here at home" (Brown, "American Negroes" 547). Similarly, as Blum reports, some radical Blacks rather naively claimed that "Hitler has not done anything to the colored people -- it's the people right here in the United States who are keeping us out of work and keeping us down" (quoted in Blum, V was for Victory 184). Yet, the official NAACP organ The Crisis took a more level course and advised its readers that wartime sacrifice should be "for a new world which not only shall not contain a Hitler, but not Hitlerism" and that "the fight against Hitlerism begins in Washington, D.C., the capital of your nation, where Black Americans have a status only slightly above that of

Jews in Berlin" (Crisis Jan. 1942, 7). In summary, The Crisis also made clear how African-Americans should situate themselves ideologically, pointing out that they should fight only for "the democratic ideal as enunciated by America and by our British ally" and not for perpetuation of "many of the practices which have been -- and are still -- in vogue here and in the British empire" (Crisis Jan. 1942, 7). The Black community realized that it faced a fight on two fronts, against a foreign and a domestic enemy. Analogous to the ubiquitous "V for Victory" slogan, Black leadership "soon advocated a 'Double V' symbolizing victory at home as well as abroad" (Buchanan 113).

African-Americans' divided loyalties and the ideological contradictions created by White racism were thrown into particularly stark relief in the segregated armed forces. Concerning racial integration, the military differed little from society at large. The brass for the most part refused to -- as they put it -- experiment with desegregation and sought to prevent all changes of the racist status quo with repeated and stubborn reference to the general mores of society. Pointing out that their job was military efficiency, officials stressed that "the Army is not a sociological laboratory" (Buchanan 67) and that "the army did not create the [race] problem, that the army consisted of people with individual views, and that an army order could not change these views" (Buchanan 67). Yet, to many Black observers it rather seemed that Southern elements in the army were "more vigorously engaged in fighting the Civil War than in training soldiers to resist Hitler" (Reynolds 289). Similarly, Black soldiers often felt that they, rather than the Japanese or Germans, were the real threat to White officers, and in turn began to redraw the battle lines for themselves. Thus, for instance, in his inquiry into the effects of the war on Blacks in America, A Rising Wind (1945), then NAACP president Walter White noted how he "was puzzled at the frequency, despondency, and bitterness of the use of the phrase 'the enemy' [and how he] soon learned that Negro soldiers referred not to the Nazis across the Channel but to their white fellow Americans" (White 18).

Initially not represented in the elite Marines and Air Force at all, African-Americans were mainly relegated to auxiliary functions in the army and navy at the outset of the war. An overall quota existed for their number in the armed forces and even before the start of the war, Blacks "were increasingly annoyed because restrictions were imposed on young men who wished to join the armed services and because of the injustices they met when they did" (Buchanan 15). By 1943, concerned about Black frustration about their role in the military, the highest ranking African-American, General Davis, advised the military leadership that Black troops be immediately used in combat functions in a forward area. By early February of the same year, the War Department recommended that Black "units be introduced into combat ... and that schedules if necessary be changed" (quoted in Buchanan 94). As Walter White points out, Blacks thus faced the absurd situation of having to "fight for the right to fight" (White 47).

Wartime and battlefield pressures in many cases effected desegregation and profoundly changed race relations in the military. But, as Ebony pointed out, "with the war over and the desperate need for manpower on the wane, cordiality between colored and white GIs has ebbed accordingly. White career officers (many of them from the South) are openly displaying their prejudices" ("Germany meets" 7). Indeed, many observers noted White resentment about the cracking of the color line, and Newsweek stressed that "in their attitude toward Negro troops, many Americans are more virulent than a large number of Germans" (Newsweek 24 Dec. 45, 50). Similarly, a sociological study about GI attitudes towards Europeans concluded that "the absence of a color line in Europe -- in particular, the American Negro soldier's freedom to associate with white civilian girls -- stirred most southern whites and many northerners to extreme anger" (Glaser 434). Yet, other Whites, who had come to appreciate the performance of Black troops during the war, condemned the relapse into racism and pointed out the hypocrisy of renewed stricter enforcement of segregation policies after the cessation of hostilities. In a letter to the editors of Life, a White GI remarked: "I had felt if the Negroes worked and proved themselves worthy of democracy they would obtain it. But now I see that I was wrong to have thought such a thing. [...] The Negro in this war has proven himself entitled to the benefits of democracy above and beyond the call of expectation. If this be denied then we are frauds" (Life 29 Oct. 45, 8). The Crisis similarly denounced the army's "unamerican treatment" of its Black troops which was made worse by the "loud voices telling him what a great honor it is to die for his country" (Reynolds 289). Frustrated about the lack of substantial positive change in race relations even towards the end of the war, Walter White charged that at least "World War II has immeasurably magnified the Negro's awareness of the disparity between the American profession and practice of democracy" (White 142).

The internationalization and export of American racial prejudices through and in the fight against Nazism provided the most telling image of this disparity between American democratic practice and rhetoric. After a tour of Europe in 1945, Walter White noted with horror that "there had been an almost complete transference of the American pattern of racial attitudes to English soil" (White 33), and that racial tensions in the Theater of Operations had resulted because "white American soldiers, particularly those coming from the South, were infuriated when some British women clearly emphasized a preference for Negro soldiers" (White 48). In spite of the questionable colonial policies of their government, the British population was mostly on the side of the Black soldiers and "resented the attitude of white American soldiers toward the Negro" (Buchanan 91). As Walter White reports, this support even went so far that in a racially motivated fight at a dance "the British took the side of the Negroes" (White 11). White concluded at the end of the war that "race prejudice and the memories of racial misbehavior by Americans have already become a part of the British concept of Americans" (White 146).

In spite of the general tendencies towards an institution of America-style racial segregation in postwar Europe, African-Americans abroad still experienced a degree of freedom and equality unthinkable at home. Black troops found things particularly to their liking in conquered Germany. Newly-founded Ebony in 1947 gave the situation of Black GIs in occupied Germany extended coverage. The report provides a welter of photographs depicting interracial fraternization in clubs, on the streets, and in the family circle, and tries to account for the popularity of occupation duty in Germany amongst Black troops by pointing out that "Army pay and working conditions are for many GIs better than what they could get back home in the South" ("Germany meets" 6). An Ebony correspondent also noted with amazement that "strangely enough, here where Aryanism ruled supreme, Negroes are finding more friendship, more respect and more equality than they would back home -- either in Dixie or on Broadway" ("Germany Meets" 5). The journalist concedes that "most [fräuleins] become friendly with soldiers out of self-interest, to get cigarettes, coffee, soap and other rare items," but also made it clear that the experiences of Black GIs in Germany did not just make a personal difference but rather had momentous political implications as well: "Many of the Negro GIs in the German capital are from the South and find that democracy has more meaning on the Wilhelmstrasse than on Beale Street in Memphis" ("Germany Meets" 5).

Although the article does not say it in so many words, it is clear that for many African-American GIs, military service and occupation duty in Germany provided an unforgettable object lesson about the difference between democratic rhetoric and practice in America. Summing up the positive effects of the war on Blacks, Walter White noted in 1945 that although American forces in general obviously took with them their racial prejudices, for many African-American GIs, their tour abroad also put into perspective for the first time the relationship between the races at home. "For many of the Negroes," White concludes, going abroad "was their first experience in being treated as normal human beings and friends by white people" (White 21).

"The Feel of Being Free": William Gardner Smith's The Last of the Conquerors

The surprisingly positive representation of Germany in African-American eyewitness accounts during the occupation, and the incipient cultural critique that they imply, is fleshed out in William Gardner Smith's The Last of the Conquerors, which constructs Germany not as dark opposite of America, but rather takes the foreign culture as a model for positive change in racial relations at home. Smith came to Germany in mid-1946 and was stationed in Berlin in a maintenance unit for eight months. His fictional account of a Black GIs experiences in postwar Germany is obviously based on his own impressions as a member of the occupation force, although he might have found a model in James Weldon Johnson, who had conceived of Berlin in similar utopian terms in his Autobiography of an Ex-Colored Man (1912).[20] The Last of the Conquerors is not primarily concerned with the discovery of another culture, but rather focuses on the invention of a cultural counter-space to American realities. Smith's protagonist and first person narrator, Hayes Dawkins, really explores America in his discovery of postwar Germany.

On the passage to Germany, Hayes gets close to two other Black GIs, the Professor and Randy, and together the three friends become complementary elements of a composite narrative consciousness. Randy is impulsive, an outspoken and ardent German-hater, and initially personifies the official wartime American stance on Germany and the Germans. The Professor functions as the author's alter ego. A journalist in civilian life (like Smith himself), his evaluations and descriptions throughout the novel provide a kind of objective commentary. Both Randy and the Professor are almost like externalized and objectified parts of Hayes' emerging consciousness who articulate many of the insights that yet escape the first person narrator .

Hayes and his two friends end up in Berlin in the office of a Quartermaster company. The unit also employs a number of German women in clerical and menial functions. It is in the interaction with these German women that Hayes slowly begins to realize the paradoxical character of his situation as a Black American GI. He finds that as an American he has to represent the values of democracy to the Germans, but that at the same time as a Black soldier he cannot fully enjoy the fruits of that democracy. Hayes and his friends thus encounter particular difficulties in trying to maintain their cultural identity in the foreign country. Two apposite incidents circumscribe this quandary.

In the first incident, Hayes's friend Randy, to whom all Germans are still "no-good bastards" and "Hitler's children" (Smith, Last of the Conquerors 35; LC henceforth), gets into an argument with a German girl who champions a more differentiated view and tries to exculpate at least

---

[20] In his autobiography, Johnsen relates how, when he was taken to Europe by a white benefactor, he experienced firsthand what it meant to live without a color line, and found that he was accepted as a fellow-musician and composer in educated white circles from London to Berlin. -- For details on William Gardner Smith's biography see LeRoy S. Hodges' study.

part of the German population. But Randy remains adamant and insists that "all of you are the same. Every damn one of you" (ibid.). The argument takes an even nastier turn when one of the German women points out the contradictions in Randy's position and slyly remarks: "How can you talk? What about the white Americans? In your country you may not walk down the street with a white woman. The white Americans hang you from trees if you do " (LC 35). Predictably, Randy is upset because the German woman ever so subtly hints that the Americans' democracy is after all not that much different from Hitlerism. Although Randy cannot but refuse to acknowledge the obvious shortcomings in American democratic practice, his argument with the German woman brings up the central conflict in the Black GIs' position. Attacked by the Germans, they have to defend their country, although it so far denied them their full rights.

The second and apposite incident that makes Hayes recognize his position outside of American dominant culture dramatizes what Walter White described as the most important experience of African-Americans in World War II, namely a rising awareness of the "disparity between the American profession and practice of democracy" (White 142). Ilse, one of the German women who work in the company, asks Hayes out on a date to go to the Wannsee lake with her. Lying in the sun Hayes suddenly realizes that here in Germany for the first time in his life he experiences racial equality. "Odd, it seemed to me, that here, in the land of hate, I should find this one all-important phase of democracy. And suddenly I felt bitter" (LC 44). Although this bitterness is probably nothing new for Hayes and many other African-Americans like him, it takes on a different quality because as a soldier in Germany he is an ambassador of democracy, a salesman for goods he cannot acquire. When Ilse, the German girl, muses that it must be wonderful in America, Hayes replies: "'America,' I said to the white woman, to the Bilbo, to the Talmadge, 'is a wonderful land where everyone is guaranteed a fair deal regardless of race, creed, religion, national origin, or parentage. It's the land of the Common Man, Mr. Pegler wincing, where all are guaranteed the right to life, liberty and the pursuit of happiness. Amen'" (LC 44f.). The emergence of a sarcastic voice in this passage marks the first step in his education and the development of the utopian vision centered on

Germany. In his little speech he also addresses a double audience: the German Ilse and White Americans at home. Hayes has begun to situate his own cultural identity in the interstices between occupied Germany and White America by articulating the contradictions arising from his position as disfranchised member of the occupation force supposedly bringing democracy to the conquered country.

Overall, <u>The Last of the Conquerors</u> can be divided into three narrative strands: Hayes's love affair with Ilse, the increasing harassment of Black GIs by their White commanders, and Hayes's re-evaluation of his country and development of a utopian vision centered on Germany.

Hayes gets a first glimpse of what is in store for him and is reminded that his tour of Germany is in some sense only a holiday from reality, when one of his friends is due to return to the States. Initially, that friend had pictured his repatriation in glowing terms, a future in college, life in Chicago, a family of his own; but it soon transpires that he has merely imaginatively constructed a better life for himself and has only poverty and misery to greet him on his return. Hayes commiserates with his friend, and tells him that he understands his desperation. His friend, however answers: "No, you don't understand. [...] You ain't been away from all that sh-- as long as I have. You ain't got the feel of being free. I like this goddamn country, you know that? [...] It's the first place I was ever treated like a goddamn man" (LC 67). Hayes' friend has disowned his country; in a sense he has been de-Americanized and identifies with the country he has come to occupy. There, in Germany, he can invent a different and ideal self. Germany affords him with the space to articulate what he has been denied at home. Germany has thus become the American "internal other," providing a vision of an alternative life and self.

Hayes's process of self-invention and definition continues when he is made to confront the idealized image that America paints of itself in the movies. When Ilse questions him on his background, his family, and life in the United States, Hayes's narrative consciousness undergoes a split that is anticipated in the earlier emergence of an ironical voice. His earlier outburst at the lake dramatized the overall denial of basic democratic rights to African-Americans. But now Hayes particularizes this denial and wistfully imagines a life different from the realities in the slums when Ilse asks him: "how is your home? Do you have a car? Did you go many times to the night clubs such as I see in the American movies? Did you have much money?" (LC 74). In answer, Hayes lies that "yes, we have a car. A very big car. I have gone to many night clubs and they have been much like the ones you see in the movies" (LC 74). But then, in an interspersed passage, italicized to denote the shift to interior monologue, Hayes remembers what life really was like in his hometown. He remembers the cramped and dirty, roach-infested house in the slums. Of course, there were no glitzy nightclubs in his neighborhood and he recalls that "I had seen such night clubs as this girl spoke of, as she had seen in the movies, as I had seen many times in the movies, as were always shown in the movies, as if everyone really went to them -- I had seen such night clubs, or night clubs nearly the same, but only from the outside in Philadelphia" (LC 76). In fact, to Hayes it seems that Germany comes closer to the good life depicted in Hollywood movies than the realities he knew at home. Originally embarked on his tour abroad as a kind of adventure, curious to learn more about the Germans and their way of life, in the meeting of the two cultures Hayes for the first time fully discovers his own country and his own origins. And in this meeting of the two cultures, Germany functions as positive counter-image that contrasts with and directly criticizes the negative cultural image of America.

The dark side of American social reality and the prevalent racism within the military find expression when the generally agreeable White commander of Hayes's unit comes to the Black GIs' social club and gets drunk. Hayes, his friends and the captain begin to discuss the occupied country and the officer remarks that the absence of democratic freedoms lead to the political and moral excesses in Germany. He goes on that "Such things as a free press, free speech, free labor -- these things the Germans have never had. Not recently. It's sad. Led to distortion. Led to mass hysteria, to sadism, to war mongering" (LC 104). But he also believes that Hitler did at least one good thing, to get rid of the Jews, and that America should adopt a similar course. Hayes and his friends realize that in spite of his agreeable character, the officer after all is not all that different from the Nazis they conquered. In this light, the captain's earlier analysis of the Nazi phenomenon also takes on a more ominous meaning. With the captain, who had earlier quite convincingly claimed that the absence of democratic freedoms led to fascism in Germany, Smith seems to imply in his novel that similarly the lack of democratic equality might eventually lead to yet another cataclysmic struggle -- in America. Even as negative parallel, Germany as the cultural other still functions as projection of the American internal other, as image of America's dark and hidden potentials.

Shortly after this episode, Hayes and all the other Black GIs are transferred to another garrison in the heart of Germany, a move intended to concentrate all Black troops in one area in order to isolate them from the rest of the occupying army. Life in the new garrison town, Bremburg, differs considerably from that in Berlin. Restricted to camp for their unit's high venereal disease rate, Hayes and his friends have in fact been ghettoized, or even worse, almost transplanted into the pre-Civil War South in a plantation-like setup under the command of a "white cracker" from Texas and his overseer, an "Uncle Tom" first sergeant. Obviously, the Black GIs are not the only American group (re)making the occupied country and inventing it as an American space. As much as the Black GIs, the White pseudo slave-masters seize on Germany as a chance to realize their social and cultural ideals.

While the inevitable conflict between the commanding captain and one of the Black soldiers, a sergeant, builds, the love story between Hayes and Ilse also develops when she comes to join him in Bremburg, staying with a civilian family. Eventually, Hayes promises Ilse that he will come back to Germany after his release from the army in the States, and that they will then live in Germany together.

The two are one night picked up by MPs, and Ilse is imprisoned for two weeks on charges of prostitution. The army is apparently trying to reeducate the German population by introducing them to American racism. Ilse later reports how when the American military official found out that she has been going out with a Black GI, he advised her that she "must know that the colored man was not like everybody else, and that an American white woman would never go out with one. He said that the colored man was dirty and very poor and with much sickness" (LC 196). The White MPs' attitude starkly contrasts with the hospitality extended to Hayes by the German friends he makes through Ilse. The episode reinforces Hayes' decision to stay on in Germany, where he thinks he can live more or less free from the dehumanizing restrictions of White racism.

Matters in the Bremburg camp come to a head when the army begins to prepare to get rid of its Black troops by discharging them dishonorably. The captain of Hayes's company asks all sergeants to sign blanks certifying the troublemaker status of all Black GIs under their command. When one of the Black sergeants refuses, he is unjustly court-martialed for insubordination. When he is about to be shipped off to serve his term, he runs amok, going after the captain and his first sergeant and killing the latter. The captain wants to get rid of Hayes, who, as a witness to the episode and its background, could jeopardize his military career. He first threatens to court-martial Hayes for a missed bed-check and then tries to bribe him with an early discharge. Disillusioned by now and realizing that opposition to the captain will only result in having his own plans for college and his future ruined, Hayes caves in and agrees to be shipped back to the States before the expiration of his term.

Before he leaves, however, the Professor, as the most articulate element of the composite narrative consciousness of Last of the Conquerors, reiterates the thematic focus of the novel and sums up the change that Hayes and his friends have undergone, how the utopian promise of the conquered country has changed their self-conception as Americans:

> I don't think I'll ever be happy at home again. [...] Before I came here I just ignored the things that went on there. I mean, I knew what was going on, I wrote about it in fact, and I hated it, but I was used to it. It had been with me all my life. Now it's different. I've gotten away from that stuff and I'll never be able to take it calmly again. [...] It'll burn me up inside and might even fill me with hate. Because I'll always remember the irony of my going away to Germany to find democracy. That's bad. (LC 238)

The Professor's evaluation of their situation is complemented and illustrated when Hayes day-dreams about and imaginatively fulfills the utopian potential of Germany by painting an idealized domestic future in a villa on the shores of the Wannsee in Berlin; the cultured dances and clubs, "everyone looking up at me in admiration, admiration, admiration ... not disdain ... because my skin is brown" (LC 239); vacations all over Europe, "with no thoughts of prejudice. Forget race. No, don't forget. Be proud because of it" (LC 240); and children, "with cocoa skin and curly hair" (LC 240). Again, and by contrast, Hayes also tries to imagine how life will be back in the States, how many lynchings, how many unemployed Blacks, how much discrimination in the unions, the schools and universities, on the streets and in politics he will encounter on his return. And summing it all up, Hayes exclaims in his dream monologue in Bremburg, projecting himself to Berlin and into the future: "Nice being here. Nice being here in Berlin. Nice being here in Germany where the Nazis once were rulers. Nice being so far away that I can wonder [about conditions in America] -- but not be affected" (LC 240). The resignation and detachment that find expression in these lines exemplify the imagined and Utopian character of Hayes's American Germany, which is conceived primarily as a projection of his own cultural hopes and desires.

"The Colored Question": Kay Boyle's View from Abroad

While occupied Germany affords William Gardner Smith with a utopian space on which to project his ideal of racial harmony and his critique of American racism, the (White) writer Kay Boyle variously uses the figure of marginalized Americans abroad in order to comment on her own culture. The protagonists of her German short fiction, collected in The Smoking Mountain (1951), are thus occupation wives, liberals in the military, children -- and Blacks, whose perspective outside the political and ideological mainstream is used for a critical view on America. The stories "The Lost" and "Home" in particular articulate a liberal critique of racial injustice in America by looking at the color question from abroad, from occupied Germany.

A less-known member of the American expatriate group in Paris between the wars, Kay Boyle only came to Germany after World War II when her husband in the diplomatic service was transferred there. In her introduction to The Smoking Mountain, Boyle admits that after having lived in France for two decades, she came to Germany "without eagerness, abhorring this country's immediate past" (Boyle 3), and that as a result of those feelings she committed herself "to a painstaking and almost completely loveless search for another face of Germany" (Boyle 4). Judging from her collected stories, the search for an alternative Germany was very much in vain. Some of her stories, and especially the journalistic introduction to The Smoking Mountain, charting a Frankfurt Nazi trial, echo widely-held contemporary American beliefs about and evaluations of the occupied country, and Boyle seems to have mainly found German hypocrisy, unwillingness to assume responsibility for the Nazi past and sheer political and ideological opportunism.

　　While Boyle's stories are to some extent a reflection of liberal American perceptions of Germany after the war, her pieces also depict the occupied country from unusual perspectives that lead to an account radically different from those written by other Americans at the time. Thus, for instance, Boyle repeatedly approaches Germany during the occupation from the vantage point of army wives, who were uniquely positioned to observe at once the traces of German monstrosity and the failures of the American occupation. The lack of political imagination and ideological intransigence that Boyle found in the occupation administration clearly foreshadow developments at home in America. (Boyle may have been particularly sensitive to the iniquities of occupation reality because of her husband's difficulties as liberal in an increasingly intolerant and jingoistic diplomatic service. Her husband was eventually suspended as diplomat during McCarthy's reign of terror). Most of Boyle's stories thus function both as an indictment of Germany in the wake of Nazism and as a critique of America on the eve of McCarthyism.

　　But most interesting for our purposes here, Boyle not only generally criticizes America in her German stories but more specifically also imagines Germany through the eyes of Black Americans in order to comment on American realities. "The Lost" and "Home," illustrate Boyle's appropriation of what could be called the promise of an African-American utopian perspective, as she describes contemporary race arrangements filtered through the uncomprehending minds of European refugee children befriended by Black GIs in the one story, and a Black GI's momentary realization of a cultural and personal "room of his own" as he takes a little German boy shopping, in the other. In both stories, however, Boyle not quite describes Germany as an alternative to and in some way superior to America, as Smith does, but rather emphasizes the redemptive function of domesticity, as it were, denied to the Blacks in both stories but possible abroad. In contrast to Smith, then, who describes Germany as African-American utopia, Boyle in her stories constructs domestic utopias which happen to be located in Germany.

In "The Lost," three children from all over Europe, who have been adopted as pets, as it were, by GIs, arrive at a orphanage set up especially for child D.P's (displaced persons), after their American protectors have been shipped home. Having lived with their soldier friends for an extended period, the three boys affect their habits of speech as well as their outlook on life. One of the boys, Italian by birth, sums up the three boys' feelings towards respective countries of origin when he claims that "I ain't no Eyetie no more, [...] I'm American. I wanna go home where my outfit's gone" (Boyle 181). As the story progresses, two of the three boys are successfully reintegrated into civilian life and activities more appropriate to their age, but the third boy refuses to give up his freedom and holds out in a nearby barn for a time, where he is fed and kept informed on developments in the orphanage by the other boys. Because he has a low opinion of the D.P. center as bureaucratic halfway house on the way to the U.S. -- "I been two and a half years in the American Army. I'm no emigrant" (Boyle 187) he remarks bitterly --he decides to hitchhike to Frankfurt and stow-away on a transatlantic flight to America. Eventually he vanishes, and the second boy is sent back to Italy, were he has a grandfather, but the third boy, Janos, is all alone it seems, except for his American friend, Charlie Madden.

Although their friends were African-American soldiers, none of the boys was aware of the complications of race yet, and in that respect still lived in a world of child-like innocence. Without surviving parents, Janos would be eligible for immigration into the U.S. -- but not for adoption by Black foster parents, as he is told by the principal of the D.P. camp. "Maybe in a combat outfit you didn't hear much talk about men being colored or men being white, or maybe you didn't pay much attention to it if you did," the woman tells him. "But over there, back home, in the States, there's the color question" (Boyle 196). Of course, Janos has trouble understanding what she means, and the principal herself feels at a loss for words to explain it as she "searched logic or history for justification of the nearly incredible story" (Boyle 196) she has to tell the boy. After waiting for a few days and asking again, if in the meantime "there wasn't no change yet in that question you was talking about -- the colored [sic!] question over there" (Boyle 197) -- Janos decides to be repatriated and to forget Charlie Madden. The redemptive power of domesticity, realized for a time between the Black GI and the orphaned war child, can only provide a glimpse of a better world and a racially integrated (American) society but not bring it about. The prototypical family (reminiscent of the relationship between Huck Finn and Jim on the Mississippi raft as space apart from and outside of America) between an African-American abroad and a lost European boy dramatizes a utopian alternative and sketches a critique of contemporary White America.

In "The Lost," both the innocent and commonsensical perspective of the boys, who are stymied by the incomprehensible realities of racism, and the social and cultural utopia afforded by the racially integrated army and wartime chaos in Europe, provide a point of articulation for Boyle's critique of her home country. Although Boyle's story is set in Germany, unlike in Smith's novel, the occupied country itself is not constructed as utopian social space, it merely serves as setting and as foreign locale apart from America that facilitates an outside view. While The Last of the Conquerors would lose much of its critical force if it were not set in Germany as "the land of evil," which paradoxically turns out to be racially more tolerant than America, Boyle could have had described events in "The Lost" against any other European background without diminishing any of its culturally critical power.

In "Home," however, the German setting more fully contributes to Boyle's cultural critique, and in the story the vestiges of German racism are depicted as a mirror image of White American attitudes towards Blacks. In the story, an African-American GI on occupation duty in Germany comes to a PX shopping center. What for White Americans is a nostalgic replica of middle America in occupied Germany, "children in their Gene Autry outfits, with rodeo holster and pistol sets strapped at their waists, and the groups of blue-jeaned high-school students passing, with their saddleback shoes, their insignia-stamped windbreakers, [that gave] this the cleavage of any Stateside town" (Boyle 150), must seem as foreign as the occupied country to the Black GI who has grown up in poverty. The PX shopping center as official space, as ideological mirage of middle America, however, is transformed into a "home" for a moment when the GI picks up a freezing little German boy and takes him inside.

Against the protests of the German shopkeeper, the soldier takes the little boy into a clothing shop. "Germans are not allowed to come in here," the saleswoman insists, but the GI answers, "Well, maybe neither him nor me's allowed to come in here [...] but he's got the right to have shoes on his feet the same as you and me got the right" (Boyle 157). His role as American soldier in Germany allows the Black GI to stand up for his own rights against White people. Moreover, in protecting the little boy as thinly disguised alter ego, he also seems to take the first steps on the road to racial and egalitarian self-determination. Clearly, Germany as foreign space in "Home" becomes the locus for an experiment in equality and the demand for equal civil rights for African-Americans at home.

The African-American GI ends up buying the German boy a whole set of new clothes. The experience provides the soldier with a glimpse of a different life, allows him to anticipate a social utopia. While he recognizes his own dejection in the tattered German child, the "temporary dignity [lent] by the uniform he wore" (Boyle 153) also enables him to assume the role of protector and to transcend momentarily the restrictions of his social position in America. The narrator sums up and characterizes this process by stating that "the soldier, who had known only leaning Negro shacks, became the provider, the protector at last" (Boyle 159). Both as soldier in Germany and in a domestic setting, the Black GI can live the American dream of equality and prosperity.

The Black GI and the abandoned German boy become a minimal nuclear family, and the shopping center has become their temporary home. To the Black GI, the shopping center is no longer alien or forbidding, but has become "home," hence the title of the story. The narrator comments how as a result of this transformation, "the soldier dreamed the bright, clear dream of love about the boy. For the duration of the dream, the boy was his, the authority of family, of country, of Occupation even, having discarded him" (Boyle 159). In the domestic sphere circumscribed by their relationship, both the boy and the African-American soldier are momentarily released from the constraints of their respective positions. Just as the German boy is removed from various official spaces and is reclaimed in the domestic, the shopping center has been transformed from an alien into a utopian space: it no longer just reflects White middle America but an America where all have equal opportunity for self realization.

African-Americans in Europe during the war found that going abroad "was their first experience in being treated as normal human beings and friends by white people" (White 21), an observation particularly true for Germany simply because Black GIs came as victors and not only liberators, as in other European countries. Firsthand experience of African-American GIs was reflected in the Black press, which noted with painful surprise that Blacks had more equality in only recently totalitarian and White-supremacist Germany than in democratic America, and used the unfavorable comparison between the two countries for critical purposes. Smith's novel even more than Boyle's stories, finally, realize the culturally critical potential of comparing a favorably depicted Germany with an America less than perfect in its treatment of minorities. Unlike most liberal critics of their country and culture, African-Americans depicted Germany as utopian space but similarly in contrast to American realities. In Germany as the land of evil, they found the promise of a better America.

Chapter Three - GIs and <u>Fräuleins</u>: Hollywood's Romance of Foreign Policy

In the previous chapters we have seen that the American image of Germany in literature served both as utopian and dystopian space for critics of America. In this chapter I will argue that Hollywood's depiction of Germany in contemporary films had its roots more immediately in a still emerging conception of America's new role as dominant world power in the post-World War II period. While liberal authors dramatized a mostly general critique of their country and culture in their works, as we have seen in the previous pages, Hollywood intervened much more directly in contemporary questions about America's global role and directly and implicitly engaged in national questions about involvement in Germany in particular and the world in general in a more specific fashion than most of American literary production concerned with Germany ever did.[21]

---

[21] To try to account for this fascinating institutional and generic difference in the relation between cultural production and foreign policy would lead the present study too far astray. However, a preliminary answer may be suggested by the fact that Hollywood in general had played an important part in the American war effort and was thus used to conceiving of its projects with reference to national foreign policy aims. In particular, Billy Wilder's <u>A Foreign Affair</u> had its beginnings in a propaganda film about -- and for Germany, as Ralph Willett has shown. While serving as Military Government Film Officer in Berlin in late 1945, Wilder proposed in a memo to his superiors "an entertainment film with Rita Hayworth or Ingrid Bergman or Gary Cooper, in Technicolor if you wish, and with a love story -- only with a very special love story, cleverly devised to help us sell a few ideological items" (quoted in Willett 13) to help in re-educating the German populace. The film would eventually turn into something else and become <u>A Foreign Affair</u>, but the nexus between Hollywood entertainment and foreign policy could not be stated more clearly. Even if nothing

In spite of a growing American assertiveness on the world stage since the Spanish-American war at the turn of the century, we will see in this chapter how the nation was torn by an unresolved conflict between its supposedly democratic mission and the realities of its foreign policy after World War II. In spite of the heated debate, however, the actual and practical course of U.S. foreign policy had long been set on an interventionist course. The brief surge in isolationist sentiment over the German question after World War II, I will argue, can thus be taken as a kind of rhetorical rearguard action, an almost futile attempt to turn back the clock on a debate that had long since been decided in favor of an assertive foreign policy. The isolationist argument was eventually smothered by the onset of the Cold War and the formulation of Truman's (anti-Soviet) containment policy. Isolationists realized that the future of Germany would be catalytic for the shape of American foreign policy in the following decades and consequently tried to influence the course of occupation policies.

Accordingly, we will see that the American approach to the German problem as well as Hollywood's depiction of Germany can be taken as bellwethers of the process of postwar American self-definition. In the depiction of Germany, isolationist and interventionist forces waged an ideological battle over the future shape of American foreign policy, while the dangers and rewards of American involvement with Germany became allegorical expressions of the implications of America's global role. I will try to show that the trajectory of this battle profoundly influenced the American depiction of Germany as Germany became the testcase and illustrating example both for isolationist and for interventionist arguments.

Only a few American films deal with life in Germany during the occupation, in spite of numerous productions dealing with the war and the Nazis. American film makers mainly took occupied Germany as a kind of exotic setting for generic Hollywood plots, and most of the resulting films merely transform Germany and the Germans into either a vague

---

comparable is known about the ideological origins and genesis of the other films considered here, their propagandistic intent and effect seems similarly transparent.

cultural "other" or into a transparent projection of the American self.[22] Yet, Hollywood also released three films about occupied Germany that seem to negotiate the opposing positions in a contemporary American debate over the future course of foreign policy. Billy Wilder's A Foreign Affair (1948), George Seaton's The Big Lift (1950) and Henry Koster's Fräulein (1958) allegorically depict the political relations between the U.S. and Germany as the romance between American GIs and German fräuleins. To highlight the changes in American filmic representations of Germany, I will also briefly consider Billy Wilder's One, Two, Three (1961) which fully articulates the Cold War consensus by depicting the romantic involvement between American and German civilians.

Since my focus here, as well as in other chapters, is on cultural history, I will approach these films as texts, as it were, trying to show how they mediate cultural concerns. Described in terms of film theory, I will not attempt a kind of "auteur" analysis, explaining a given film by examining the political and ideological affiliations of its writer, director and producer. Instead, I see popular films as a site of contest where different cultural needs and visions are articulated. Or, in the words of recent "ideology critique" film theory, I will read films "not as aesthetic acts but as modes of cultural exchange" (Zavarzadeh 5) that construct political and historical meaning and intelligibility.[23] Accordingly, I move

---

[22] The resulting films were, for instance, pseudo-political dramas dealing with a growing neo-Nazi underground like Berlin Express (1948) and The Devil Makes Three (1952); familiar explorations of crime and justice in court dramas such as The Sealed Verdict (1948), Town without Pity (1961), or even Judgement at Nuremberg (1961); sentimental melodramas about the price of war like The Search (1948); crime dramas such as Subway in the Sky (1960); and even comedies like I Was a Male War Bride (1949) and musicals such as G.I. Blues (1960). The Red Danube (1949) about the occupation in Vienna, and the final reels of the war film The Victors (1963) might loosely be classified as American depictions of life during the occupation.

[23] In Seeing Films Politically (1991), Mas'ud Zavarzadeh proposes a critical methodology that moves beyond currently dominant poststructuralist film theory, which ignores "the political economy of signification and focus[es] instead on the 'immanent' formal strategies of signification" (4), without returning either to the

freely between film, history and ideology, using formulations like "the film says" or "the film can be taken to illustrate" and "the film allegorically depicts" interchangeably.

As I will situate the few films about GIs and fräuleins within the political debate about foreign policy, a brief survey of its history will be necessary. In my introductory account in the next segment and in the sketch of Cold War changes later in this chapter, which are both intended as historical background for the readings that will follow, I will mainly rely on the work of "revisionist" historian William Appleman Williams and on recent reinterpretations of foreign policy by Thomas J. McCormick and Michael H. Hunt. Obviously, neither of these accounts have gone unchallenged, but they reflect very well, I think, the current state of American diplomatic history.[24] Williams, the most influential advocate of "revisionism" as the New Left's challenge to historiographical orthodoxy in the 1960's and 70's, is generally regarded to be "the most influential American diplomatic historian of his generation" (Hess 499). However, the 1980's saw the "emergence of a genuine synthesis of previously

---

earlier "auteur" approach or a kind of psycho-sociological criticism attempted by Kracauer in From Caligari to Hitler. A Psychological History of the German Film (Princeton: Princeton University Press. 1947). Although it may seem as if I embark on a Kracauerian analysis since I will talk of the allegorization of politics as sexual drama, I am not trying, like Kracauer, to analyze a culture's "collective mentality" (6) and a country's "deep psychological dispositions" (v). Instead I propose several historical and cultural discourses as the forces shaping the films I analyze.

[24] For authoritative reflections on the state of the art in diplomatic historiography over the last decade see John Lewis Gaddis, "The Emerging Post-Revisionist Synthesis on the Origins of the Cold War" (Diplomatic History Vol. 7 No. 3 [Summer 1983]. 171-180); Gaddis, "The Corporatist Synthesis: A Skeptical View" (Diplomatic History Vol. 10 No. 4 [Fall 1986]. 357-62) and Michael J. Hogan, "Corporatism: A Positive Appraisal" (ibid. 363-72); Gaddis, "New Conceptual Approaches to the Study of American Foreign Relations: Interdisciplinary Perspectives" (Diplomatic History Vol. 14 No. 3 [Summer 1990]. 405-23) and Thomas J. McCormick, "Something Old, Something New: John Lewis Gaddis' 'New Conceptual Approaches'" (ibid. 425-32).

antagonistic viewpoints" (Gaddis 171) in a "New School" or "postrevisionist" diplomatic historiography. The accounts of McCormick and Hunt describe the new interdisciplinary directions taken by the "New School," both clearly departing methodologically from the tenets of New Left historiography. But at the same time, their thought is also heir to the theses of revisionism inasmuch as McCormick and Hunt insist on the importance of economic factors and a kind of structural imperialism in American foreign policy formulation respectively.

After a general historical introduction, I will examine contemporary evaluations of American involvement in Germany in the chapter's second and third sections, before moving on to a similar survey of contemporary American concern about fraternization between GIs and German women. Unlike the first part of this chapter, which is concerned with historical interpretations, the following two parts -- and similar short discussions throughout my analyses of the films -- will provide a sense of American opinions as voiced in contemporary newsmagazines and book-length accounts, illustrating my readings rather than serving as a historically explanative framework. The main part of the chapter in the final three sections will explain the four films as mediations of a foreign policy debate.

Isolationism and the Melodrama of Beset Nationhood

For the U.S., World War II had been a smashing success. With only minimal casualties, compared to the horrifying numbers of dead of the other nations involved, America had emerged as the only true victor of the war and the predominant world power, eclipsing for the first time in history all of its European rivals for global hegemony. Yet, in spite of the successful global interventionism during World War II, America seemed ready for a global withdrawal of its forces, relapsing into isolationism almost by reflex towards the end of hostilities. Politicians like Robert Taft "opposed not only American involvement in 'power politics,' but also the continuing expansion in presidential power" (Yergin, Shattered Peace 171). The Morgenthau plan for the de-industrialization of Germany, proposed early in 1945, seemed to provide the champions of isolationism with a viable blueprint for American disengagement from European politics. But the American foreign policy establishment realized that the former basis for an isolationist posture, the impregnability of fortress America, had been shattered with the attack on Pearl Harbor, becoming increasingly convinced that "America's safety and security were also now measured by what took place far beyond its borders" (Yergin, Shattered Peace 85). Critics of Morgenthau also pointed out that Germany was the key to the recovery of the European marketplace (for American goods), thus favoring economic and industrial reconstruction of Germany instead. "Successfully integrated into the world-system, West Germany's industrial production and consumptive capacity could make Europe a viable, competitive unit in the world economy" (McCormick 106). Consequently, American foreign policy soon shifted from the isolationist Morgenthau to the interventionist Marshall plan, from the planned de-industrialization to the industrial reconstruction of Germany.

American foreign policy in the wake of the second world war, and particularly its relation to conquered Germany, however, was not only determined by the technological and economic contingencies (the "shrinking" of the world due to technology and the increasing importance of international trade), it was also profoundly shaped by a historical conflict between American isolationists and interventionists, who had done battle since the early days of the republic.

The phenomenon of American isolationism is difficult to understand, first because of the split between the noble rhetoric and the opportunistic realities of U.S. foreign policy, and, second because it exists in three parallel and intersecting dimensions: foreign policy, domestic politics, and a moral sphere. As we will see presently, notions of American moral exceptionality led to the supposed practical need for non-involvement in world affairs so that republican achievements in democracy would be left unsullied. In addition, an assertive foreign policy raised the domestic political specter of a strong centralized government, which had been anathema to republican zealots like Jefferson. But at the same time, the political necessities of geographical expansion rather than the traditional moral self-conceptions of being a righteous and chosen people seemed to dictate the course of foreign policy, creating internal contradictions that are left unresolved to this day.

Revisionist historians since the 1960's have claimed that in spite of a seemingly strong anti-imperialist tradition originating in the spirit of 1776, the U.S. has always pursued an essentially imperialist foreign policy. In Empire as a Way of Life, William Appleman Williams describes how the well-being and safety of the republic have constantly been defined in terms of spatial expansion and a policy of conquest, but nevertheless couched in terms of a rhetoric of freedom and democracy. "Empire became so intrinsically our American way of life," Williams claims, "that we rationalized and suppressed the nature of our means in the euphoria of our enjoyment of the ends" (Williams, Empire ix). Be it the winning of the West, the Monroe doctrine, the Truman doctrine or Carter's involvement in the Middle East, the expansion of American influence was hidden under a cloak of liberatory rhetoric. Whether one agrees with the details of Williams' argument -- and obviously there is the problem of an independent Canada and Mexico which his thesis cannot fully account for -- both the United States' quest for hegemony first in North America and later the world, and the curious discrepancy between liberatory rhetoric and imperial posturing seem incontrovertible facts. And not surprisingly, as Williams points out, the rhetorical transformation of imperialist conquest into a democratic crusade, "that process of reification -- of transforming the realities of expansion, conquest, and intervention into pious rhetoric about virtue, wealth, and democracy -- reached its culmination during the decades after World War II" (Williams, Empire ix).

Revisionist accounts highlight a curious discrepancy between rhetoric and action in U.S. foreign policy, emphasizing that the traditional conception of American exceptionality was never reconciled with the political needs of the growing nation. Ideologically, America tried to cling to its self-conception as a small nation beset by adversity while acting more and more like a colonial power. The Puritan pilgrims had defined their settlement as a beacon of hope and a New Jerusalem. A hundred and fifty years later, the founding fathers perpetuated both the idea of radical (historical, geographical) discontinuity and the promise of now secularized salvation. "We have it in our power to begin the world all over again," proclaimed Thomas Paine on the eve of the American revolution (quoted in Hunt 19). Through the decades America held on to that vision of itself; American self-conceptions were frozen, as it were, sometime after the revolution while the nation expanded westwards across the continent and later extended its influence on a global scale.

Michael H. Hunt's account of the ideological continuities over two centuries of U.S. foreign policy in <u>Ideology and U.S. Foreign Policy</u> (1987) makes clear that conceptions of American greatness and exceptionality informed both the isolationist and interventionist positions. Over and over again, interventionist policy-makers attempted to justify adventures abroad by recourse to America's democratic mission. The democratic world-revolution, begun in the New World, had to be completed with a little help here and there. The world had to be made safe for democracy. Isolationists, by contrast, saw these interventions in the affairs of other nations as perversions of the democratic revolution of 1776; to them it seemed as if the U.S. was behaving no better than a latter-day British empire. America should be a shining example to the world, but play no direct role in its actual salvation. But overall, both the proponents of an assertive foreign policy and the isolationists took visions of American political exceptionality as a point of departure.

Hypothetizing the emergence of a morally superior political subject in their country, American isolationists also allegorized foreign policy as drama of moral hygiene (in itself a symbolic conflation of medicine and philosophical principles), positing the need for isolation so as not to be infected by the contagious political diseases of the Old World. Convinced about the righteousness of their cause and their moral superiority, the Founding Fathers were afraid that this new animal, the republican subject, and the new republican institutions, would be compromised by too much contact with the vice-ridden and slothful Old World. The birth of the American nation was also meant to be the "birth of a virtuous people" (Takaki 5), and "patriot leaders [...] felt at once an intense need for the people to be free from external authority and a severe lack of confidence in their ability to control themselves" (Takaki 9). Isolationism thus became a moral necessity. First as secretary of state to George Washington and later as president, Thomas Jefferson held that isolationism was "the best way of preserving the liberties Americans had achieved and of allowing them to develop still further as a free people. Geographic distance from a rapacious and turmoil-prone Europe [...] promised peace" (Hunt 22).

Hunt's chapters on the "hierarchy of race" informing American foreign policy and the American reception of the French revolution illustrate how the moral necessity of isolation from the Old World translated directly into practical political terms -- and anxieties. The young republic, as much as its individual budding democratic subjects (the perennial American innocent abroad), were threatened both with losing their innocence or with being taken advantage of by cynical and un-democratic operators. Consequently, early U.S. foreign policy attempted to avoid entangling alliances. Thus "Adams argued that [they colonies] 'should avoid all Alliance, which might embarrass Us in after times and involve Us in future European Wars'" (Varg 15). Historical experience time and again seemed to bear out those fears, probably most prominently after World War I and the dubious behavior of the European allies. America could not but ask itself whether it had fought the war for British imperial causes after all.

Finally, isolationism also had what might be called domestic political aspects intimately related to the agrarian ideal. Hunt also charts the trajectory of republican (Jeffersonian) discontent with an assertive foreign policy throughout the late 18th and the whole 19th century. With Jefferson, leaders of the then emerging Republican party feared in the late 1790's that extensive involvement in world affairs would put "liberty at risk by concentrating power in the hands of the executive" (Hunt 25). Concentrated federal power, those critics feared, would undermine not only freedom at home but also eventually unravel America's role as beacon of democratic hope (Hunt 30). Ironically enough, Jefferson's own drive for westward expansion effectively curbed the debate over foreign policy; the interventionist side seemed to have won by default since its main opponent had reversed his views.

The Mexican-American war of the late 1840's again raised republican dissent and critics feared that President "Polk threatened to cast the United States irrevocably -- and to its eventual sorrow -- in an imperial role" (Hunt 34). Again, the demands of empire would only strengthen executive power, lead to high taxes and a standing army; in short, they conjured up the specter of imperial Britain. Indeed, the union seemed to have bitten off more than it could chew. In addition, the issue of slavery in the new territories might directly lead to Civil War, as indeed it did a decade later.

The foreign policy debate flared up once more on occasion of McKinley's drive for expansion in the Pacific and the Caribbean at the turn of the century, and critics warned that "'adventurous policies of conquest or ambition' would transform this special 'democratic republic' into 'another empire just after the fashion of the old ones.' [...] The net effect of foreign adventures would soon be seen at home in the form of a burgeoning state apparatus that would dispense patronage and control a large military establishment" (Hunt 40). The rewards of empire, however, seemed to outweigh its costs, and "the combined appeal of liberty [from Spain for the Philippines and greatness [for the U.S.] easily triumphed over a narrow, cautious, self-limiting conception of national mission. [...] By the turn of the century the keystone of U.S. foreign-policy ideology had fallen securely into place" (Hunt 41) and subsequently intervention was regarded as the best means to further the democratic cause.

Isolationist forces, however, could mark up a small victory for their cause after World War I and the rejection of U.S. membership in the League of Nations. Influential western agrarians, in a variation on earlier anxieties of executive power, saw interventionist forces in the eastern establishment as a threat to their independence. Antagonistic towards "Great Britain, the international bankers, and the eastern metropolis [... they] viewed any international political organization as a hostile alliance of these three groups" (Smith, "Republican Policy" 267). But the momentary relapse into isolationism after World War I ended with America's entry into World War II. The threat of German world domination provided ample reason for American intervention in world affairs on behalf of liberty.

Predictably enough, republican critics (most of them agrarians like Morgenthau or New Deal reformers) once again rehearsed the familiar formulas first raised in the Hamilton-Jefferson debate.[25] Once again they

---

[25] Interestingly enough, the demise of the Soviet empire and the war with Iraq sparked yet another round in this recurring debate, roughly a half-century after the last one.

objected to what they saw as American imperial pretensions and the threat of undue concentration of power in Washington. The interim period between the end of World War II, which had obviously made necessary American intervention abroad, and the onset of the Cold War, which once again left America no choice but to intervene on a global scale, saw yet another flare-up of isolationist sentiment. The ideological battle over the future of Germany was one of the major skirmishes in this debate.

As so often before, arguments against intervention and continuing involvement in Europe sprang from fears about the adverse diplomatic and domestic political implications of foreign involvement. Increasingly, reports from Germany painted a grim picture of GI behavior reminiscent of a colonial force and in stark contrasted with the avowedly democratic purpose of the occupation.

GIs in Germany: Ambassadors of Democracy or Poobah Sahibs?

Many firsthand accounts of the occupation in articles and books provide a clue to contemporary American sentiment about involvement in Germany, furnishing a sense of the climate of opinion which existed when the first of our films, Wilder's A Foreign Affair, was released in 1948. Moreover, these obviously biased reports also illustrate the relationship between general American anxieties about foreign involvement traced above and the specific fears about the dangers of Germany which will occupy us for the rest of this chapter.

Even to impartial observers of occupation-time realities it looked as if republican critics of U.S. interventionism had been right with their admonitions against a continued involvement in Germany.[26]

(Cf. a symptomatic series of articles in the July 1991 issue of The Atlantic, with titles ranging from "What is the national interest" to "Interventionism vs. minding our own business").

[26] For an overview of sources on the American occupation of Germany see Barbara Dotts Paul's bibliography mentioned earlier and the first section in Gisela Hersch, A

Suddenly the erstwhile American colonials with a formidable tradition of anti-colonial rhetoric behind them found themselves in the role of a colonial administration, with all the trappings and seductions of nearly absolute power. The writer Kay Boyle, a firsthand observer to that quasi-colonial rule as the wife of an occupation staff member, described the degradations of the colonizer as well as the colonized in one of her stories about Germany under American rule. Impersonating the American General Consul, the only person who can grant a visa overnight, one member of the occupation force at a party has cruelly made the 73 year-old German Hausmeister the butt of a drunken joke, playing with the janitor's desperate dream of escape from bombed-out Germany. As the old man breaks down in tears, obviously not realizing that he is the victim of a cheap practical joke, the party's host, an American major, contemplates their situation: "What are we doing here, any of us? he asked in sudden bewilderment, almost in fright. What has become of the lot of us here?" (Boyle 115).

Similarly, an Army wife noted with some uneasiness that the "needlessly extravagant practices [...] undermine the real purpose of the occupation" (Berry 120). "I feel guilty about such wealth of food amid so much hunger, but I don't know how one person can correct it. Nevertheless, I can't help feeling depressed about it" (ibid.). The Army wife's account of her life in Germany highlights the unresolved contradictions of the American occupation of Germany. Noting that her neighbor's dog was put on a high calorie diet by a vet and got a daily ration of sugar equaling the total Christmas bonus for German children, the author wonders somewhat peevishly,"how this sort of occupation can teach them our brand of democracy" (Berry 25; author's emphasis). As one historian of the period summarized, "strangely enough the Americans, in spite of their long history of anticolonialism, were not far behind the British when it came to playing the role of colonial governor" (Botting 210). Moreover, even then Assistant Secretary of War John McCloy remarked after a visit to Germany that "military governor was a pretty heady job. [...] It was the nearest thing to a Roman proconsulship

---

Bibliography of German Studies 1945-1971 (Bloomington: Indiana University Press. 1972).

the modern world afforded. [...] Benevolent despotism" (quoted in Yergin, Shattered Peace 374).

Initially, American forces had come to Germany as conquerors of Nazism but also as missionaries for a new society. GIs were to be live exhibits of Democratic Men for the barbaric enemy to contemplate. The military's Pocket Guide advised GI's to "give them [the Germans] a glimpse of life in a Democracy where no man is master of another, where the only limit of success is a man's own ability" (Pocket Guide 3). Yet, many GIs in Germany seemed to embody the rapacious spirit of venture capitalism rather than that of democracy. Similar to many enterprising young men who had a century earlier jumped on the bandwagon of British colonial expansion and made a fortune, numerous GIs made their fortunes on the black market in America's Germany.

The scale to which occupation troops enriched themselves in Berlin (and in their zone of occupation) was described by Julian Bach in a chapter entitled "The Berlin 'Millionaires'" in his eyewitness account of the occupation, America's Germany (1946). He computed that on a total investment of roughly $100, used to purchase weekly cigarette, candy and liquor rations only, an average American soldier could realize a yearly return of $ 12,000. More enterprising GIs easily increased their profits by reinvesting in watches, jewelry and lingerie for the black market. What thus took place in the conquered country was the systematic and ruthless exploitation of German "resources," the barter of every conceivable item and service for consumerist "baubles," the bulk of them candies and cigarettes. Of course, the colonialist economy of exploitation also brought its own currency, and Time observed that "wherever there were Americans, Europe had a new medium of exchange, subject to all the lamentable fluctuations that affect legal tender. The medium: cigarets" (Time 13 Jan. 47). The magazine summed up the situation when they laconically captioned a photo of the black market in the Berlin ruins "For a watch, $ 500; for a girl a chocolate bar" (Time 6 Aug. 45, 47).

According to one observer, "what the ordinary BTOs [Big Time Operators] did with watches, jewelry, stamps, leather goods and liquor, [American industrialists] could do with whole factories, whole industries and whole cartels. Unlike the GIs with their petty 'operations,' however, the large corporations and banking houses in America were also concerned about their investments and holdings in Germany" (Kahn 109). The corporate colonization of Germany, paralleling the military occupation, is nowhere more poignantly illustrated than in a Life photograph of two heavily laden military signposts at a crossroads in Germany, one of them prominently topped with a "Coca-Cola Plant" sign (Fig. 2; Life 10 Feb. 47, 85). Critics sensitive to international antitrust issues also could not but notice that near heavily bombarded Cologne, the Ford plant had been left practically untouched (cf. Kahn 87); or that the British dealt severe blows to the German fishing, ship construction, steel and watch industries, and individual companies went as far as Unilever, who (without success) "tried to extinguish the Henkel soap factory" (Botting 226f.). Although Washington and the occupation administration tried to deflect such ambitions and probably also succeeded in the most egregious cases, what occupation historian John Gimbel has called "postwar carpetbaggers," scientific consultants to the military or scientists in uniform, "transferred substantial amounts of technical know-how directly to their own firms and for their own purposes" (170).

Figure 2 Occupation Power Lines: the Way to the Coca-Cola Plant (Life)

Liberal critics, scandalized by the behavior of the occupation force, were probably not fully off the mark with their observations.

Subsequent historical research has shown that like the individual GI "carpetbagger," the American military-industrial complex as a whole moved in a similarly imperial fashion with its unprecedented -- and to this day unparalleled -- exploitation of German know-how and skills.[27] In fact, in internal communications the military described their program of transferring technical know-how with the very term, "exploitation," and must have been quite aware of the implications of their behavior because even decades later they still felt uneasy enough to censor the term in a historian's research notes (cf. Lasby viii). At the time, however, an American observer reveled that

> the greatest 'brain-picking' in history is being carried out by a large number of agencies, which are literally snooping out every technical, military, scientific, medical, industrial, agricultural, diplomatic and financial secret that the Germans had. If the enemy had a new stretcher for wounded, or a new fertilizer for farms, or a better way to build a mouse trap, it is by now almost certainly known to us. (Bach 42)

Moreover, Military Intelligence did not just rest content with collecting technical information in Germany, but instituted what even disgusted American observers described as a kind of modern day slave trade (cf. Lasby 101), bringing many German scientists to the U.S. The group of rocket engineers around General Dornberger (later Vice President of Bell industries, a major defense contractor) and Wernher von Braun, settled in the 1950's on "Sauerkraut Hill" in "rocket-town" Huntsville, Alabama, was to become most famous among these more intangible spoils of war.

---

[27] For an authoritative general account see John Gimbel, Science, Technology, and Reparations. Exploitation and Plunder in Postwar Germany. Clarence G. Lasby, Project Paperclip. German Scientists and the Cold War concentrates on the exploits of the American military-industrial complex. Linda Hunt, Secret Agenda. The United States Government, Nazi Scientists, and Project Paperclip, 1945 to 1990 (New York: St. Martin's Press. 1991) covers the same ground in a less focused piece of "investigative journalism."

Critics of these importation programs probably slightly overstated their case when they spoke of a modern slave trade; after all, the German scientists were paid and had signed contracts to work for the U.S. government. But clearly, the American occupation force undertook the planned and systematic exploitation of German scientific resources. Overall, experts estimated that "American industry had saved billions of dollars and advanced its research by several years" (Lasby 164).

The realities of the military occupation of Germany (before the founding of the two German states in 1949) thus seemed to justify its critics' anxieties about the bad influence of foreign involvement on American democratic traditions. And indeed, to many contemporary observers, American behavior in Germany displayed all the characteristics of the "dominant" phase of colonialism: "While the covert purpose is to exploit the colony's natural resources thoroughly and ruthlessly through the various imperialist material practices, the overt aim, as articulated by colonialist discourse, is to 'civilize' the savage, to introduce him to all the benefits of Western cultures" (JanMohamed 62). While the military-industrial establishment was busy in exploiting the conquered country, the media disseminated the ideological framework for that replay of high colonialism.

Official American policy stipulated the de-barbarization and "civilizing" of Germany, as it were, but the language and imagery of the media betrayed the underlying jingoistic attitudes of the occupation force. Writing about the role of German courts in the denazification process, a Saturday Evening Post correspondent, for instance, pointed out that "the fact that Germans, not Americans, are in charge of the house cleaning is in line with our occupation policy of 'giving the country back to the Indians as fast as we can'" (Hauser, Germans Resist 17; my emphasis). The same article provided yet another telling image for the historical continuities in American treatment of the cultural "other," a metaphor which only highlights the underlying condescending paternalism informing the depiction of Germans as "Indians": "Like an impractical-minded godparent who presents a three-month-old baby with a complicated electrical railroad set, Uncle Sam has presented his Germans with all the trappings of self-government before they can say 'mamma' and 'papa' in a nice, democratic way" (Hauser, Germans Resist 122).[28]

In spite of the massive media effort that tried to depict the occupation as a civilizing enterprise, repeated soul-searching in the press attests to widespread American anxiety over the success of the troops' ambassadorial mission. Even the avowedly interventionist Luce press voiced concern that re-education on the basic level of everyday interaction would fail. A Life editorial opened with the observation that "the conqueror's robes look silly on Uncle Sam. He has been stalking through Germany with a stern look on his face and a stick of chewing gum in his hand" (Life 28 Jan. 46, 32). By contrast, the Saturday Evening Post tried to reassure its readership of the moral integrity of the occupation force, and under the heading "G.I. Joe Wouldn't Play Herrenvolk," an editorial exclaimed that the average GI was "the best salesman democracy has" (Saturday Evening Post 4 Aug. 45, 112). But in spite of repeated assurances, the contradictions in occupation policy were too obvious. One member of Military Government summed up popular fears about the detrimental influence of continued involvement in Germany when he confessed: "we became 'India Service' -- poobah Sahibs -- masters of a conquered people, rulers of an occupied colonial state" (Kahn 114).

Even before revisionist historians analyzed similar patterns in U.S. foreign policy two decades later, liberal critics in the late 1940's felt that American involvement in Germany seemed to give rise to American imperialist behavior while displacing its realities into a pious discourse about global liberty and democracy. They also maintained that U.S. military government in Germany had deteriorated into a colonial administration -- presumably instituted in the global fight for democracy. While Washington persistently heralded the GIs' role in Germany as part of the democratization process, the American public continued to worry about the costs of empire. The media and entertainment industry, both as expression and shapers of public sentiment, staged these specific anxieties as the almost archetypal American drama of frail national character beset by the evil temptations of the Old World. They found a

---

[28] Cf. ch. 3 of Hunt, Ideology and U.S. Foreign Policy on the tradition of American paternalistic attitudes in foreign relations, especially with Caribbean nations.

convenient symbol for Americas darkest fears about beset innocence in "fraternization," the sexual relations between American GIs and German women.

"Fraternization": Contagion and the Conquest of the Fräulein

Reports about fraternization between American soldiers and German women first surfaced in mid 1945, when Time and other newsmagazines reported on "occupational semantics," noting that "among G.I.s the word 'fraternization' had acquired a meaning not included in family dictionaries. 'How's fraternizing down your way?' was a standard conversational gambit" (Time 2 July 45). In trying to answer the question "Why Americans [sic!] like German women," a correspondent to the American Mercury was more blunt, if somewhat archaic in his word choice, when he wrote that "in Army usage 'fraternization' came to have the exclusive signification of fornication" (Padover 354). Another observer noted dryly that "troops, who have the knack for calling a spade a spade, promptly called Non-Fraternization, 'non-fertilization'" (Bach 72). However, and more importantly, by 1947 the "fräuleinwunder" dominated American impressions of Germany. Thus, for instance, Newsweek covered fraternization and nothing else in a status report on the occupation, and put an American soldier with a beautiful German actress on its cover (Fig. 3 Newsweek 16 June 47).

To many critics of continued involvement in Germany it must have appeared that youthful Americans, seduced by the (sexual) charms abroad were abandoning virtue in droves, leading lives of sloth and dissipation. One concerned observer complained that fraternization was nothing but "widespread adultery" (Padover 355). Similarly, a correspondent to The New Republic warned that "sexual promiscuity and prostitution have become the normal pattern of boy-and-girl [sic!] relationships," and asked, "if [war veterans] become 'diseased,' what can be expected to happen to the teen-age recruits?" Apparently, innocent republican subjects were ill equipped to deal with the temptations in the zone of occupation. Overall, the critics' main worry was the breakdown of American moral superiority, the crumbling of the virtuous subject under the onslaught of European vice: "The picture is one of large numbers of men accepting crooked dealing, dishonesty and promiscuity as a way of life -- and apparently liking it" (Slatoff 687), summed up one critic. Obviously, virtuous republican subjects were being compromised through contact with the morally depraved German population.

But fraternization not only raised questions about the moral rectitude of innocent American GIs, it also seemed to have more practical political implications. If soldiers got too friendly with the population, the occupation would lose its character as punishment and political policing of Germany. In spite of these fears, most American officials probably did not share British Field Marshal Montgomery's paranoid conviction that "German girls seemed to be carrying on an organized strip-tease campaign to break down the will of British soldiers" (Newsweek 2 July 45, 45). But still, many Americans feared that a sympathy for German women would

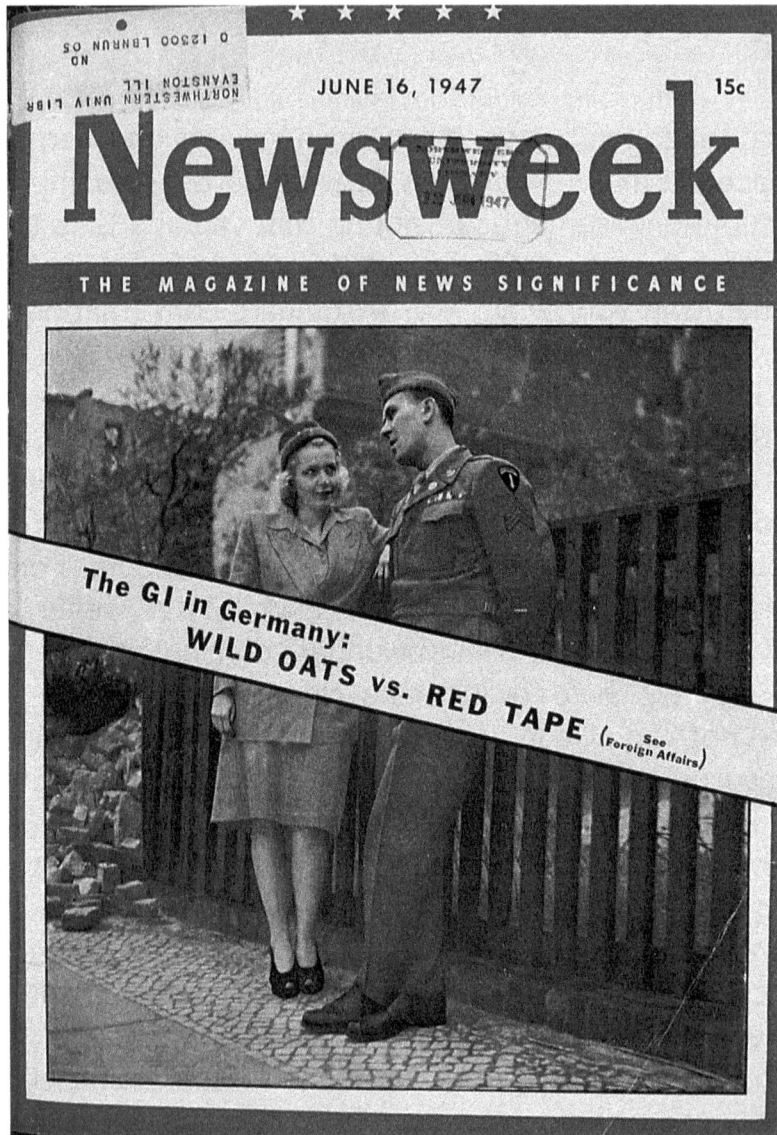

Figure 3 The Romance of Foreign Policy: GI and Fräulein (Newsweek)

translate "into political terms of not being too harsh with the Reich as a whole" (Padover 357). Unlike the French and British allies who soon after the beginning of the military occupation eased restrictions on contacts between their soldiers and the German populace, fraternization became a major cause for concern both in the American public and the executive branch in Washington.

The Defense Department and Military Government came up with their own way to allay American fears about the detrimental influence of contact between American "boys" and the German population in general by instituting a de facto system of apartheid between the two groups. In spite of their role as ambassadors of democracy, American military personnel and their dependents in Germany lived very much in isolation and had little contact with Germans outside of institutional settings (a practice that remained unchanged as long as American soldiers were stationed in Germany!). "We realize we have no real contact with the German people. Our relations are pretty well confined to our servants" (Berry 122), observed an Army wife. The official Army account of the occupation states that "the concentration of large numbers of Americans in the various tactical units or community centers provided sufficient social life so that there was little incentive to seek it outside American circles. [... Moreover,] the traditional cohesiveness of the armed forces at home or abroad, [...] induced them to look for companionship among their own numbers in the occupation as in the zone of the interior" (Frederiksen 137f.).

But clearly, Military Government enforced cultural segregation, even if it was made easier by the traditional self-sufficiency of military communities. Looking back on the earlier days of the occupation from the perspective of the Cold War, Time noted that Military Government had risked alienating the German population by raising an invisible wall between them and American soldiers: "It is built of a thousand tiny brick-hard facts," the report stated, and consists of "the OMGUS documents that never speak of Germans but only of 'indigenous personnel'; the terse little signs in official buildings that designate which toilets the 'indigenous' shall use" (Time 17 May 48). Similarly, Life revealed in the legend of one picture in a photo-report about a GI's daily routine that "the [depicted] shop, which sells mostly junk, has one entrance for civilians, another for GIs" (Life 22 Oct. 45, 144). Obviously, "civilians" here is a euphemism for "Germans," who had to use a separate entrance from American occupation personnel. Moreover, the ban on fraternization stipulated that "local entertainment facilities were to be taken over for exclusive use at all times or at specified hours by Allies [, and that] Americans were to be forbidden to enter German theaters" (Frederiksen 129). Non-fraternization, which meant apartheid, extended to all spheres and included "segregation at religious services" (Frederiksen 132). Desegregation only set in once the fraternization ban was lifted, and "after some hesitation, the entry of Americans into German motion picture theaters was permitted" (Frederiksen 132).

Ultimately, however, even the institutionalization of apartheid could not prevent contact between well-fed, amply provisioned, and sex-starved American soldiers and hungry and lonely German women, especially since the official logic that saw German women as a political threat was too brittle for the average GI. Reporting on fraternization, Life noted, in the caption of a picture showing two German girls on an Autobahn overpass waving to GIs in a Jeep, that many soldiers "find it hard to see connection between Nazi war crimes and a smiling girl on a bridge" (Life 23 July 45, 36). Commenting on the inevitability of the lifting of the fraternization ban, Newsweek pointed out that "the hard-peace zealots had stretched the doctrine of collective guilt beyond the breaking point" (Newsweek 16 June 47, 48).

The ban on intermarriage between Germans and Americans was notoriously ineffective and counter-productive. The military found themselves with a law on their hands that could not be enforced effectively, a situation analogous to the political debacle of Prohibition, and gradually eased the rules governing fraternization. Officials also soon realized that the ban on fraternization was backfiring dangerously, undercutting the credibility of Military Government more than fraternization ever could have done. The military feared that to the Germans it must appear as if the military administration was not even in control of its own soldiers, and so could not possibly be credible as occupiers. The ban practically pitted the average GI against the officers, who were relatively immune from enforcement of the ban, a fact that immediately re-drew the lines within the occupation forces, as it set "many an American soldier and the German community in a united front on one important issue against the Army command itself" (Newsweek 16 June 47, 48). Most observers agreed that "Non-Fraternization had been strictly a 'Brass Hat' idea, made necessary by the intensity of public opinion in Britain and the U.S" (Bach 75), and even before Secretary of State James F. Byrnes officially announced a softer peace for Germany in September 1946, many fraternizing GIs had already done what the Secretary was asking for, and had helped at least the female part of the German population to "win their way back to an honorable place among the [...] nations of the world" (in Frederiksen 131).

But even after fraternization was taken off the books as an offense by Military Government, public opinion continued to struggle with what Newsweek had called the "unpalatable fact [of] growing sympathy of the Americans for the Germans" (Newsweek 3 Sep. 45, 44). The specter of American GIs seduced by designing German "frowlines," remained troublesome and in their efforts to take the moral and political sting out of fraternization, the media tried to convince the American public that GIs' liking of German women was only a result of their dislike of French women, and that politics played no role at all in these relationships. Most American observers agreed that "accustomed as they were to the predatory French girls or to domineering-demanding ones back home, the GIs found the fräuleins in possession of enough qualities to make many a male wax eloquent" (Padover 356). As to the fears of political seduction, an observer summarized: "Fraternization is strictly a matter of sex. An American with a German woman is with her because she is a woman, not because she is a German" (Bach 71), and Newsweek concluded in an article headlined "Do the Fräuleins Change Our Joe? Not a Bit of It, He's All Wised Up" that "from the beginning [the GI] has displayed a distinct apathy, if not allergy, to almost all the political issues of this war" (Newsweek 24 Dec. 45).

Although fraternization was legalized in October 1945, rules for international marriages remained highly restrictive. Until the end of 1946, marriages between Americans associated with the occupation and Germans remained illegal, and resulted in discharge from the military if found out. German women soon realized that they were being sexually exploited on a grand scale and with official sanction. Newsweek pointed out that "there is no quicker way to reap a psychological whirlwind in any nation -- defeated or not -- than to imply that its women are good enough to sleep with and to breed with but not to commit matrimony with" (Newsweek 16 June 47, 48). Beginning in 1947, MG changed the rules so that "American personnel [...] would be allowed to marry Germans during their last month of duty with the occupation forces in Germany but only after a 3-month waiting period" (Frederiksen 136). The union also had to be authorized first by general officers and later by military post commanders. This rule only left a small window of opportunity for German-American marriages, especially considering all the red tape involved in the required screening of the American wife-to-be. As Newsweek described, the process involved checks "by the chaplain, then by the unit commander, then by the denazification Spruchkammer, then by the Counterintelligence Corps, then by the medics, and finally by the combined travel security board. By this time [the German bride] is not only lily-white, she is practically bleached" (16 June 47, 49). Although not legally forbidden, for all practical purposes a ban on marriage thus existed until mid-1948 , when all restrictions were lifted.[29]

As the selected examples of contemporary sentiment make clear, American anxiety about fraternization only pointed to a more general -- and in many cases vague -- fear about the effects of intense foreign involvement. Critics of American involvement in Germany feared that the inevitable and extended idleness of the troops once the fighting was over would compromise them as subjects of a virtuous republican people. They would develop a taste for luxury, dissipation and vice through their involvement in the black market and their contact with the Germans, who practically prostituted themselves to garner favors from the victors. The cultural (and military) superiority of Americans abroad would only put them into an imperial role; at worst, they would be

---

[29] This is the sense conveyed by contemporary accounts. Frederiksen's official history of the occupation only mentions that "statistics are incomplete, but apparently 3,500 legal German-American marriages had occurred in Germany by 30 June 1948" (137). More detailed raw statistical data probably exists somewhere in the records of Military Government, but they have yet to be recovered and evaluated.

infected by the depravity of the "natives," at best, they would develop a taste for authoritarianism and lose their libertarian virtues. And also, by assuming the role of strict but essentially well-meaning father to the Germans, America would be restricted and restrained in her foreign policy, get more and more entangled in European affairs. The individual soldier's entanglement with the population he was meant to police merely illustrated that threatened loss of effectiveness: how can you crack down on the people you fraternize with? Overall, fraternization nicely seemed to sum up the political and moral dangers lurking abroad.

Moreover, American observers may even have focused on fraternization to articulate their doubts about American involvement in Germany because the curious displacement of political fears about the loss of innocence in the international arena into sexual allegory has a long tradition in American history. For instance, cultural historian Ronald T. Takaki reports that

> Jefferson warned that American studying abroad would acquire a fondness for European luxury and dissipation, and would be led by "the strongest of all human passions" into a "spirit for female intrigue" or a "passion for whores." Thus [...] young men of the republic should be kept away from European women with their "voluptuary dress and arts." (40)

Jefferson here not only contributes to a uniquely American self-conception, but also has recourse to the Biblical manichean schema that juxtaposes the "whore Babylon" with holy Jerusalem. The iconography of isolationism represented the drama of young America in the international arena as the melodrama of beset innocence, displaces foreign relations into sexual politics. Henry James and his preoccupation with the "international theme," of course, provided the most thorough representation of cultural and political foreign relations as the war between the sexes. In Portrait of a Lady, for instance, American innocence and idealistic naiveté are personified by Isabel Archer, who is seduced and abused by the European Gilbert Osmond. Although the later The Ambassadors complicates the equation somewhat, reconceptualizing presumed American innocence and moral rectitude as New England narrowness in the figure of Strether, the central question of the novel again involves the perennial American innocent, Chad, who is sexually compromised and seduced in the old world.

In 1947, a brief Time piece, interestingly enough in the "Foreign News" section, contained all the elements of the Jamesian international sexual drama and provided a glimpse of American anxieties vis a vis postwar Germany:

> Lovers. In the snack bar of Frankfurt's Rhein-Main airport, a German girl sits with her G.I. fiancé. He is a slight blond boy of perhaps 18; she is a blonde, bulging, overbearing, with a broad, white face, narrow, calculating eyes and a smile like the flat glare of an electric light switch. She leans with both elbows on the table and in a loud and domineering voice orders ice cream from the tired German waitress, while the boy follows her movements with a young dog's eyes. Outside, in the lounge, is a group of German war brides who will take off in two hours for America. Among them is a mother with a baby in her arms. She sits and dreams with a slight half-smile on her lips, her eyes on the plane outside, one hand caressing the baby's downy hair. (Time 28 July 47, 24)

The sexual threat of the blonde (German) bitch, the voracious lover, the castrating woman, masks a political threat. The German girl has her "narrow, calculating eyes" obviously firmly set on the land of plenty; the German mother also anticipates her own and her child's bright future in America when she dreams with her predatory eyes on the plane that will carry her abroad. Sexual politics thus becomes an image for international relations and illustrates the perceived threats of American involvement in Germany. Like the boyish GI, innocent America would be taken advantage of by the Germans if it got too closely involved. Just as the German woman who is obviously in love not with the unsuspecting GI but with his privileges and lifestyle, Germany supposedly coveted the material rewards the U.S. could offer. Like the German woman, the occupied country would probably leave its American protector to pick up the pieces of the relationship as soon as circumstance would allow it. Obviously, what is played out here in sexual terms is the American anxiety about the characterological advantage of cynical Old World operators over democratic American innocents.

Nowhere is the displacement of political into sexual fears more strikingly illustrated than in a propagandist cartoon campaign in the army publication Stars and Stripes. Beginning in early 1946, the military daily produced for the American occupation force occasionally featured cartoons by young cartoonist Don Sheppard, intended "to discourage soldiers from taking their fraternization ... too seriously" (Life 17 June 46, 12). The cartoons revolve around "a bovine fräulein character dubbed Veronica Dankeschön (VD), whose dirndl skirt was decorated with cute little swastikas and who was always out to hornswoggle some shining example of democratic American manhood into her bed" (Newsweek 16 June 47, 48). Thus, for instance in one cartoon a swarthy pimp-like civilian introduces sprawling and smirking Veronica with a lot of leg to a Dagwood-like, obviously gullible American GI with the words, "Meet the sweetest little gal in Deutschland, Veronica Dankeschön" (Fig. 4). In addition to her swastika-adorned hemline, Veronica also wears big bows with even more conspicuous swastikas in her braids. Just to make sure even the most unsophisticated reader understand the meaning of Veronica's name, she touts an oversized handbag with the initials "VD." The "VD"-cartoon campaign's fetishization of the Nazi symbol echoes the soon to be abandoned official fraternization ban, which outlawed intimate relations between GIs and Germans supposedly for security reasons. It is obvious that the VD cartoon aimed to reinscribe the increasingly tenuous cultural "color line" segregating Americans and Germans. As many observers continued to notice, "GIs find it hard to see connection between Nazi war crimes and a smiling girl" (Life 23 July 45, 36), and failed to perceive Germans as fundamentally different and threatening, so the "VD" campaign sought to ensure that perception. Since Germans lacked visible signs such as skin color to differentiate people into dominant and subservient social positions, invisible expressions of that alterity had to be posited. Both the threat of venereal disease, which oftentimes only manifests itself long after the "fact" and when contagion has already taken place, and the Nazi threat, Veronica's swastikas which imply an elusive political threat, denote an invisible enemy and point to an otherness that is hidden and cannot be perceived outright.

Figure 4 The Threat of Contagion: Veronika Dankeschön Cartoons (Stars and Stripes)

The "VD" cartoons show that even after the lifting of the official ban, intimate relationships between American GIs and German women continued to be taken as a metaphor for the relation between the U.S. and Germany, expressing American anxieties: by ingratiating herself to her American conquerors, it was felt, Germany might yet snatch victory from the jaws of defeat. Isolationists feared that an interventionist foreign policy would endanger American democracy, and American innocents abroad would be bamboozled by cynical German operators.

"Women's politics": Fraternization and Emasculation in A Foreign Affair

Billy Wilder's A Foreign Affair (1948) takes up the problem of fraternization and tries to show what will happen if America gets involved too deeply with corrupt Germany. The film argues for a careful and essentially isolationist American attitude towards Germany, and is concerned with the question how Americans best approach the German problem. Capitalizing on the comic potential of the politically as well as morally illicit love affair between an American GI and a German nightclub singer, A Foreign Affair caricatures the ideological anxieties over American foreign involvement and the dangers of the new global hegemonic role as the trials and tribulations in the war between the sexes. The relations between GIs and fräuleins in Wilder's film dramatize the political relation between Germans and Americans in particular and Americans and the world in general.

In the opening scene of the film, we see a congressional committee of six men and one woman in a plane over Berlin, discussing what is to be done with the country. Suggestions range from reconstruction to democratization, even Americanization, and thus one congressman, obviously from Texas, suggests to "move in longhorns." The only female member of the group, Phoebe Frost, representative from Iowa, follows the heated debate of her fellow committee members with interest and then calmly cuts them down to size by reminding them of the real purpose of their German tour:

> We're here to investigate the morale of American occupation troops, nothing else. Twelve thousand of our boys are policing that pesthole down below and according to our reports, they are being infected by a kind of moral malaria. It is our duty to their wives, their mothers, their sisters, to find the facts. And if these reports are true, to fumigate that place with all the insecticides at our disposal. (A Foreign Affairmy emphases)

Congresswoman Frost's little speech not only exemplifies the ethnocentric paranoia of American exceptionalism and isolationism run wild, but also redefines the political and cultural problems of the occupation as questions of hygiene and morals. Phoebe Frost polemically redefines the actual _political_ failure of the occupation as the presumed _moral_ failure of preventing fraternization between GIs and German women. The feared political failure of the occupation -- finding expression in a burgeoning black market and GIs the biggest operators on it instead of reforming the country to righteous democratic ways -- this failure to implement foreign policy decisions thus becomes the moral failure to prevent fraternization between GIs and German women. Moreover, the moral failure in turn finds expression in the failure to contain the spreading of a portentous disease, the "moral malaria." The point of transmission of the disease is the relationship between American soldiers and German women. When Phoebe Frost says that the committee's "duty [is] to [the soldiers'] wives, their mothers, their sisters, to find the facts," it is sex not politics or even culture (a non-American way of life) that she sees as a serious threat to the moral health of American occupation troops. Phoebe Frost sees -- and _A Foreign Affair_ stages -- the political drama of the American occupation of Germany, with all its undemocratic nasty details of exploitation and domination, as the sexual melodrama and comedy of the American conquest of the German _fräulein_.

As expected, Congresswoman Frost soon discovers that black-marketeering, fraternizing and a general breakdown in discipline are rampant in the American occupation force. She becomes especially enraged when she finds out that nightclub singer Erika von Schlütow (Marlene Dietrich, with distinct echoes of _The Blue Angel_), a member of the former bigwig Nazi coterie, obviously has a protector somewhere in the upper echelons of Military Government. Thus Phoebe Frost sets out to find that officer and solicits the help of Captain John Pringle (John Lund), also from Iowa. However, unbeknownst to Phoebe, Pringle also happens to be Erika von Schlütow's protector. Although Phoebe does not instantly realize it, her search for the hidden protector is thus also a fight for Pringle's love, an attempt to break Erika's evil spell on him. Her political crusade becomes a romantic quest.

On the surface, _A Foreign Affair_ seems to be concerned with the question whether Captain Pringle can be saved for American womanhood. Is bleached and starched Republican Congresswoman from Iowa Phoebe Frost going to save Pringle from the claws of seductive nightclub singer Erika von Schlütow? And will radical innocence and down-home values win the day over sophistication and moral cynicism? Yet, what is really at stake in this imperialist allegory about the colonization of Germany is the democratic integrity of America, and whether America, personified by Captain Pringle, can make the right choice between the dark lady and the fair maiden, between political opportunism and democratic integrity respectively, and whether America will emerge unscathed and culturally superior from the encounter with the German savages, from involvement abroad.

A Foreign Affair's overall plot reflects the displacement of political into sexual relations enunciated in the opening scene of the film described earlier. After her first day in Berlin, Congresswoman Frost feels that nowhere are the moral and political problems of the occupation better epitomized than in nightclub-singer Erika von Schlütow. Thus Phoebe's part of the congressional investigation concentrates on Erika and on trying to find out who in MG covers her. The potential suspense-plot of the hunt for the invisible American behind Erika, however, does not become romantic suspense, as it does, for instance, in Alfred Hitchcock's North by Northwest. In that film, the search for the unknown CIA agent whom Cary Grant has been mistaken for, is linked with the romance between him and Eva Marie Saint, who turns out to be that agent. In Hitchcock's film, the audience is as much in the dark about the unknown third man as the protagonist, Cary Grant, himself. In Wilder's film, by contrast, the audience knows far more than the protagonists, and as a result the overriding question is not the identity of the mysterious man in the background, but rather how and when Phoebe is going to realize it is Pringle. Since the eventual and inevitable unmasking of Pringle will break the spell that Erika has over him, the search for the elusive hidden protector finally also becomes Phoebe's quest for Pringle's love.

Nowhere is this shift from suspense to comedy, from politics to sex thrown more into relief than in the encounters between Erika von Schlütow and Phoebe Frost. Erika continually shifts the focus of their conflict away from the political -- who is her American protector? -- to the sexual: who is more attractive? And of course, the bleached and ungainly duckling-cum-executive from Iowa is no match for the seductive Erika, who thus effectively silences her opponent.

At one point, Erika spells out the implications of that shift in focus from politics to sex. Questioned by Pringle about the degree of her past involvement with the Nazis, Erika answers:

> Erika: Oh Johnny, what does it matter? Women's politics. Women pick out whatever is in fashion and change it like a spring hat.
> Pringle: Yeah. Last year it was a little number with a swastika on it. This year it's ostrich feathers. Red, white, and blue. Next year it's gonna be a hammer maybe, and a sickle.
>
> (A Foreign Affair)

Here the sexual comedy and the abortive political morality play intersect, and Erika's "women's politics" and their sexual opportunism point to real-world American fears about German political fickleness. Isolationists were convinced that, like Pringle, America would get entangled in the affairs of foreign countries, unable to extract itself and similarly unable to act independently. In short, American foreign policy would be emasculated by too much involvement abroad. Concerning Germany, isolationist critics also believed that deep American involvement would yield little but embarrassment for the U.S. because eventually Germany, like Erika, would invariably "cuckold" its transatlantic protector and turn to whoever else did the most political courting.

Significantly enough, Germany and the Germans, fickle and opportunistic as Erika, are thus depicted as female, weak, unreliable, cynical and potentially threatening, while Americans appear as principled (even if idealistic), effective, and male, in pursuit and out for conquest of the German fräulein. Obviously, Captain Pringle does not fit this description of American rectitude -- because, as we will see, he has already been infected by women's politics, and is de-Americanized as well as emasculated in the process. The fear of contagion, overshadowing

Phoebe's mission in Germany, is thus charged politically as well as sexually. Isolationist anxieties about involvement abroad find expression in male fantasies about female "uncleanliness" and the threat of emasculation through (sexual) intercourse with women. To contain the threat of contagion through "women's politics" that Erika poses, Phoebe, as the representative of (male) America, has to enforce cultural segregation.

Before she finds out that Pringle's democratic integrity has already been compromised by "women's politics" through his involvement with Erika, Phoebe realizes that the occupation itself -- and not only its individual members -- has been thrown off track. In the same way that Pringle has been corrupted, the occupation as democratic enlightenment has become colonial-style exploitation and resulted in moral decay in the American troops. And like the audience, Phoebe Frost finds out on her tour of conquered Berlin that America's Germany exists in two parallel worlds, the world of official policy and the world of colonialist reality. Thus, in the second scene of the film, after we have watched the the congressional committee in the plane approaching Berlin, we see a Colonel give a prep speech to his troops. While the colonel advises his troops that "this committee is going to be around for five days. Let's give them as good an impression as possible" (A Foreign Affair), we also see Captain Pringle with a nylon stocking dangling out of his pocket, which he has just acquired on the black market for a few candy bars, as he points out to a friend. And similarly, we follow the circulation of Pringle's Iowa-imported birthday cake, brought by Congresswoman Frost, from the airport to the black market, to a nightclub and back to Pringle, which puts him into a tight spot when he has to explain its curious movement through the two worlds. The audience, however, is in the know about the existence of two parallel realities in this comedy of errors, and one of the narrative objectives of the film is to bring Phoebe Frost's perceptions in line with those of the audience, to disabuse her of her illusions about the nature of the occupation.

This process begins when Colonel Plummer takes the committee on a tour of the occupied city. While they are driving through the ruins, the colonel gives a glowing report on the morale of his troops and on the effectiveness of their relations with the German population. The colonel points out that "one family already christened their child DiMaggio Schultz. That's when I started believing we really won the war" (A Foreign Affair), but this observation takes on a different and more ominous meaning as Phoebe Frost observes fraternizing GIs left and right, and even a girl with a perambulator adorned with two American flags, unmistakably denoting the nationality of the baby's father. Obviously, the occupying force has not just gotten hold of German hearts, but of their bodies as well.

While the rest of the group watches German boys in a neighborhood baseball game sponsored by American GIs, Phoebe wanders off for a moment and is picked up by two carousing GIs on a tandem who take her for a German fräulein. While her colleagues continue to watch sanitized and "official" fraternization between American men and German boys at work, Phoebe finds out about the realities of German-American relations with the two GIs. She invents the name Gretchen Gesundheit for herself, and after she has fended off initial clumsy advances, being offered chocolate bars and cigarettes in exchange for sex, she is taken to a nightclub. There she first sees Erika von Schlütow, a singer in the club. She also finds the birthday cake she brought Pringle from Iowa. But unlike before, when she saw through the many ruses of the colonel who was trying to mislead the committee about the real state of affairs in the zone, Congresswoman Frost is unable to see the reason for the circulation of the cake, namely that Pringle is involved in the black market. She also fails to realize why Pringle himself shows up in the nightclub, namely that he is Erika's protector. Assuming him to be as guileless and morally strict as herself -- after all he is a fellow Iowan, his family staunchly Republican -- she falls for his excuses and continues to believe that he is in the nightclub merely to check the spreading of vice. The moment Pringle is concerned, Phoebe Frost loses her acute sense of reality and replaces it with idealized preconceptions.

Phoebe fails to see that the one person she thinks is immune from it, fellow Iowan Captain Pringle, has in fact been infected with the moral malaise she has set out to combat. She even solicits his help in trying to find who in Military Government protects Erika. A Foreign Affair, however, is a comedy and not a thriller, and thus the search for the hidden man takes a farcical turn when Pringle not only feigns ignorance about Erika and her background, but seeks to protect her by romancing Phoebe, making her believe that he loves her although he does not really feel anything for her.

The pivotal scene takes place in the filing room of MG headquarters, when Pringle and Phoebe go looking for Erika's file at night. While Phoebe frantically searches through the filing cabinets, Pringle tries to arouse some sympathy in her for the mysterious officer by appealing to her pity, trying to make her realize how hard it is to keep up the role of unforgiving conqueror as battle-weary soldier in the defeated country. She only quips that "everyone who forgets he's an American [has to be taken] out of service"(A Foreign Affair). Pringle keeps on trying to evoke some human compassion in her, provoking her to relate the story of her one and only love-affair that ended in disaster when she realized she was being used for political reasons. But still, Phoebe continues to look for Erika's file and when all fails and she finally gets close to it after having first tried to find it under "Sch" instead of "von" for her last name, von Schlütow, Pringle pursues Phoebe along the filing cabinets declaring his love, under heavy protestations from her, until he finally corners her and they kiss. Phoebe is transported with happiness, having finally been de-Frosted by Pringle. Pringle in turn has achieved his ends, and without her noticing slips Erika's file behind a cabinet before they leave to turn in for the night.

Although the scene is pure romantic comedy, it also fully establishes for the audience that Pringle is infected by the contagious disease of "women's politics." Pringle had earlier objected to Erika's opportunism, her sexual and political fickleness and inconstancy. When Pringle romances Phoebe and makes her believe that he is in love with her in order to protect Erika, he is as opportunistic as the nightclub singer; but even more so, the film seems to say that while such behavior could be excused in a woman for a man it is taboo, and that his becoming sexually opportunistic, his using a woman's weapons, his resorting to "women's politics" is tantamount to his emasculation. The moral malaise has infected him and he is undone because of his foreign involvement, which A Foreign Affair depicts as a sexual adventure. It is important here not to be misled by the scene's manifest content, but to see the larger picture. One could object that by the standards of stereotypical masculinity, Pringle's simultaneous relationship with Erika and Phoebe makes him more virile instead of emasculating him. However, most striking about this scene is that Pringle opportunistically romances Phoebe, not because he loves her but because it is his only defense. Again by the stereotypical standards of masculine and feminine behavior, this kind of emotional blackmail is effeminate, constituting "women's politics."

The scene in the filing room powerfully underscores the never-ending complications resulting from dangerous entanglement abroad. Initially probably innocent and virtuous, Pringle practically has to prostitute himself in order to "honor" his commitment to Erika. It is hard to imagine a more graphic illustration of the isolationist fear of entanglement in foreign affairs, an entanglement that all too quickly could turn into a major embarrassment and thus would compromise every attempt to conduct political business guided by democratic ideals. Pringle's involvement with Erika and the resulting embarrassments must be taken as an allegorization of isolationist critics' nightmare scenario of extensive American involvement abroad.

The film reiterates and underscores the isolationist message in showing that not even Phoebe is impervious to the dangers of foreign entanglement. Like Pringle, who is unmanned through his relation with Erika, Phoebe too is compromised in her emotional involvement with Pringle, having lost her virtuous astuteness and thus failing to recognize Pringle as the mysterious officer protecting Erika. Although she realizes that Erika sums up the moral problems in the zone, she fails to realize Erika is her rival for Pringle's love. But most importantly, because she is helplessly in love with Pringle, she succumbs to the siren song of the black market and underworld entertainment -- the Puritan republican anathemas luxury and dissipation -- and is thus infected with the very "moral disease" she had come to combat. Although she feels uneasy about it, Phoebe purchases an evening dress for herself on the black market in order to look more beautiful to Pringle. She then begs him to spend their last evening not at an official embassy reception, but at the "Loreley" nightclub. "You don't wanna go to that sewer," Pringle tries to dissuade her. "Yes, I do. I want it dark, and gay, and with music" (A

<u>Foreign Affair</u>) swoons Phoebe. Never has she been farther removed from her initial attitude of moral absolutism and her belief in American cultural superiority. In fact, she is about to "go native."

Phoebe's entanglement in affairs foreign to her moral universe soon threatens to end in the inevitable embarrassment. Phoebe and Pringle go to the "Loreley," where they watch Erika perform and where Phoebe gets drunk. Pringle is called away on urgent business, but Phoebe stays in the "Loreley" and is taken to a police station when American MPs and German constables raid the nightclub. Erika, however, takes care of her, and since she has leverage with the German police through her association with Pringle, gets Phoebe out without questioning and without revealing her identity as American politician. Although Phoebe has thus avoided the political problems -- she already tried to imagine the headlines about a Republican Congresswoman from Iowa being arrested in a notorious Berlin nightspot -- her moral corruption has manifested itself. Given the choice between turning to her arch-rival for protection and persecuting her enemy, Phoebe has given in and chosen the easier path, but has also broken with her principles in the process. Her entanglement in the affairs of foreigners has deprived her of her freedom; she has become unable to act in line with her beliefs.

Erika realizes what has happened and intuitively understands that Phoebe's integrity is compromised and that she is at her mercy. Jealous about Pringle's massive efforts to distract Phoebe from her mission by making her fall in love with him, Erika knows her moment for revenge has arrived. She bluntly reveals to Phoebe that Pringle is her protector and in love with her. She concludes and spells out the implications of Phoebe's transformation: "Four hours ago you were in a position to have him court martialed, to send me to a labor camp. Not now. Not any more. Now you're one of us" (<u>A Foreign Affair</u>). Clearly, Phoebe, like Pringle, has lost her democratic superiority and her efforts to reform are rendered ineffective precisely by the involvement abroad. Or, conversely, the film seems to say that even someone as principled as Phoebe Frost would be compromised without fail by the moral malaria, and that the only way she could have preserved her moral and democratic integrity would have been never to venture abroad. The isolationist case could not be stated more clearly.

Pringle and Phoebe, both from Iowa and both American radical innocents, have been infected by the German moral malaise, transmitted by Erika. But more importantly, both Pringle and Phoebe are rendered unable to act, "unmanned" as it were, by that infection. Pringle becomes opportunistic, resorts to "women's politics" when he practically prostitutes himself romancing Phoebe in order to protect Erika. Phoebe, in turn, has to leave her arch-enemy untouched and the problem of moral disease unsolved, because she has deprived herself of her position of moral superiority. Intervention will only lead to corruption of American virtue, and the film illustrates what happens if America continues its involvement in the moral and political twilight in Germany, summed up by the seductive atmosphere of the "Loreley" nightclub and the Marlene Dietrich character. Congresswoman Frost's introductory speech advertising the committee's goals as "We're here to investigate the morale of American occupation troops, nothing else" (A Foreign Affair), could be rewritten as "We're here to investigate the influence of our global interventionist attitudes on our domestic democratic traditions." Captain Pringle's fate is the fate of American democracy, his malaise that which threatens republican traditions at home. A Foreign Affair tries to defuse that threat and to solve the problem of "moral malaria" by proposing strict non-involvement in German affairs.

The film has made its ideological case and concludes with a rather conventional and almost deus ex machina dénouement built around Erika's Nazi protector. Trying to avoid a political scandal when Congresswoman Frost alerts him to Pringle's involvement with Erika, Pringle's superior, a colonel, tries to rationalize his actions by inventing a sting operation intended to flush out Erika's fugitive Nazi consort, Hans Otto Birgel. The colonel then tells Pringle either to cooperate in the plan or be court-martialed. The final showdown takes place in the "Loreley," where Birgel comes, trying to shoot Pringle. Birgel is killed in the ensuing gunfight, and Erika is taken to a labor camp for Nazi criminals. By redefining Pringle's involvement with Erika not as a lapse of military discipline but as part of an ingenious plan, the colonel effectively solves the political problem created by Pringle. As authorial alter ego, the colonel similarly resolves the complications of Wilder's plot by removing Erika from the romantic triangle. But more importantly, as much as

Pringle's emasculation was depicted as dangerous and negative, the eventual "emasculation" of Congresswoman Frost means that she is restored to her natural position as woman. The un-Frosting of Phoebe Frost and the loss of her moral superiority has thus made her fit for the resolution of the romantic and comic plot in marriage. Yet, the formulaic resolution of its romance plot still underscores A Foreign Affair's isolationist message: only with his withdrawal from Germany (Erika) can America (Pringle) find happiness.

In reality, however, the disentanglement of American and German affairs proved far more complicated, if not impossible. By the time the Berlin crisis broke in 1948, the U.S. had firmly committed itself to the protection of a democratic Germany, and thus gotten even more involved in Germany than before. While Wilder's A Foreign Affair could still assume at least in theory the viability of an isolationist withdrawal from Germany, Seaton's The Big Lift no longer even considers that option. Fully embroiled in the emerging Cold War, the question has now become how America can avoid being undone by the irrevocable involvement in world affairs. The Big Lift thus both articulates familiar fears about interventionism while trying to formulate a position distinct from isolationism.

Foreign Relations as Sexual Tragi-Comedy in The Big Lift

While A Foreign Affair proposes a stringent isolationism, George Seaton's The Big Lift (1950) advocates a kind of careful interventionism and explores the question of the relationship between American conquerors and German subjects. The film examines the political alternatives for the treatment of postwar Germany in the contrasting sexual relations of a disillusioned and an idealistic GI with their German "Schatzis." Thus the film warns about the adverse effects resulting from political idealism in a U.S. foreign policy that by then was interventionist almost by default because of the global Soviet threat (The Big Lift takes the first Berlin crisis in 1948-49 as its historical backdrop and topic). In contrast to A Foreign Affair, which advised Americans not to venture abroad, The Big Lift thus paints the dangers of idealistic American involvement in global affairs, yet argues for the need of (level-headed and realistic) American intervention in world affairs.

All-American boy and Jimmy Stewart-like innocent Danny McCullough (Montgomery Clift) and gruff Polish American ex-POW Hank Kowalski (Paul Douglas) are buddies. Both are flown into Germany from Hawaii as reinforcements for the year-long Berlin airlift in 1948/49. Danny is a tech sergeant on one of the transport planes stationed in Frankfurt, Kowalski a radar operator, who talks incoming planes to the ground at crowded Berlin-Tempelhof airport. One of Danny's flights happens to be the one-hundred-thousandth airlift mission into the blockaded city, and in a ceremony commemorating that event, he meets beautiful Friderica Burckhardt (German actress Cornell Borchers), who is there to thank the crew in the name of the women of Berlin. The two exchange addresses, and when Danny gets the chance to spend a few days in Berlin, the two meet again.

Before his date with Friderica, however, Danny meets Kowalski. Kowalski's estimation of the Germans is not high -- in fact he hates them and makes them feel as much as he can that theirs is a vanquished nation. Danny finds, to his surprise, that his friend is seeing a German woman in spite of his reservations. Kowalski, however, makes clear that his relationship with Gerti is nothing personal and only part of enjoying the spoils of war and the conveniences that come with being a GI in America's Germany: "With Gerti it's different. I wanna see her, I see her. I feel like talking, she talks, and if I don't feel like it, she keeps her mouth shut. Anyway, she gives me one-day service on my laundry. PX takes a week" (The Big Lift). In spite of Kowalski, who urges him to treat Germans as he does and repeatedly warns him against Friderica, Danny inevitably falls in love with the German woman when he sees her again. He finds out that she works as a Trümmerfrau, doing hard manual labor cleaning up bricks for re-use and moving them amidst the ruins.

While Kowalski obviously uses and even abuses his German girlfriend, it soon becomes clear that Danny is prone to be manipulated and exploited because of his innocence and good faith. What must be understood as the compromising of the innocent democratic American abroad, or even his emasculation through the loss of his uniform, comes about when Danny doles out cigarettes to two Germans posting billboards, one of them on a ladder with a bucket of glue that he accidentally empties on Danny. The change in outward appearance that he undergoes, paralleled by the psychological change resulting from the loss of his privileged position, is thus depicted as a direct outcome of Danny's softness toward the Germans. The situation takes on a nightmarish character when he cannot get back his uniform from the cleaners, and is thus deprived of the mark of difference and his identity as conqueror and forced to live "on the other side" for a day and a night. Kowalski is sensitive to the implications of Danny's change in appearance, commenting on it in unmistakable terms: "You sure went native in a hurry"(The Big Lift).

For different reasons and in quite a different fashion, Kowalski also begins to sympathize with the Germans, although he never goes as far as Danny. Danny's emasculation is depicted as his de-Americanization, and his deepening uncritical emotional-sexual involvement with Friderica takes its predictable course towards a marriage proposal. By contrast, Kowalski changes from unforgiving conqueror to ambassador of democratic goodwill, a course that mirrors American public attitude towards Germany in the immediate postwar period. Kowalski can be taken as a dramatization of the observation by a Life editorial that "the conqueror's robes look silly on Uncle Sam" (Life 28 Jan. 46, 32).

Kowalski begins his indoctrination of Gerti in a series of democratic question-and-answer sessions when he is challenged for his unforgiving and essentially paternalistic attitudes. Many of these scenes, of course, are rather transparent and clumsy propaganda moves in a Cold War movie; yet they are interesting as an example of the construction of Germany as junior partner in the worldwide American enterprise for democracy and containment of the Red Scare. At one point Friderica challenges Kowalski on his view of the Germans when the two couples discuss the tradition of paternal authoritarianism as explanation of German totalitarianism. But as Friderica points out, Kowalski only perpetuates that tradition by bossing Gerti around. Kowalski is somewhat taken aback, but after a brief pause agrees and encourages Gerti to disagree with him instead of accepting his every word. Just to make sure, Gerti asks him whether she can disagree with him "out loud" or just in principle, and then enthusiastically exclaims: "I want to find out so much about America" (The Big Lift). While Kowalski gives Gerti the first installment of the primer on American democracy, Danny and Friderica go off to dance. The discursive democratization of Gerti by Kowalski has its counterpoint in the emotionally induced de-Americanization of Danny by Friderica. While Kowalski begins to educate Gerti in American civic virtues, Danny strays more and more from the proscribed path of American involvement abroad in his entanglement with Friderica.

Although The Big Lift warns of an idealistic and uncritical American involvement abroad by criticizing Danny's unquestioning sympathy for the Germans, it does not sanction Kowalski's unrelenting rancor. Illustrating the Pocket Guide's admonition to GIs not "to carry a chip on your shoulder or to brutalize the inhabitants [because] we are not like the Nazis" (5), Kowalski receives his object lesson when he accidentally comes across the German camp-guard who mistreated him when he was a POW in Germany. The guard made Kowalski learn German, and Kowalski now jumps at the opportunity to repay the favor, nearly killing the German in the process. The fight is broken up by Allied MPs, and Kowalski returns to Gerti's apartment, only to feel remorse instead of satisfaction about having lived out his revenge fantasies in an excess of brutality. Thus realizing that he is neither all that different, nor really inherently superior morally to the Germans, Kowalski is reconciled to the Germans and profoundly changes his attitude, no longer pushing and bossing them around whenever he can. Instead he tries to understand and get along with them. This change in attitude finds expression in Kowalski's acceptance of the German hand-shaking habit, which so far he has doggedly ignored.

Through the example of Kowalski, The Big Lift thus seems to argue for a modification of the (Rooseveltian) blanket indictment of the Germans, implying that they did not have the advantage of democratic institutions to prevent them from falling into barbarism. More importantly, however, the movie also provides a model for the American attitude towards Germany between unforgiving zealotry in the unreconstructed Kowalski, and uncritical acceptance in Danny, an attitude of well-intentioned democratic proctorship from a respectful distance. Thus The Big Lift departs from A Foreign Affair's unquestioning support of an isolationist position. Instead, The Big Lift argues that

American ideals will only be corrupted if the foreign nation is approached without any reservations, as allegorized in Danny's uncritical attitude toward Friderica. However, if approached carefully and realistically, The Big Lift seems to say, interventionism can succeed and is a viable alternative to isolationism and an American withdrawal from Europe which would leave the continent at the mercy of Russia.

Kowalski finally proves to Danny that Friderica lied about her husband and her family's background. A checkup in the Document Center reveals that both her father and her husband were Nazis. Instead of leading to a realistic and more distant attitude in Danny, this discovery only further deepens Danny's identification with the Germans. Predictably enough, when Danny confronts Friderica, she appeals to his pity in defending her blatant opportunism: "When you have to live by the generosity of others you lie to make yourself pitiful and brave. When you live in a sewer you soon discover that the sewer-rat is best equipped to survive" (The Big Lift). Friderica's evasive explanation interestingly enough also contains an implicit critique of the hard-peace approach to Germany and a defense of the newer line. With Friderica, the film seems to say that subjugation of the conquered country's population only engenders opportunism, and worsens rather than rectifies the apparent moral decay. Friderica's confession opens Danny's eyes -- to the suffering of the German population, but not to Friderica's deceit. In dejection he walks the streets of the battered city, suddenly becoming aware of all the misery around him. He notices a woman with only one shoe and rags around the other foot, watches a bride and groom all dressed up arrive on one bicycle for their wedding, an old man who lives in a shabby construction caravan and people scavenging from the refuse of an Army mess hall. Danny returns to Friderica, moved with pity.

Danny has thus crossed the "color line," he has "gone native" for good, and although still (and again) in American uniform, he sees with German eyes. Since he will be punished eventually for his leniency, as will become clear presently, Danny has failed in his ambassadorial mission. The film shows that instead of cultivating democracy in the occupied country, Danny has been infected by the moral decay, having been de-Americanized. But significantly enough, The Big Lift does not argue for an unqualified isolationism as the example of Danny might lead us to expect. In fact, as we will see, in the depiction of Kowalski The Big Lift clearly advocates interventionism that does not rely on the political immunity of American democratic subjects abroad but instead seeks to prevent infection and decay of democratic rectitude by converting the "natives" to democratic values.

At the same time that the film shows Danny straying from his colonizing mission, it also depicts the battle of the sexes as a travesty of the democratic conflict of ideas in the exchanges between Kowalski and Gerti. At one point Kowalski gets furious when Gerti decides to have plans of her own and bluntly tells him that no, she will not join him right now:

> Kowalski: What's the matter, you plastered or something. What have you been drinking?
> Gerti (pamphlet "Things to know about the United States" in hand): Words, good words. I've been reading this. Your constitution. The Bill of Rights. What Lincoln said. And Wilson. And Roosevelt. [...] You are a disgrace to America, and they shouldn't send people like you here. [...]
> Kowalski: Now wait a minute. You're not yelling to some crummy kraut, you know. I'm the guy that brings you the cigarettes, and the candy, and the soap, and the stockings.
> [Gerti hurls various household items at him, screaming, telling him to take back all his presents and stop bossing her around]
> Kowalski (conciliatory, from behind a door): You're right, baby. Don't let anybody push you around. That's democracy.
>
> (The Big Lift)

The Americanization of Gerti, who in a sense has finished her cultural apprenticeship when she begins to boss Kowalski around in best Laurel and Hardy fashion, parallels Danny's loss of cultural and political identity when he finds out, only minutes before they are to be married, that

Friderica has an (ex-)Nazi husband who has made it to St. Louis, and that Friderica herself is only using Danny to get to America.

The emotional pain of being jilted and the loss of his youthful innocence are thus the price Danny has to pay for his crossing of the cultural "color line" in this drama of displaced American anxieties about political involvement abroad, again expressed as sexual melodrama. Kowalski spells out the lesson of this imperialist morality play when he sees Danny off on his return to the States and Danny concedes that Kowalski probably had been right in his reservations about Friderica and in warning him about her. But Kowalski retorts: "No. We were both wrong. You were too easy, and , like Gerda said, I was acting like a stormtrooper. I suppose the answer lies somewhere between it" (The Big Lift).

The Big Lift thus seeks to define the emerging Cold War attitude towards Germany, and it is important to remember that the film takes the first Cold War crisis, the Berlin blockade, as its historical backdrop; the film also criticizes the pre-Cold War Rooseveltian approach to the German problem, intimating that a hard peace for Germany would only turn out to hurt American interests in the long run. At the same time, the film also illustrates anxieties about the breakdown of cultural and political difference between Americans and Germans, rehearses familiar American fears about entangling alliances abroad that find expression in images of seduction and emasculation. Squarely within the tradition of exceptionalist self-conceptions and republican fears about an assertive foreign policy outlined earlier, Danny's trajectory in The Big Lift both dramatizes the loss of innocence and the abuse at the hands of foreigners threatening unsuspecting and idealistic Americans abroad. But although the film again paints a picture of foreign guile and American innocence, it also qualifies the traditional indictment of European depravity by showing that the drama of American loss of innocence and democratic integrity abroad has as much to do with American lack of realism as it is the result of foreign cunning.

Finally, The Big Lift tries to show that cautious interventionism can be successful as a strategy for involvement abroad. Interestingly enough, the film does not supply a very sophisticated reason for the need for American intervention and takes it for granted, so to speak, with reference to the Soviet threat. Unlike later Cold War rhetoric, however, The Big Lift does not fully dramatize what would happen if America left Germany and Europe to fend for themselves and does not paint the picture of an impending rape of European freedom on the hands of the Soviets. Similarly, the film makes no effort to justify America's (hegemonic) global mission, but rather assumes that everybody agrees that level-headed Americans like Kowalski have to spread the gospel of democracy across the world. Looking back at the film from today's perspective and in light of later examples, the Soviets in The Big Lift come across as curiously unthreatening and rather clumsy at the game of power politics. Without resorting to the all too familiar demonization of the Soviets and assuming that the promise of democracy is reason enough for American involvement in world affairs, The Big Lift is perhaps more optimistic, but certainly more naive than later examples of Cold War ideological work.

Although, as we will see, Hollywood continued to depict German-American relations in terms of the romance between GIs and German women, the whole framework of the American depiction of Germany changed with the redrawing of old battle-lines in the Cold War. Instead of dramatizing the threat of American involvement abroad, the threat of political emasculation articulated in sexual terms, the Americanized fräulein now stood for the helplessness of the new democratic (West) German state. Clearly, threatened by rape at the hands of the Red boors, the newly discovered political innocence and democratic frailty of the German maiden called for quick and decisive action by the American officer and gentleman. The Cold War not only effectively smothered remaining traces of doubt about the need for an interventionist American foreign policy, it also began profoundly to change the American image of Germany. A half-decade after the end of the war, Germany and the fräuleins were at last conquered on the ideological as well as the military front.

Germany as Persecuted Maiden: Cold War Transformations

The emerging confrontation with the Soviets provided a convenient occasion for silencing any lingering isolationist doubts about interventionist American foreign policy. In America's Half-Century, diplomatic historian Thomas J. McCormick has shown that the Democratic Truman administration opted for a rhetoric of confrontation with the Soviets in order to sell an interventionist program of economic aid for Europe to a Republican Congress and American public with isolationist leanings. Only by reconstructing Europe as a viable market for American goods could the so-called "Dollar gap" of the postwar years, the inability of the Europeans to pay for American imports, be solved; similarly, only by subsidizing and redeveloping European economies could the United States perpetuate its newly-attained hegemonic role. Yet, the only way to convince a reluctant Congress and traditionally isolationist public of the need of large-scale involvement in foreign economies, was to emphasize the Soviet threat. McCormick shows how Truman's message to Congress changed accordingly, and how an earlier draft that, according to Under Secretary of State Acheson, "sound[ed] like an investment prospectus" (77) was refocused around the image of the Communist menace. All in all, Truman's message to Congress and the Truman "containment" doctrine in general were "intended not simply to pry $400 million out of a Republican Congress but to prepare the proper political climate in which that Congress would be asked [...] to approve a revolutionary economic aid program for Europe that would ultimately cost forty times that sum" (McCormick 77; author's emphasis).

That the linkage of European economic reconstruction to containment of the Soviet threat struck a receptive chord with the American public is made clear by John Dos Passos' impressions from a tour of Europe, serialized in Life throughout late 1945 and published as Tour of Duty in 1946. Dos Passos combined his European pieces with earlier wartime reportages from the Pacific. But "in contrast to his experiences in the South Pacific, Dos Passos was bored by much of his European tour of duty" (Carr 439), and probably as a consequence the European part of his reporting turned into a fervent polemic against Communism instead of a more objective account of the postwar situation on the continent. Of course, Henry Luce's Life, long since one of the vocal advocates of anti-Soviet American policies, all too gladly printed

Dos Passos' pieces.[30] Dos Passos raves about Military Government's confusion and the vengeful character and the hypocrisies of American liberal rhetoric that persecuted Nazi war crimes but looked the other way concerning Soviet civil and human rights violations. Dos Passos already begins the ideological reconstruction of postwar Germany and thus asks "What have the Nazis done that compares with your handing-over of Poland, your own ally, into the hands of the darkest tyranny in history?" (309). Like many other American critics of social revolutions since John Adams, Dos Passos, witness to Stalinist terror in the International Brigades in civil-war Spain, resorts to polemical oversimplification when he complains about the barbarism of the Communists, charging that they have destroyed the fabric of society and "made a clean sweep of civilization" (329). Clearly, to equate the admittedly monstrous methods of the Stalinist terror with a general fall of civilization seems a bit exaggerated. But more significantly, after all the ideological hyperbole in his report, Dos Passos concludes that in order to secure democracy in America, the foreign policy establishment would have to concentrate on reconstruction instead of revenge in their approach to Germany:

> The only way the United States can remain prosperous and keep up a high standard of living is by full employment and full production. Isn't that true? Well, the only way we can do that after we've saturated the domestic market is to play for foreign markets. To keep going we've got to have a high standard of life in the rest of the world. We have got to have democracy and high wages in the rest of the world. (Dos Passos 335)

Roughly a year before Truman went before Congress and defined his policy of containment of Soviet expansionism, Dos Passos described the economical and hegemonic underpinnings of what came to be known as

---

[30] As a contrast, Margaret Bourke-White's Dear Fatherland Rest Quietly (1946) provides a much more accurate and perceptive (narrative as well as photographic) picture of the postwar situation in Germany. Significantly enough, Life published Bourke-White's photo essays but not her exhaustive commentary.

the Truman doctrine. While Truman soft-pedaled the economic motivation in the final version of his speech, placing the emphasis instead on the Communist threat, Dos Passos' argument in Tour of Duty takes the opposite course, moving from ideology to economic self-interest and describing in no uncertain terms the reasoning underlying the Cold War consensus. In addition, Dos Passos in Tour of Duty was as critical of isolationism and as interventionist as any radical proponent of the emerging Cold War could have been.

The changed relationship between the U.S. and Germany at the beginning of the Cold War is nowhere clearer than in the continuities and discontinuities between Billy Wilder's A Foreign Affair of 1948 and his One, Two, Three of 1961. This later film is also set in Berlin, but A Foreign Affair's occupation officer Captain Pringle has become One, Two, Three's Coca Cola executive MacNamara (James Cagney), and the object no longer is to clean up Germany, which has been sufficiently Americanized as the wall chart mapping Coke sales shows, but to enlighten the Soviet savages by extending the civilizing influence of sodapop eastward. Like Wilder's earlier film, One, Two, Three depicts foreign policy and the ideological conflict between the two systems, the U.S. and the Soviet Union, as sexual farce between the daughter of MacNamara's boss in Atlanta and a young East German communist. One, Two, Three not only inverts the gender positions in relation to A Foreign Affair and makes Scarlett Hazeltine a silly Southern belle instead of another incarnation of American innocence abroad, it also redefines the process of contagion by making East German Otto Ludwig Piffl get entangled in the trappings of (American) capitalism. As much as Wilder seemed to warn against the threat of German political and ideological contagion in A Foreign Affair, in One, Two, Three American capitalism and democracy are infectious and thus a hope for the world.

One, Two, Three thus illustrates the hegemonic phase of American domination of Germany, in which Germans are no longer depicted as the threatening "other," but as extensions of the American self, either as Americanized as MacNamara's German secretary, Ingeborg, or as personifications of American stereotypes about the Germans as MacNamara's heel-clicking staff and his apparently ex-Nazi private assistant, Schlemmer. But both the allure of Ingeborg, who precipitates a domestic crisis in the MacNamara household, as well as the ingrained militarism of Schlemmer and the staff are depicted as a lark and running gag instead of a formidable threat as in A Foreign Affair. Both the German sexual and ideological threat have been blunted, presumably by a process of assimilation, by the Americanization of Germany, the process that turns the other into an extension of the self.

This process of cultural assimilation was laid out in allegorical fashion in the evolving relationship between Kowalski and Gerti in The Big Lift. Only as Gerti assimilates Kowalski's (American) values, does she also acquire a voice and begins to be taken seriously by him. Thus, for instance, in their heated discussions about democracy, Kowalski begins to listen to Gerti and to answer her, instead of just bossing her around. A similar process of assimilation and change in perception can be seen in the depiction of Germany in the American press. After almost a decade of American evaluations of and pronouncements about Germany and the Germans, something like a German voice emerged in a special issue of Life magazine (10 May 54) entitled "Germany - A Giant Awakened" on the eve of West German integration into NATO. Then chancellor Konrad Adenauer wrote a preface to the issue, but more importantly, several photo essays as well as a long article also featured German social, historical and political evaluations -- as well as some criticism of the American mentors. Commenting on the initial hard peace approach, Germans are thus quoted as questioning the contradiction between democratic pretensions and summary justice against a whole people. Life also has Germans comment on the American shift in political standards from strict anti-Nazism to excessive anti-Communism. And finally, Life also reported Germans as appealing to be absolved from history: "You should be wise enough to know that if a people is to live, to work, to believe, it cannot be sentenced to live in a chamber of horrors of its own past" (Life 10 May 54, 170). These comments obviously also function as a Cold War commentary on the hard peace approach to Germany, and it could be argued that again American representation of German concerns here is thus highly selective at best and the seemingly German concerns are only thinly veiled American ones. But then, even the mere appearance of dissenting credible German voices in this article marks a departure from earlier practice that relegated the cultural other to absolute silence.

Overall, Kowalski's trajectory in <u>The Big Lift</u> from unquestioning hate of the Germans to a more moderate attitude, reflects the changes in the American approach to Germany as the occupation progressed. The isolationist paranoia of <u>A Foreign Affair</u> has become an attitude of careful rapprochement. Similarly, the mainly punitive measures of the early months of the occupation gave way to a program geared towards the economic reconstruction of Germany. Then Secretary of State Byrnes made this policy change official in a speech delivered in Stuttgart in September 1946. "His declaration that the American people wished to help the Germans win their way back to an honorable place among the free and peace-loving nations of the world was followed by a campaign of troop indoctrination intended to emphasize the fact that the negative phase of the occupation was at an end and that the constructive phase was emerging" (Frederiksen 131).

But in spite of the changed and more positive attitude, the American media (and public) as well as politicians were still wary of a potential German threat and advocated caution very much as Kowalski does in contrast to Danny's innocent sympathy in <u>The Big Lift</u>. In a lengthy report on the occupation early in 1947, <u>Life</u> summed up the prevalent American mood by pointing out that "security from Germany remains a prime aim of U.S. policy because there is still a German menace," but also by making clear that the German threat no longer emanated just from Germany itself, but from the country's pivotal role in the European balance of power: "Germany's chief danger is in its value as a junior partner." Consequently, America found itself in the curious role of having to temper its approach to the German problem and side with the former enemy to contain Soviet ambitions. "While few Americans would look with much relish on entering into a partnership with Germany, it is equally clear that the U.S. does not want Germany to become a member of an Eastern bloc" (<u>Life</u> 10 Feb. 47, 96). Like Kowalski in <u>The Big Lift</u>, the American public was ambivalent about their country's involvement with Germany, and viewed the recent and almost inevitable rapprochement as a kind of necessary evil.

The eruption of the Cold War changed that ambivalence to almost unqualified support. In contrast to its earlier reticence towards the emerging German-American alliance, <u>Life</u> described the reconstructed country as "the Germans on our side" (Life 7 June 52, 104) less than a decade after the war, indicating changed American attitudes. Although the Cold War had been going on for some time, according to some accounts since the emergence of American atomic diplomacy and the breakdown of Four Power agreement at the Potsdam conference in July 1945 (Gar Alperovitz), it only fully came to the American public's attention with the Soviet Berlin blockade and the Anglo-American airlift between June 1948 and May 1949 (cf. Yergin, Shattered Peace 390). Finally, the long smouldering conflict had erupted, and with the Berlin airlift the previously invisible emerging postwar global order had at last found its symbolic and pictorial expression. Indeed, the Berlin crisis constituted "the 'great divide' in the history of the Cold War" (Yergin, Shattered Peace 366), as Daniel Yergin has noted.

Washington Cold War hardliners, in the ascendancy for some time, could not have invented a more perfect script than the Berlin blockade for the dramatization of Soviet expansionism. Over against the belligerent Soviet military blockade, the U.S. (with the help of the British) mounted a supposedly humanitarian campaign to help the civilian population, appropriately named "Operation Vittles." Of course, the American military "big stick" was always in the background of the airlift. Thus, for instance, shortly after the beginning of the airlift, a Newsweek cover depicted an American armored car in Berlin with the caption: "Berlin: 'We will not be coerced'" (Newsweek 2 Aug. 48). Two weeks later, Newsweek commented on the picture of American B-29 bombers and a squadron of airborne jets overhead by pointing out that "American jets and B-29s in Germany put firepower behind the Berlin air lift" (Newsweek 16 Aug 48, 28). Similarly, Life commented in a photo essay on a jet fighter group recently stationed in Germany that "their transfer to southern Germany was designed to strengthen the arm of U.S. diplomacy" (Life 11 Oct. 48, 101).

In spite of these unsubtle hints, the imagery and rhetoric of this first Cold War confrontation tended to stress the the humanitarian effort of the American-led airlift, and media coverage of the effort came to be dominated by pictures of expectant groups of German children in the ruins, heads raised up to incoming American transport planes. National Geographic provided a clue to the motivation of this iconography when they commented in a photo essay on civilian Berlin under siege: "Millions of such children [as in the pictures] represent the material from which the Allies hope to build a democratic, self-supporting nation" (National Geographic May 49, 612). The blockade as attack on democracy was thus visualized as an attempt by the Soviets to starve Germany's children, symbolic of the budding democratic state, into submission . American images of Germany had come a long way from the rabid SS stormtrooper and malignant hun out to kill brave American boys of wartime propaganda, to the threatening fräuleins waiting to corrupt American GIs sexually of the early occupation, and finally to the starving and expectant German children in dire need of American help.

For the German population, who still remembered the endless and relentless streams of Allied bombers and raids during the war, the herculean task of supplying a city of more than two million inhabitants with everything from coal to coffee redefined the role of the occupiers, who were seen no longer as conquerors but as guarantors of freedom. At the same time, the American perception of Germany changed in a similar way. With the Berlin airlift Germans were no longer the enemy, but rather the ally of the United States, even in the public mind. Realizing that their two nations were facing a common enemy, average Americans suddenly reconsidered their evaluation of Germany and began to pay more attention to that new and unlikely ally. A throwaway line in Time makes clear that the Berlin blockade marked the watershed in the German-American relationship: "It was one of history's consummate ironies that, to stand firm, the West now had to consider the mood and mettle of the Germans" (Time 12 July 48, 19). Obviously, the Germans here have changed from being radically different from Americans and have become an extension of America and the democratic free world . Their position on the frontline of the Cold War made "our Germans" and especially the Berlin population the spearhead of the righteous fight for democracy. John F. Kennedy over a decade later canonized this American projection onto Germany and the identification of a common German-American cause. Visiting the beleaguered city at the height of yet another confrontation between the superpowers over missiles in Cuba and the wall in Berlin, he declared "Ich bin ein Berliner" ("I am a Berliner"), highlighting the position of Berlin as outpost and beacon of democracy.

Once identified as standing firmly on the American side, the Germans had to be proven fit for freedom and as good democratic subjects. In best ethnocentric fashion, the media thus increasingly described Germany as a kind of model America. In describing "The Germans on our side: what are they like today?" Life approvingly noted the tidiness of the country: "On the streets of most German cities one is as safe at midnight as one is in New York at noon" (Life 7 June 52, 109), and although, according to the same report, German crowds and life in the reconstructed country in general lacked verve and were rather boring, the magazine noted that Germans also "display the mulelike steadiness and stamina that have carried them through disaster so far toward recovery" (Life 7 June 52, 109). In fact, the Life report tried to effect something like the "Babbitt-ization" of Germany, the depiction of that country as a kind of oversized enterprising midwestern town dominated by middle-class boosterism, like the fictional Zenith described in Sinclair Lewis' Babbitt. "Postwar Germany is the businessman's country," Life declared; "it is governed by his temper and geared to his ambitions" (Life 7 June 52, 110).

But most importantly, this new Germany is no longer described as the heavily cartelized industrial collossus that uses economic might to project grandiose nationalistic designs on the world, but rather as a reformed country that fully subscribes to the precepts of entrepreneurial capitalism. Thus Life assured its readers that the new generation of capitalists had finally shed their militaristic bent and now were "sober believers in private enterprise, all thinking in the same cool, practical terms," having "decided that arms were not profitable" (Life 7 June 52, 105). Obviously, these captains of industry were a far cry from the traditional nationalistic business leaders in Germany since Bismarck's time. They had been passionate believers in German greatness and superpower ambitions instead of sober business technocrats; they had defended state-sanctioned cartelization and resource pooling instead of independent private enterprise; they had also always opted for heavy industry instead of consumer goods. In short, traditional German economic elites had only provided subsequent generations of political leaders with the warmaking capability for their increasingly disastrous foreign policy adventures. But this newest generation of business leaders

Figure 5 Cold War Transformation: Alfried Krupp 1945 (Time)

was different.

The pictorial representation of Alfried Krupp, heir to the world famous industrial empire and one of the premier armament makers crucial for the global ambitions of both the Kaiserreich and the Nazis, dramatizes the American efforts to present German industry as reformed and thoroughly pacified. In 1945, Margaret Bourke-White had photographed Alfried Krupp for Life and made his portrait into a historical commentary on the ties between German industry and the military (Fig. 5). As first picture in a section contrasting the neo-feudal comportment of the monopoly industrialists with the hardship of the workers, the untouched Krupp family mansion with the bombed-out factories, Bourke-White presented an almost Expressionist wide-angle low perspective shot of Alfried in front of a painting of his great-grandfather, the founding Krupp, with the heading "Krupp: Where the War Cancer Grew" (Bourke-White 135). The harsh flash lighting and resulting threatening shadows, as well as the extreme perspective and the massive frame dominating the photo let young Krupp appear with all the demonic force that wartime America saw in the Krupps.

Figure 6 Cold War Transformation: Alfried Krupp 1954 (Time)

Less than a decade later, Bourke-White again photographed Alfried Krupp for Life as part of a photo essay entitled "Boom City of the Ruhr. Düsseldorf is a glittering citadel for Germany's newest tycoons" in the special issue on Germany (Life 10 May 54, 135). Although the report makes passing reference to the humble circumstances of the many workers, the emphasis is on the new prosperity of the bosses. And again, although an introductory note mentions Western fears about the resurgence of coal and steel production in the Ruhr and the military implications, the pictures tell a different story, depicting shop windows full of luxuries and the wealthy manufacturers of consumer goods. Similarly, the photo of Alfried Krupp allegorically visualizes the discontinuities between the old and the new Germany, with the heir to the former armaments empire no longer depicted in front of an ancestral painting but with a camera endlessly reflected between double mirrors (Fig. 6). Clearly, the underlying message here is that the new Krupp and his empire are somehow disconnected from their troubling past (the illusion of depth in the self-referentiality of the facing mirrors), are an integral and quite normal part of the new level-headed business culture (both in the infinite duplication of the reflected image and in the figure's similarity to the other businessmen), and are receptive to the requirements of the modern age (photography instead of neo-feudal painting).

The depiction of the new Germany as a somewhat boring but righteous nation of entrepreneurs, no longer interested in military world conquest but in expansion into global export markets and economic reconstruction at home, was complemented with a depiction of formerly mercurial German politics as rather soporific. Life correspondent Emmet John Hughes stated that instead of radicalism and ideological upheaval, the new Germany and its towering Chancellor, the conservative Konrad Adenauer, stood for "a pure, uncomplicated and unsophisticated clarity of mind" (Hughes 178), and Germany's political leaders had finally acquired a degree of level-headedness. "He is a genius of that rarest of God's gifts to Germans, common sense" (Hughes 178), as a close friend of Adenauer was quoted as saying in Life. Indeed, "from the somber gray of Bonn's conservatism to the cloudy torpor of the German left, the political panorama of the new Germany seems less than glittering," commented Life (Hughes 177), but then, Germany also had the "most stable parliamentary government in Western Europe" (Hughes 168).

The Cold War and the new transatlantic alliance between the former enemies fundamentally changed the American image of Germany, but because the eastern part of the reduced German Reich did not partake in this change, the older demonization of Germans was partly perpetuated in the depiction of the emerging East German state. With Cold War hysteria concerning Communism emerging in the United States, one of the foremost anti-Soviet ideologues of the new era, the American theologian Reinhold Niebuhr, noted in Life in late 1946 that "in the western zones [of occupied Germany the conservatives] claim 75% to 80% of the votes and the Communists about 10%. That is the measure of the German rejection of Communism, a much more complete rejection than in France for instance" (Niebuhr 68). Niebuhr might have added that in this respect Germany was the most "American" of the European countries. By the same measure, the emerging Cold War consensus tended to compare and even equate Communism with Fascism, Stalin with Hitler. According to Cold War historian Michael Hunt, by 1948 Truman was convinced that "the 'Frankenstein dictatorship' in the Kremlin was 'worse than any of the others,' including (Truman explicitly noted) Hitler's Third Reich" (Hunt 157). Similar to the categorical condemnation of Nazism in the later war years, ideological warriors such as Niebuhr now depicted Communism as pagan and cynical (Niebuhr 72). And predictably enough, Cold War hardliners attacked American liberals by comparing their moderate and conciliatory handling of the Soviets with the Western powers' appeasement of Hitler on the eve of World War II. But most interestingly, with the actual division of Germany into two satellite states, each oriented towards their respective superpower, and each in a sense fashioned in the image of its superpower parent, the depiction of Germans was split into good and bad Germans, into champions of American-style democracy in the West and perpetrators of "Red Fascism" in the East, as Newsweek poignantly put it in a headline on its 29 May 1950 cover, commenting on a photograph of marching paramilitary Communist police troops.[31]

The assimilation of Germany as an extension of the American self with the emergence of the Cold War consensus, finally, as well as the interventionist conventional wisdom are perfectly illustrated by yet another film, the deservedly unknown Fräulein (1958). Similar to A Foreign Affair and The Big Lift, the film questions America's involvement in Germany and recreates the emergence of (West) Germany as ally of the United States in allegorical fashion, in this case dramatizing foreign policy as pure melodrama. As much as A Foreign Affair stated the isolationist case, Fräulein dramatizes the by then canonized interventionist approach to U.S. foreign policy.

American flyboy Foster MacLain is shot down over Germany, during an air-raid escapes from his band of POWs, and finds temporary shelter in the house of a German professor, who also has a beautiful daughter. Out of basic decency rather than for ideological or political

---

[31] Of course, this was not an exclusively American formulation and used widely in contemporary West German political discourse even by members of the left-leaning social democrats.

reasons, the Angermans save MacLain from his Nazi jailers. Here the film already supplies an indirect justification for the postwar rapprochement between America and Germany by insisting on the irrelevance of ideology in the behavior of the Germans: although Erika has a Nazi fiancé, she readily hides MacLain in her bathroom when the SS come to search the Angerman house for the escaped prisoner. Given a German greatcoat, MacLain leaves the house and continues his flight.

The professor is killed in a subsequent air-raid. Erika moves in with her uncle in Berlin, where she also witnesses the fall of the city and the occupation by the literally raping and pillaging Russians. Trying to protect Erika, who is hidden away in the attic of the house requisitioned by the soldiers, her uncle is killed; Erika herself is almost raped by a drunken Russian soldier. Following Erika to the roof when she manages to escape through a window, the Russian soldier falls down and is killed. Erika is taken to the Soviet headquarters where she is charged with his murder, and can finally only be saved from immediate doom by being taken up by a Russian colonel, who falls in love with her when he sees her. He is soon ready to marry her, and for the time being, fulfills her every wish. Rather put off by the boorish advances of the colonel and realizing that she has ended up in the wrong sector of the divided city, Erika eventually flees to West Berlin. There she is taken up by a friendly couple, but as she soon finds out, they only want her as the latest addition to their family-run brothel. As soon as she realizes where she is, she tries to leave, causing a fight that is finally broken up by an American patrol. In the meantime, however, MacLain, who has returned to Germany as an occupation officer, has been trying to locate Erika and her father to thank them for saving his life. He finally finds her -- now a diving board model in a nightclub. Expecting him not to be any different from all the other men beleaguering her, however, she spurns his advances. Predictably enough, MacLain finally succeeds in winning her heart and the two plan to settle in the States. Obviously, Erika's innocence, threatened by the opportunism of her friends as well as the sexual threat posed by the Russians, can only be safeguarded and defended by the bright American knight. Germany, like Erika almost without friends, would only be raped by Russia or sold down the river by political opportunists if not protected by Uncle Sam.

Two obstacles remain, however, to Erika and MacLain's marital bliss. There is still a Nazi fiancé in the background and Erika is also registered as a prostitute, which bars her from getting a visa to the United States. These two threats obviously signify the burden of the German (Nazi) past and the leftist opposition (the Social democrats, who severely criticized Adenauer's ardent West-orientation at the time and who were accused of being a front for Soviet interests), which both seemed to stand in the way of the sacred union between Germany and America. With MacLain's help Erika finds out that her ex-fiancé is a cripple and lives with another woman. Unlike the potent threat posed by Bergel in A Foreign Affair, who almost succeeds in killing Captain Pringle, the inevitable Nazi "in the background" is no longer to be taken seriously in Fräulein. The handicap of being listed in Military Government records as prostitute, however, is a little harder to overcome, but here again the film stresses that basic human decency has priority over ideological concerns. Of course so far only the audience knows that Erika is innocent and was only lured into signing the registration form by her designing friends; yet, she is lucky and the same sergeant who helped her during her escape from the brothel now has to handle her papers, and, with a wink, gives her a clean bill of health. Obviously innocent and only blemished through unfortunate circumstances, Erika as well as Germany are fit for American protection and the sacred Cold War union. The defense of the beleaguered maiden has precedence over bureaucratic procedures. To save Germany from the Soviet threat, America has to re-evaluate its formally correct hard peace approach to the conquered country.

Shot on location in West Germany and in Berlin, a contemporary reviewer faulted the film for its episodic character (New York Times 9 June 58, 27), and indeed Fräulein is a far cry from the dynamism created by the ideological conflicts underlying Billy Wilder's and George Seaton's films about Americans in Germany. Indeed the curious lack of energy in Fräulein might be explained by the absence of a true conflict; the film only seems to reiterate and illustrate the solutions to an ideological conflict long dead. The isolationist position advocated by A Foreign Affair and to some extent The Big Lift was by now no longer a viable alternative, and to argue for interventionist policies and for the rapprochement between Germany and America had become a moot point by 1958. Instead of testing the limits of American global involvement, the logic of superpower rivalry, and the containment doctrine, as for instance Stanley Kubrick's Dr. Strangelove did only a few years later, Fräulein chooses to reaffirm the American foreign policy position towards Germany and the Cold War consensus. At the same time, Fräulein also illustrates the assimilation of the German cultural other to the American self. Again, and in contrast to A Foreign Affair and The Big Lift, Fräulein is devoid of the displaced cultural anxieties that fueled the two earlier films. In McLain, America is personified at its paternalistic worst and as no longer anxious about any threat of infection or emasculation abroad. In Fräulein the only anxiety depicted is the familiar female reticence in the face of male advances, an anxiety that -- although it might be taken to express real contemporary German fears about cultural domination by the big American brother/lover -- is discounted and depicted as a mere diversion on the inevitable road to cultural marriage.

The four films considered here more or less directly engage in contemporary foreign policy debates. Apart from the obvious reference to specific problems of the occupation and the relations between America and Germany, what is at stake in them ideologically is the attempt to formulate a workable postwar approach to American involvement in global affairs. All four films play through different policy scenarios by allegorizing foreign relations as sexual relations, by deflecting political drama into romantic melodrama or comedy.

The four films as Hollywood productions also clearly partake in what cultural critic Antonio Gramsci has described as cultural hegemony, constructed in the ideological "complex of trenches and fortifications of the dominant class" (390). At the same time, it is clear that the battle-lines in this cultural conflict are constantly shifting and that they are hotly contested. As a result, the four films constitute not so much a coherent political statement but rather illustrate the process of ideological entrenchment and fortification, the effort to arrive at a kind of foreign policy consensus. And as the example of Fräulein shows, once that conflict has crystallized into a set of clear-cut positions, the fortifications have already begun to lose their ideological effectiveness once the real conflict has moved on to other newly contested areas.

In the same way, after the creation of the West German state in 1949 and the incremental political normalization at least in America's Germany, that country as a foil for the process of American political self-definition increasingly lost ground. With the Korean war, attention eventually shifted away from Germany to other parts of the globe, and the drama of public foreign policy formulation and debate was accordingly be played out in films (such as, for instance, The Manchurian Candidate) focusing on those foreign parts. But for a time, Germany was at the center of ideological attention and catalytic in the articulation of a changed American role in the world.

Chapter Four - "Industrial Counter-Revolution": The New Deal in Germany

In the previous chapter we have seen how Hollywood's depiction of postwar Germany articulated a critique of contemporary foreign policy and projected American concerns on the foreign country in an even more specific manner than comparable literary engagements. Surprisingly enough, American politicians and administrators similarly conceived of Germany as a foil and mirror image after World War II, as we will see in this chapter. New Deal reformers, I will argue, conceived of Germany both as a key symbol by which different economic alternatives could be imaginatively tested and as a practical laboratory for their plans for industrial reorganization. New Dealers intended the reconstructed Germany to become an object lesson in the politically redemptive power of trustbusting. Consequently, the plans for the political and economic reconstruction of Germany were designed as a practical commentary on and even critique of America, just like the American novels and films analyzed in the foregoing chapters. But while literary accounts, films and the press only intervened imaginatively and/or rhetorically in Germany, the American military government abroad and policy-makers at home in Washington directly shaped material reality in the occupied country.

Just as Hollywood's depiction of Germany in the immediate postwar period must be seen as an attempt to influence the future shape of American foreign policy, as I have tried to show in the last chapter, New Deal plans for the economic reorganization of Germany can be seen as the desperate attempt to come to terms with the legacy of the industrial revolution that had transformed America in the wake of the Civil War. I will argue that, on the one hand, the architect of President Roosevelt's policy for defeated Germany, Henry Morgenthau, attempted to turn back the clock to pre-industrial times and meant to refashion Germany after an ideal of economic innocence and agrarianism that had been lost in America with the coming of modern industry. On the other hand, the reformist lawyers of the Justice Department tried to continue instead in Germany the domestic trustbusting campaign that they had had to abandon when the U.S. entered the war. Prevented from interfering with big business in the name of the war effort, the Economic Warfare Section at the Justice Department and later the Decartelization Branch of Military Government in Germany attempted to continue abroad what they could not do at home, namely their work against the threat posed to democracy by the concentration of productive power. The New Dealers' plans for Germany only fully make sense, I will argue, if they are understood as the product of displaced reformist zeal directed against Germany but intended for America. The "industrial counter-revolution" proposed by the New Deal in Germany, as we will see, is thus not only an attempt to solve the German problem, but also part of the struggle to change the course of economic and political development in America.

The New Deal reformers had in mind a critique of America when they addressed the problem of German reconstruction. They conceived of Germany as a mirror-image of America and intended to reform the occupied country in order to provide a visible and practical example of the viability of their socio-economic ideas. Indeed, the antitrusters came to Germany in a spirit somewhat similar to that which had brought the Puritan founding fathers to America. John Winthrop and his fellow Puritans had conceived of America as model city upon a hill and example to Christendom in general and the Anglican church in particular. The antitrusters had similar ideas about their German experiment and hoped to inspire the democratic forces in America with their model of government talking back to big business in Germany.

In this chapter, then, we will see that writers, journalists and film makers were not alone in turning to Germany in order to see or criticize America, but rather that even on the level where foreign policy is formulated and implemented, we can detect the same -- and by now familiar -- perceptual pattern of taking the cultural other as a commentary on the self.

It seems necessary to remind my readers that I am not trying to write history here, but rather to engage in cultural critique, interpreting the history of American antitrust in Germany by examining its ideological origins and its structural similarity to imaginative encounters with the foreign country. In my reading of the New Dealers' approach to Germany, I rely not only on the published recollections of involved parties such as Henry Morgenthau and James Martin, but also on the accounts of various historians. I will draw on business historians to highlight the conceptual challenges facing the New Deal trustbusters, use historical accounts of trustbusting and the New Deal in order to show the roots of American ideas and motivations for the industrial reconstruction of Germany, and quote from the work of diplomatic historians who have traced the trajectory and evaluated the success of New Deal antitrust in occupied Germany. Yet, although it will be necessary to reconstruct a number of particular historical contexts, I am not providing any new historical evidence, exploring instead how the tradition of Populist protest against industrial capitalism shaped the American approach to the problem of German reconstruction.

In the following, in a necessarily somewhat circuitous route, I will first trace the influence that earlier Populist protest against the concentration of industrial power had on the plan for the economic reorganization of Germany advanced by Henry Morgenthau. In the second part of this chapter, I will then show how the checkered history of New Deal approaches to the problem of industrialization eventually brought New Deal reformers to Germany in order to continue abroad their abortive domestic trustbusting campaign, and how they rhetorically constructed Germany both as a promise of liberal reform for America, and as a warning against the political dangers posed by big business to American democracy.

Back to the Farm for Germany: Henry Morgenthau's Agrarian Nostalgia

In contrast to the other allied powers, who had far less idealistic political agendas for the reconstruction of the defeated Reich, the U.S. intended to shape the new Germany in its own image and as a model democracy. A decentralized and decartelized economy was to be part of that political package. Unlike the Americans, the Soviets, with a badly war-damaged economy, were content to have lived to see the demise of their arch-rival for European hegemony. Mainly interested in reparations, they simply disassembled everything from workshops to whole factories and ferried the material east. The British, without a trustbusting tradition, and under Labour rule pursuing the nationalization of domestic industries at the time, failed to view cartelization as a problem and were primarily interested in quick economic recovery in their zone anyway. But for American reformers, Germany provided a kind of laboratory to test their ideas for an ideal democratic society. The architect of President Roosevelt's plans for the shape of post-World War II Germany, Henry Morgenthau had in mind a Jeffersonian, pre-industrial agrarian state, a distinctly American socio-economic ideal. As the idealized vision underlying various trustbusting programs in the past, agrarianism had also been the traditional and customary American response to the pressures of industrialization since the late 19th century. The element of tradition was so obvious in the American approach to German reconstruction that British occupation officials derisively characterized the trustbusting efforts of their transatlantic counterparts as "a kind of American hobby" (Taylor 35).

      As Roosevelt's Secretary of the Treasury, Morgenthau would normally only have been concerned with questions of occupation currency, and thus have at best marginal interest in American policies for defeated Germany. However, a staunch believer in a hard peace for Germany since he had witnessed the German "buzzbomb" V1 terror attacks on London, Morgenthau objected to plans for economic reconstruction of the defeated enemy prepared by the War and State Departments. He was in a unique position to sidetrack the policies of his rivals in those two departments. Friends with Roosevelt since 1914, when he bought an estate next to that of the Roosevelts in upstate New York, Morgenthau was also one of the president's staunchest political allies. Their political partnership began when Morgenthau in 1928 organized the Agricultural Advisory Commission for Roosevelt, then governor of New York (cf. Carter, New Dealers 106ff.). As a result of their long association, Morgenthau had easy access to and more direct influence on the president than the officials in the State and War departments. His plans for defeated Germany thus prevailed for a time over those of the foreign policy experts.

      Morgenthau was steeped in agrarian ideology and pre-industrial values, and had been a successful farmer even during the Depression. But while he obviously was a shrewd businessman, he lacked broader economic understanding. Indeed, when he became Secretary of the Treasury in Roosevelt's administration, the political establishment was a little puzzled about the choice. "Whether he is anything more than [a good organizer] -- except a country gentleman -- is not revealed by his shy taciturnity," wrote an observer about him in 1934. "Certainly, no one has accused him of incubating economic ideas of any sort" (Carter, New Dealers 106). Morgenthau's lack of modern economic understanding, paired with his easy access to the president, led to the adoption of an impractical plan for the de-industrialization of Germany and an American policy that stipulated that country's return to an agrarian society as the price for aggression. In Germany Is Our Problem (1945), Morgenthau aptly described the nature of his plans for a peaceful Germany as "industrial counter revolution" (the title of his fifth chapter) and declared: "My own program for ending the menace of German aggression consists, in its simplest terms, of depriving Germany of all heavy industries" (Morgenthau 16). As the only alternative to a fully industrialized and thus threatening Germany, Morgenthau proposed a reconstructed agrarian German state.

The pastoralized Germany that Morgenthau constructed was clearly a utopian space rooted in the tradition of American anti-industrial sentiment. Needless to say, his vision was an inadequate response both to the needs of postwar Germany, and to the foreign policy objectives of the United States, which focused on European political stability. Rather, Morgenthau clutched on the need for a democratic reconstruction of Germany and used it as a chance to try to realize his agrarian ideals, to build a Germany in the image of pre-industrial America. The Germany that Morgenthau envisioned in his plans thus cannot be seen but as a kind of counter-image and indirect critique of industrialized America. An agrarian Germany had its roots not in a level-headed analysis of the political and economic situation, but in a particularly American conception of democratic society that had hardened into dogma as a response to the process of industrialization.

The Morgenthau plan employed one of the most effective and time-honored strategies the young American republic had developed for dealing with its anti-democratic enemies within and without, agrarianism.

In young America, the health of the new republican institutions had been founded on the role of the farmer, the independent and proud yeoman idealized from Hector St. Jean de Crèvecoeur to Thomas Jefferson. Moreover, as Ronald T. Takaki reports in Iron Cages, Jefferson even proposed to contain the Indian threat by making the savages into farmers. Thus Takaki:

> To civilize the Indian meant, for Jefferson, to take him from his hunting way of life and convert him into a farmer. As President of the United States, [Jefferson] told the Potawatomies: "We shall ... see your people become disposed to cultivate the earth, to raise herds of useful animals, and to spin and weave, for their food and clothing. These resources are certain: they will never disappoint you: while those of hunting may fail, and expose your women and children to the miseries of hunger and cold." (Takaki 55f.)

Jefferson's humanitarian rhetoric, however, only masks his imperialist intentions in this passage. The Indian tribes stood in the way of the westward progress of empire (Jefferson thus, for instance, instructed the Lewis/Clark expedition, exploring a water passage across the continent, to collect information on Indian tribes), and with horses and an abundance of wild buffalo, they had ample resources for their survival. Rather, the native Americans only posed a threat as hunters; usually, one buffalo would supply a family with enough food for a year, which left the hunting parties too much time to spend on the warpath. By contrast, if they had to meet their subsistence needs as farmers, they would have to spend a lot of time cultivating the land and would thus be pacified.

Morgenthau's solution of the German problem followed an identical agrarian logic. The industrial revolution made possible the creation of an enormous surplus value, and at least theoretically, freedom from material want. It also made possible extended wars. Morgenthau, like Jefferson thinking about the Indians before him, thus concluded that the easiest way to shackle the German beast was to deprive it of its ability to create material surplus; let it be busy with feeding itself instead. Consequently, the transformation of Germany into a pre-industrial agrarian society is Morgenthau's solution and he summed up his plan by saying, "Germany's road to peace leads to the farm" (Morgenthau 48).

For Morgenthau, the best way of dealing with Germany would be to reconstruct the country in the image of pre-industrial America, with individual entrepreneurs and small industry. In the new German state, an economic ideal that had been canonized in the long (populist) tradition of industrial discontent going back well into the 1880's would be put into reality. Although it is hard to imagine a different course for industrial progress nowadays, the return to a kind of Jacksonian economy and democracy to Morgenthau still seemed a possible solution to the political problems of the industrial age. Yet, not many of his contemporaries shared that optimism, probably realizing that at the close of World War II, concentrated industrial power was so firmly established and had already transformed American society so much as to preclude a realization of Jeffersonian social ideals for all practical purposes. Yet, firmly rooted ideologically in an bygone age, Morgenthau still believed in the viability of pre-industrial ideals in an industrial age. His plan for a reconstructed Germany and his implicit polemic against American industrialization are informed by what can be called the tradition of American industrial discontent, a tradition that created a distinctive rhetoric, images and concepts.

Diversion on the Rhetoric of Industrial Discontent

The industrial revolution not only created unprecedented national wealth, it also gave rise to Populism which focused grassroots discontent with the new developments. However, faced with new industrial giants like railroads or big oil, Populist critics faced as much a political as as a conceptual challenge as they both had to find ways of checking the power of the new concerns and to find the terms and concepts that would adequately describe the organizational revolution that had taken place, as we will see in more detail shortly. For a long time, they failed in both tasks, mainly because they remained oblivious to the qualitative change brought about by the industrial revolution. But in spite of the inadequacy of its conceptual economic framework, the following short diversion in my main argument will make clear that Populist protest became almost a reflex and an ingrained American tradition because it seemed to demand a return to the hallowed political and economic traditions of the revolutionary founding fathers.

The onset of industrialization revolutionized traditional economic practices. The coming of the railroad, the widespread use and availability of coal as energy source, and the introduction of the telegraph, transformed the way America did business. The railroads and the telegraph not only spearheaded what was known as the course of empire, the westward expansion across the continent, they also created new markets, and allowed hitherto local manufacturers to distribute their goods across the nation. New methods of communication and distribution in turn profoundly altered production patterns, since bigger markets allowing higher output demanded mass production. For the first time in human history it became possible for industrial societies to produce more than enough material goods for everybody and for modern populations to raise significantly above the subsistence level.

The industrial revolution also led to increasingly big business enterprises. Heavy industries like railroads were inordinately capital intensive and thus needed enormous scale economies. Unit costs could only be lowered by long production runs, or, in the case of railroads, only long networks could make them profitable, since the unit cost per mile decreased with every additional mile served. Many firms thus could become competitive through sheer size, by mass producing for big markets, markets created by the distribution revolution of the railroads. The growth of business enterprises in turn sparked an organizational revolution, heralding what business historian Alfred D. Chandler has called "managerial capitalism": "Greater speed and volume in the production and movement of goods [...] necessitated the creation of managerial hierarchies to supervise, monitor, and coordinate the new processes" (Chandler 15). Expanding railroads were the first enterprises to employ several layers of managers, who no longer could be recruited just from the family of the owners. But the trend soon spread. The growth of modern enterprise, triggered by industrialization, thus meant a growth in size, the birth of managerial hierarchies, and the coming of managerial capitalism, with its division of ownership and responsibility for operations.

The rise of managerial capitalism profoundly altered the shape of the American economy. Depending on their capital-intensity and scale economies, two kinds of firms crystallized, so-called center and periphery firms. Capital intensive and usually technologically advanced and with significant scale economies, center firms such as steel and oil manufacturers, machine producers such as Singer or International Harvester, or even consumer goods firms such as Quaker Oats or Pillsbury Flour, grew to enormous size and remained large, as Chandler points out. Periphery firms, by contrast, were small and never grew large successfully; usually labor-intensive and not highly technologized, without the advantage of scale economies, and grouped in such industries as printing, textiles, clothing, or building materials, periphery firms also lacked managerial hierarchies. Obviously, center firms were a creation of the industrial revolution, and periphery firms characterized an older, pre-industrial capitalism. The point is crucial because most of the American populist and trustbusting critics of industrial development, including Morgenthau and the New Dealers, did not herald a return to pre-capitalist modes of production, but rather idealized a pre-industrial capitalist system made up of individual and independent entrepreneurs of Benjamin Franklin vintage as described by Adam Smith. But more importantly, proposing a return to a market as that proposed by Adam Smith, these critics of big business failed to grasp the implications of the qualitative change brought about by the industrial revolution, the creation of center industries that defied the logic of traditional (pre-industrial) economics.

The new center firms profoundly threatened the most cherished precepts of free market economics, namely the concept of competition, and even seemed to challenge the very concept of a free market. Theorists and legislators soon noticed with bafflement that "if scale economies were sufficiently great, then competition in the accepted sense of the word simply did not apply" (McCraw 9). Thus, for instance, in the case of railroads, competition and cheapest possible transportation were impossible to reconcile. Competition meant larger capacity, and thus resulted in higher average cost because of unrealized scale economies. Moreover, the emergence of center firms also made obsolete Adam Smith's model of the market as guided by the invisible hand of supply and demand. Chandler stresses that "in sectors dominated by the new, large enterprises, the top-level managers of a few modern multiunit companies made the decisions that had previously been made by the owners of thousands of small firms" (Chandler 15). Smith's pre-industrial invisible hand of market mechanisms had become the visible hand of salaried managers in the modern business enterprise.

Most contemporary observers saw the very size of the new business concerns as unnatural. In 1871, when the number of government employees was roughly fifty thousand, almost thirty-seven thousand of them (over seventy percent) in the postal system, American railroads had many times that number of people in their pay (McCraw 67, 4). For people who lacked the concepts necessary for a realistic understanding of the technological, organizational and economic changes, "in the early years of industrialization, the trusts seemed to be mysterious mutations, the consequences of some evil tampering with the natural order of things. A kind of conspiratorial view is thus an integral part of the rhetorical strategies of industrial discontent. Lacking a vocabulary to describe the new economic forces, and furthermore failing to realize that a profound structural revolution had taken place, critics of economic concentration could only demonize trusts and big concerns. The substitution of radical rhetoric for a lacking sophisticated economic analysis is one of the defining characteristics of Populist antitrust sentiment.

Antitrust sentiment was a reaction against industrialization. The transformation of the American economy to a fully industrialized state caused severe social hardship as the productive power of new industrial processes led to cyclical booms and busts, the inevitable adaptation struggles of a new economic system. Over-investment, over-expansion and over-production led the crashes of 1873 and 1893. Especially hard hit by the busts were farmers and the emergent factory proletariat. Organizational and political responses ensued, be they the alliance of farmers that started with the Grange in the 1870's and resulted in the Populist party two decades later, or the violent strikes and rise of labor unions during the same period.

The industrial revolution and the emergence of concentrated economic strength challenged the traditional distribution of power within civil society. Populist critics felt that "cartels were not merely economic freaks but also sinister new political forces -- powers that had to be opposed in the name of American democracy" (McCraw 77). Originally, monopolies had meant royal privilege and the granting of exclusive rights by the crown, and thus "symbolized the corrupt, absolutist powers against which the founding fathers had fought their revolution" (McCraw 10). They constituted a threat to the American dream and to cherished republican traditions, and many people saw large corporations as parallel governments of an evil, essentially neo-feudal, nature. The trajectory of industrialization towards ever increasing concentration of productive power seemed to defy the logic of America's historical progress towards democratic perfection and a throwback to an earlier time. To concerned observers the power and influence of the captains of American industry seemed like a return of colonial rule.

The rise of managerial capitalism and the process of industrialization consequently were seen as a threat to the democratic ideals of the republic and a challenge to the achievements of the revolution. Populist critics thus stylized their political complaint into a "world-old war between Freedom and Tyranny" (Norris, Octopus 820). Clearly, the advent of heavy industries and the rise of big business necessitated a rethinking of the distribution of power in civil society. Yet, not fully realizing the implications of their demands, which would have meant a significant drop in the average level of technological accomplishment and the newly acquired higher standard of living, critics of industrialization mostly rested content with demanding a return to older, pre-industrial values, or with arguing for the breakup of concentrated economic power.

Parallel to political activism, a heated conceptual debate ensued about the meaning of big business, a debate that tried to square the old assumptions about the marketplace with the new industrial realities. Novelists and journalists, together with progressive legislators, waged an ideological battle against the conditions of industrial capitalism. Yet, most of the thinking and terminology of the critics of industrialization was inadequate to the new situation and rooted in pre-industrial concepts. The common "lament about the decline of autonomous individualism [...] was the conflict between the small producer's values, which had characterized nineteenth-century American culture, and the emerging consumerist values of a twentieth-century mass society" (McCraw 106). The discourse of industrial discontent often proved to be nostalgic and not very effective in bringing about change. Thus Alfred Kazin has argued that American realism "was rooted in those dark and still little-understood years of the 1880's and 1890's when all America stood suddenly, as it were, between one society and another. [...] It was rooted [...] in the sense of surprise and shock that led to the crudely expectant Utopian literature of the eighties and nineties, the largest single body of Utopian writing in modern times, and the most transparent in its nostalgia" (Kazin viii-ix; my emphasis). Antitrust sentiment has its roots in the same nostalgia, the same estrangement "on native grounds" from the realities of industrial capitalism that Kazin is concerned with.

Populist criticism and trustbusting created their own rhetorical conventions and images resulting in what might be called the poetics of industrial discontent. Let us examine two examples, William Dean Howells' The Rise of Silas Lapham (1884) and Frank Norris' The Octopus (1901).

The Rise of Silas Lapham illustrates the nostalgia for pre-industrial values inherent in Populist critiques of industrialization; interestingly enough, the novel also directly anticipates Morgenthau's prescriptions for postwar Germany. The novel about a paint manufacturer's business success and eventual undoing through the vagaries of financial speculation and mis-management could be read as a wholesale indictment of the forces of capitalism and a battle cry for the return to pre-capitalist self-sufficiency.[32] Yet, the Laphams' return to their personal and economic origins towards the end of the novel rather seems to signify a return to the business-ethic of an earlier and simpler age, where America could do without the perversions of finance, which are characteristic of industrial times. Like all of the anti-industrial rhetoric, Howells thus does not indict capitalism as such, but industrial capitalism. The return to pre-industrial enterprise reverses the process of social fragmentation, expressed through the fragmentation of the

---

[32] As Walter Benn Michaels has argued in The Gold Standard and the Logic of Naturalism (Berkeley: University of California Press. 1987. 38-41; 50-51)

Lapham family. "In the shadow of his disaster," Howells writes about Lapham and his family in the wake of his bankruptcy, "they returned to something like their old, united life; they were at least all together again" (Howells 367). Lapham's return to Ben Franklinesque pre-industrial industry and frugality also restores his "manhood," reverses the process of self-alienation dramatized as emasculation: "Adversity [...] restored him, through failure and doubt and heartache, the manhood which his prosperity had nearly stolen from him" (Howells 374).

Howells allegorically charts the course of the post-Civil War industrial revolution in America in the depiction of the Laphams. Lapham himself pinpoints the watershed when he muses for an interviewer at the beginning of the novel about the change on his return from the war, and remarks that "the day of small things was past, and I don't suppose it will ever come again in this country" (Howells 15). The novel also depicts the independent dynamic of industrial growth, the mind-boggling fact that suddenly there was more than enough for everybody. Mrs. Lapham recalls that, "suddenly the money began to come so abundantly that she need not save; and then they did not know what to do with it" (Howells 24). This logic of excess would also turn out to be the undoing of Silas Lapham. Although he insists that all his wealth was "honest money -- no speculation -- every copper of it for value received" (Howells 214), Lapham himself, and his wife even more so, constantly doubt the moral integrity of their success, since they still believe they gave their early (financial) partner a rough deal when they crowded him out of the growing and successful paint business. Finally it is the return of this earlier rough deal, in the logic of excess of industrial finance itself, that makes Lapham a victim by inducing him to speculate financially, to gamble and to lose it all. As one character in the novel speculates at some point, "there's no doubt but money is to the fore now. It is the romance, the poetry of our age" (Howells 64). If money is the poetry of the new times, the trajectory of Silas Lapham's career and the inevitability of his rise, suffering, fall and eventual redemption constitute the poetics of discontent with the industrial age, which saw new economic practices and thus depicted them as leading to a tragic outcome.

While The Rise of Silas Lapham mostly extols the virtues of

pre-industrial capitalism and describes the dangers of the industrial logic of excess, Norris' The Octopus dramatizes the neo-feudal threat that big business poses to democracy, further illustrating the rhetoric and images of industrial discontent. Norris makes the octopus as one of the most pervasive images of antitrust sentiment the reigning metaphor of his narrative, and symbolically equates the railroad's threat to life, liberty and the pursuit of happiness with the horror of the sea monster. In the novel, he describes the fight of the San Joaquin valley farmers against the Pacific and Southwestern Railroad in terms of the eternal struggle between good and evil, dark and light, but also as parallel to the Revolution and the Civil war as the momentous struggles for (political) liberty in American history. Transported by the murder of his farmer friends, the protagonist of the novel and authorial alter ego, Presley, exclaims, "and this is America. We fought Lexington to free ourselves; we fought Gettysburg to free others. Yet the yoke remains; we have only shifted it to the other shoulder" (Norris, Octopus 1017). Obviously, to conceive of the fight against the big trusts as a fight for democracy and against neo-feudalism had practically become a common-place and integral part of the rhetoric of industrial discontent by the turn of the century. It would remain part and parcel of the trustbusters' self-conception for at least another half-century, when the New Dealers depicted the threat of concentrated economic power in identical terms.

In the same way that the manichean struggle between farmers and the railroad attains epic proportions in Norris' novel, the people aligned with the farmers or with the railroad become incarnations of pure good and evil. The railroad itself and all the people connected with its operations are thus transformed into monsters, unnatural creations. Railroad agent S. Behrman's obesity and unnatural features, the stereotypically Populist characterization of big business as fat man with a cigar, metonymically describe the voraciousness of the freakish economical monster he works for. "He was a large, fat man, with a great stomach; his cheek and the upper part of his thick neck ran together to form a great tremulous jowl, shaven and blue-grey in color" (Norris, Octopus 629). And even the railroad-train itself as personification of big business, becomes a giant killer with an "enormous eye, cyclopean, red" (Norris, Octopus 615), a cannibalistic force and "gigantic parasite fattening upon the life-blood of an entire commonwealth" (Norris, Octopus 806), and Presley pays trembling homage to it as "the leviathan, with tentacles of steel clutching into the soil, the soulless Force, the iron-hearted Power, the monster, the Colossus, the Octopus" (Norris, Octopus 617). Big business as monster, as unnatural and as a freakish threat to man, woman and child, of course, is a prime example of trustbusting rhetoric that recasts the struggle of the classical tragic hero as the fight between a free and a centralized market, between individual entrepreneurs and centralized business enterprises, as it would be described by Brandeis and later the New Dealers.

The opposite of the unnatural and monstrous cartels, and the shining hero to the bogeyman of concentrated economic power, is the individual businessman. Like Howells, Norris glorifies the farmers as entrepreneurs in the tradition of personal capitalism. Moreover, in best Populist fashion, the economic world is divided into small struggling businesses and a few monster concerns which drink their lifeblood. Thus on occasion of the raised freight rate, now ruined hops-farmer and ex-railroad engineer Dyke fumes that

> constantly this sort of thing must occur -- little industries choked out in their very beginnings, the air full of the death rattles of little enterprises, expiring unobserved in far-off counties, up in cañons and arroyos of the foothills, forgotten by every one but the monster who was daunted by the magnitude of no business, however great, who overlooked no opportunity of plunder, however petty, who with one tentacle grabbed a hundred thousand acres of wheat, and with another pilfered a pocketful of growing hops. (Norris, Octopus 861)

But the railroad as enemy stands for industrial and managerial capitalism, and again, as in Howells and in subsequent formulations of the trustbusting faith, the ideal of a bygone age in The Octopus is the entrepreneur of personal and pre-industrial capitalism. With only slight changes, by substituting the monster IG Farben or DuPont concerns for the railroad and by enlarging the arena of struggle to international proportions, Dykes' protracted complaint would function equally well as a mid-century American critique of chemical cartels.

Overall, trustbusting as much as Howells' and Norris' novels was inspired more by nostalgia than by an analysis of underlying economic realities. Populist critics refused to acknowledge that the concentration of economic power was an almost inevitable result of the industrial revolution and that the rise of a modern economy had closed the door for good on an agrarian democracy in spite of habitual official lip service to its traditions. In spite of the Sherman antitrust act, in spite of the breakup of Standard Oil, and even in spite of Justice Brandeis' great campaign of 1912 (more on the topic later) that had only achieved mediocre results, by the 1930's it had become clear that trustbusting as a practical response to industrialization had not fulfilled its promises for economic reform. At the same time, trustbusting had clearly become an American tradition and as much part of the national self-conception as the American Revolution.

Shortly before he was made head of the antitrust section -- an appointment that many observers regarded as somewhat paradoxical given his recent attacks on trustbusting -- Thurman Arnold described antitrust laws as ineffectual rhetoric in The Folklore of Capitalism (1937).[33] Arnold argued that antitrust legislation resulted from the contradiction between industrialization and the traditional image of an economy of individual entrepreneurs. Quite perceptive and realistic in comparison with other trustbusters in the analysis of the process of industrialization in America, Arnold claimed that "specialized techniques made bigness essential to producing goods in large enough quantities and at a price low enough so that they could be made part of the American standard of living" (207). Arnold avoids the basic mistake underlying Populist attacks on big industrial concerns and clears the conceptual muddle informing the rhetoric of industrial discontent.

More importantly, though, Arnold also debunks trustbusting as

---

[33] Because he had painted such a detracting picture of antitrust efforts, Arnold's nomination led to lengthy congressional hearings in which he was able to explain away the apparent irony and contradiction of making its most savage critic head of the trustbusting program (cf. Hawley 421-24).

one more American myth and as a fantasy of a pre-industrial economy oddly out of touch with the realities of the day. According to Arnold, America failed to adjust its agrarian self-conception to the changed reality and continued to describe and approach its now fully industrialized economy with pre-industrial terms and ideals. Arnold thus explains trustbusting as the symptom of an unacknowledged and displaced social transformation. He argues that "in order to reconcile the ideal [of a pre-industrial economy] with the practical necessity, it became necessary to develop a procedure which constantly attacked bigness on rational legal and economic grounds, and at the same time never really interfered with combinations" (207). In short, instead of adapting inadequate concepts of the marketplace to changed conditions, America had thought up trustbusting. For illustration, Arnold compares the Sherman antitrust laws to the ridiculously ineffective prohibition of alcohol, the criminalization of prostitution, and to moral preaching in general, moral crusades "which were entirely futile but enormously picturesque, and which paid big dividends in terms of personal prestige" (217).

Arnold thus practically conceives of trustbusting as yet another "American ideology," so to speak, as an element of an almost mythical account of national character. Arnold's caustic criticism of trustbusting is also the most lucid description of trustbusting as a rhetorical -- and not practical -- reaction to the pressures of technological and social change brought about by the industrial revolution. His description practically redefines the nature of anti-trust action and shifts its relevance from the realm of political regulation to that of purely ideological work. "The antitrust laws were the answer of a society which unconsciously felt the need of great organizations, and at the same time had to deny them a place in the moral and logical ideology of the social structure. They were part of the struggle of a creed of rugged individualism to adapt itself to what was becoming a highly organized society" (Arnold 211). Given Arnold's description of trustbusting as the "folklore of capitalism," every resurgence of Populist sentiment in time of crisis can be seen as an imaginary return, as it were, to the mythical origins of the erstwhile agrarian American republic that rehearses nostalgia for pre-industrial values and is a self-assuring national reflex. Not surprisingly, with the shape of the postwar America and the world at stake and prefigured in the new Germany, Morgenthau had recourse to this tradition when he formulated his practical plans for the defeated country's economic reconstruction.

For Morgenthau, the reconstruction of Germany also promised a revision of the historical development of industrialization and a return to a pre-industrial society. He hoped that if his program for the deindustrialization of Germany worked and resulted in a truly democratic society, it might be taken as blueprint for reform in America, which had been grappling with the industrial threat to democracy since the late 19th century.

Back to the Farm for Germany: Morgenthau's Agrarian Nostalgia (contd.)

Writing about the future of Germany -- clearly intended as model for America -- Morgenthau essentially only employed the established conventions, images, and solutions of the trustbusting tradition in a kind of formulaic way. The yearning for simpler, pre-industrial values and the invisible hand conceptualized by Adam Smith, the indictment of absentee ownership and managerial hierarchies, big business' threat to democracy and the perennial fight for liberty and against tyranny, as well as the well-stocked arsenal of bestiary metaphors for big business all can be found in his account and grow out of the rhetorical tradition of industrial discontent. As generations of agrarian critics before him, Morgenthau attempted to tackle a problem of a highly industrialized society with the concepts and vocabulary of pre-industrial times. As a result, squarely within the tradition of trustbusting and without consideration for the real needs of the country, he imagined a reconstructed Germany as a kind of Jeffersonian pre-industrial agrarian state.

Morgenthau is most indebted to his Populist forebears when, in best muckraking fashion, he depicts German industry as colossus and -- octopus! "At least as early as 1920, [...] German industrialists began their campaign of building up heavy industries [...]. Typical of them, and one of the first, since it was organized in 1919 [sic], was the octopus-like I.G. Farben" (Morgenthau 123). The metaphor bears out Morgenthau's ideological origins. An objective analysis of the problem of German cartels would have shown that economic concentration is to some extent unavoidable in the process of industrialization; furthermore, Morgenthau must also have realized that cartel-like structures were neither restricted to nor originated in Germany and that the international relationships of German industry were far from unilateral. Morgenthau's undifferentiated and polemical depiction of the cartel problem raises many serious questions that economists

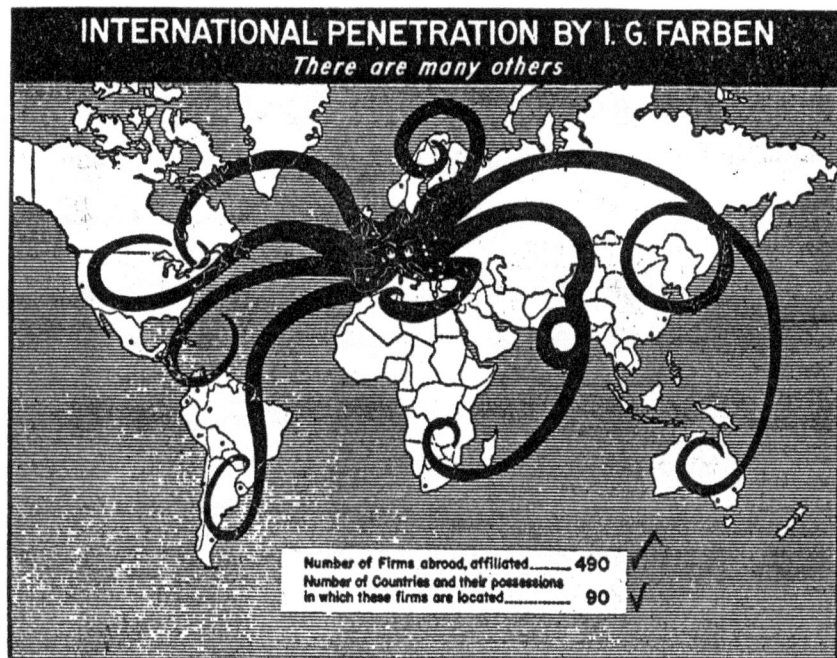

Figure 7 Henry Morgenthau's Trustbusting Rhetoric: The German Octopus (Germany is our Problem)

were then beginning to address. But surely, his recourse to the old Populist rhetoric was inadequate in any case. Morgenthau constructs an image of Germany that is defined by the commonplace assumptions of American trustbusters since the late 19th century. His Germany only bears faint resemblance to the Nazi state, and is instead another barely changed incarnation of Norris' monster-railroad, another version of the American industrial critics' colossus of big business. Morgenthau's presumed German octopus is a curiously American animal.

Morgenthau also included a little graph detailing "International penetration by I.G. Farben," which visualizes the Populist metaphor (Fig. 7). The graph depicts the reach of I.G. Farben interests as the tentacles of an awe inspiring, Germany-based octopus, which obliterates Central and Eastern Europe and North Africa with its malevolent blackness. The graph is framed by a description of the monster's deadly power:

> No matter where the heart of the cartel octopus was -- in Germany or England or Holland or the United States -- the result was the same. The tentacles reached out into all countries, squeezing the natural, beneficial growth of industry and commerce, crushing the independent manufacturer, the small trader, the truly competitive businesses which are the life of commercial and industrial progress. (Morgenthau 38)

Like Norris in his muckraking classic, Morgenthau paints the unnaturalness of cartels and evokes the picture of two economic worlds, one made up of small, independent businesses, an economic world guided by the invisible hand, the other populated by monster cartels, trying to shirk competition and to smother small entrepreneurs. Yet, the easy categorization of bigness as bad per se that still seemed to hold in earlier Populist attacks on big business, is tenuous here at best. Certainly Morgenthau did not want to imply that while Germany was dominated by big cartels, the economy of the United States consisted of innumerable small and "truly competitive" businesses. But then, why only reform Germany if all the other countries have similar industrial structures? And again, would a global return to smallness be feasible and desirable?

The difference that Morgenthau perceives between the ideal world of small businesses and competition, and the evil counter-world of cartels originates not in some German military-industrial plot; instead, it is the inevitable difference between center and periphery industries, resulting from industrialization. Although Morgenthau seems concerned with undue concentration of economic power, his conception of two economic worlds, one good, one evil, reveals that his critique is primarily aimed at the process of industrialization, and only marginally relevant as workable solution to the German problem.

In the final analysis, Morgenthau's ideas suffered from an unresolved contradiction at the heart of his project like traditional trustbusting plans for a return to a pre-industrial marketplace of small-scale entrepreneurs guided by the invisible hand. Critics of earlier trustbusting campaigns saw that in order to be successful, these reforms would have to be implemented by autocratic rule: the power of big business could only be checked by big government, and the fight against trusts thus would result in the same kind of centralized and absolutist power it was meant to combat. The Morgenthau plan implied a similar trajectory leading to autocratic rule. Morgenthau proposed to relocate German industries into other European countries, partly as reparations, partly as a way to balance the distribution of industrial power on the continent. He anticipated his critics' objection that such a relocation program would be impossible by pointing out historical parallels:

> There have been transfers of industry quite as spectacular and as difficult as this. Germany herself moved a whole group of war industries from her western borders into Silesia and behind the Sudeten mountains in an effort to escape air raids. [...] Russia took many plants apart in the face of advancing German armies and put them together again hundreds of miles away in places whose people had hardly known what a factory looked like. (Morgenthau 19f.)

Yet, the historical parallels seem to be particularly unfortunate. Morgenthau did not really want to compare totalitarian Nazi Germany and Stalinist Russia at war with the democratic American occupation force in postwar Germany, or did he? Such a rhetorical position would have been impossible, both in the domestic and in the international political arena. In the wake of postwar shift in the balance of power in American politics with the Republicans steadily gaining influence, and with U.S.-Soviet relations chilling over issues such as the "liberation" of Poland, and later questions of reparations and the bleeding of the Soviet zone of occupation in Germany, America could not risk losing the high moral ground by resorting to totalitarian methods of industrial planning and re-organization, even in dealing with conquered Germany. The plan for the pastoralization of Germany thus essentially self-destructed because of unresolved inherent contradictions.

The president himself finally shelved the Morgenthau plan in late 1944. Details of it had been leaked to the press (Morgenthau published Germany Is Our Problem the next year, trying to exonerate himself), and critics from Democrat as well as Republican ranks denounced its vengeful character. Roosevelt, in the middle of a campaign for re-election, was concerned about negative publicity and chose not to defend Morgenthau and his ideas for reform. To defuse the situation, the president tried to disentangle policy-making responsibilities between the different executive branches and "sent a memorandum to the Secretaries of State, War, and Treasury that suggested a division of functions in planning for Germany which restricted the Treasury to questions of finance" (Blum, Roosevelt and Morgenthau 604). Morgenthau had fallen from grace as informal foreign policy advisor.

Morgenthau's plan for the future of German industry not only meant another return to pre-industrial ideals and what Thurman Arnold had called the ineffectual and totally impractical preaching of the antitrust tradition, it also was another, and probably the last, move in a long smouldering feud between different government agencies. Republican Senator Kenneth Wherry noted in 1946 that the "bitter rivalry between Mr. Morgenthau's henchmen in the Treasury Department and representatives in the War and State Department [... dates] as far back as 1942; [...but] Mr. Morgenthau finally won his battle ... and forced the incorporation of his plan into the new infamous document J.C.S. 1067 despite the repeated warnings ... of Mr. Stimson and of many high officials in the State Department (Ambruster 388; author's ellipsis). But it was only meant to be a brief victory, because as much as Morgenthau's political career came to an end with Roosevelt's death, a changing geo-political balance made his plans for the industrial dismemberment of Germany superfluous.

What is important for our purposes, however, is that the Morgenthau plan must be seen as yet another instance of American discourse creating Germany as a counter-space and as commentary on America. It is obvious that Morgenthau's ideas about reform in Germany were not based on a particular critique and analysis of that country, but had its origins and motivation in a critique of industrialization in general. Consequently, it must be seen not as a way to contain German aggression, but rather as a way to contain the spread and reverse the development of industrialization in America. The critique of German industry is a thinly veiled critique of American industry. Similarly, the prescription of agrarianism as antidote against German totalitarianism is an argument for the American return to pre-industrial structures in order to preserve democratic traditions, an appeal almost identical to that of Howells, Norris, and that of the Populist critics of industrialization. In this context, Germany becomes a metonymy for the evils of industrialization, and a dark mirror-image of America, as much as the reconstructed agrarian Germany is a utopian space and positive counter-image of contemporary America.

The "Vital Defense" of New Deal Antitrust: Industrial Reform for Germany

The New Deal trustbusters approached Germany in a way similar to that of Morgenthau, even if they had other plans for the defeated country than the outright dismantling of its industrial base. Even hardline New Deal trustbusters had to concede that the Morgenthau plan was unrealistic because it "showed too little concern for the economic needs of Europe as a whole" (Martin, All Honorable Men 156). Instead of industrial dismemberment, the Decartelization Branch and other divisions of Military Government tried to carry out a policy of industrial deconcentration in Germany.[34] As we will see in more detail in a moment, unlike Morgenthau, the trustbusters thus did not propose a

---

[34] Ironically, the Decartelization Branch had to fight against being associated with "Morgenthauism" by its detractors (cf. Taylor 29; Martin 185). Obviously it was easier to attack and dismiss Morgenthau's industrially destructive plans than the trustbusters' ideas for reform.

return to agrarian times for Germany, but had in mind something like a full implementation of their antitrust plans of the late 1930's, which had called for a reshaping of the industrialized economy along the lines of a pre-industrial ideal of small and decentralized producers in a competitive marketplace.

More importantly, however, New Deal reformers saw the occupation of Germany as their last chance to implement their trustbusting ideas, after the constant oscillation of the president on matters of industrial organization, as we will see shortly. Their promising trustbusting campaign of 1937 was suspended in the name of the war effort in 1941. Given the chance to make plans for a postwar Germany, the New Deal trustbusters saw the occupied country a laboratory and test case for their economic model; initially conceived as a way to contain German aggression, the New Dealers' plans for the occupied country became instead a last-ditch effort to continue the industrial reform they had earlier envisioned for America. The decartelization of Germany became a vital defense of American trustbusting rather than a realistic contribution to American military defense, I will argue in this section.

In the New Dealers' plans for Germany, the earlier tradition of industrial discontent is overlaid with the specific conceptions of Brandeisian and Rooseveltian trustbusting. Like Morgenthau, the New Dealers imagined and constructed Germany in the tradition of industrial discontent. But their imagined Germany is doubly determined: by the older Populist tradition and the more recent experience of New Deal trustbusting. In this second part of the present chapter, I will trace the Populist roots of the New Deal's approach to big business and the vacillation between contradictory political solutions to the problem of concentrated industry and show how the military occupation can be seen as a continuation of New Deal reform with other means.

The American trustbusters who came to Germany imagined themselves to be the true Rooseveltians; yet, their business-planning opponents could equally claim to be the heirs to Roosevelt's plans for industrial reorganization, because the New Deal's approach to the problem of industrial organization was far from straightforward and even outright contradictory. The New Deal's approach to the problem of big business changed dramatically from the regulated monopolies of the early national recovery efforts to the regulated competition of the later antitrust campaign and back again to the state-sanctioned monopolies of the war effort. The plans for occupied Germany are a direct continuation of this roller-coaster t

rajectory of American trustbusting. As much as the business planning of the early New Deal had been abandoned for the trustbusting campaigns after 1937, the trustbusting advocates in Military Government hoped to counter the collusion between American business and government necessitated by the war and reinvigorate the antitrust cause through their campaign in Germany.

The New Deal's political heritage seemed to predetermine its approach to economic planning. As a contemporary observer pointed out, the New Deal's roots "consisted largely of the ideas which encouraged our forefathers to survive the crude hurly-burly of the 1880's and '90's" (Carter, New Dealers 4). To begin with, "President Roosevelt himself had a strong preference for rural values and Jeffersonian ideals" (Hawley 289), and he conceived of the modern economy precisely like 19th century Populist critics of industrialization when he cried that "it is time to make an effort to reverse that process of the concentration of power which has made most American citizens, once traditionally independent owners of their own businesses, helplessly dependent for their daily bread upon the favor of a very few" (quoted in Hawley 281). Obviously, Roosevelt's rhetoric is heavily indebted to the traditional concepts and images of American industrial discontent, from the threat of neo-feudalism, to the yearning for pre-industrial entrepreneurship, and the curse of bigness. The president also "had a number of friends who had served their political apprenticeships under Wilson's New Freedom and had not changed their minds much since the campaign of 1912" (Hawley 290). In Congress there were the Western agrarians, "who drew their intellectual precepts from the old Populist tradition" (Hawley 290), and soon the Southern agrarians around Allen Tate would take their stand, denouncing industrial capitalism as self-destructive, and declaring a neo-Jeffersonian rural democracy their common ground. Moreover, Roosevelt's administrative staff was heavily influenced by the tradition of industrial regulation, since the president had relied over the years on Harvard's law Professor Felix Frankfurter as a kind of "unofficial employment agency for the government service" (Hawley 283). And finally, the champion of trustbusting, Justice Brandeis, perceived as "the John the Baptist of the New Deal, [who] has been crying in the wilderness of Big Business of a generation" (Carter, New Dealers 310), was still a sitting Supreme Court Judge by the time of FDR's presidency.

Brandeis' name and trustbusting had become interchangeable in the American public's mind in the presidential campaign of 1912 when he profoundly influenced Wilson's economic platform and formulated the antitrust program of the New Freedom. Brandeis more than anybody else personified the "popular revolt against the sudden domination of the nation's life by big business" (McCraw 82). Like the Populists, Brandeis, proposed government regulation of big business and a return to more broadly defined pre-industrial economic structures. And like the Populists he also failed to recognize that the emergence of center firms during the industrial revolution had meant a qualitative change. Until 1916, when he was nominated to the Supreme Court,[35] he practiced law as a litigator. Significantly, "his typical clients were not center firms, but peripherals" (McCraw 87), industries and businesses in which large size was not crucial for economic survival. Consequently, Brandeis never fully grasped the relation between size and competitiveness in the newly emerged center industries and was convinced that large size and competition were mutually exclusive.

In a campaign that climaxed before World War I, Brandeis railed against the "curse of bigness"[36] and advocated a return to markets controlled by an invisible hand. He charged that big concerns were economic and organizational freaks, that "there are no natural monopolies today in the industrial world" (Brandeis 105). He claimed that monopolies only come into being when "competition has been

---

[35] Brandeis was not given a post in Wilson's cabinet mainly because of his Jewish ethnic background. His nomination to the Supreme Court had similarly faced tremendous resistance from business interests.

[36] A collection of his writings was going to be published in 1934 under that title, which sums up his project very well.

suppressed either by ruthless practices or by an improper use of inordinate wealth and power" (Brandeis 105), both in violation of the rules of the free market-place and due to a lack of restraint. Brandeis thus did not see large size and scale economies as a way to defray the burden of heavy capitalization, but rather as the attempt to avoid competition by all means. Brandeis also eyed with suspicion the rise of managerial hierarchies and the coming of managerial capitalism, which superseded private or family capitalism. He arrived at the conclusion that the permanent separation of ownership from control must prove fatal to the public interest" (Brandeis 110). As a result of recent economic and industrial developments, Brandeis was convinced, America had propelled itself backwards into a kind of feudalism. "The civilized world today believes that in the industrial world self-government is impossible, that we must adhere to the system which we have known as the monarchial system, the system of master and servant, or, as now more politely called, employer and employee" (Brandeis 35). He asked, "can this contradiction -- our grand political liberty and this industrial slavery -- long coexist," and concluded that "either political liberty will be extinguished or industrial liberty must be restored" (Brandeis 39). Clearly, Brandeis' critique of bigness was steeped in the rhetoric of industrial discontent, and so were his solutions to the problem.

To remedy the ills of industrial concentration, Brandeis proposed a return to entrepreneurial competitiveness as described by Adam Smith. This he hoped to attain through a partial return to local self-sufficiency, a balancing of agriculture and industry -- instead of a return to an agrarian economy, as the Populists had advocated -- and a return to ownership-control of business. Clearly, the ideal he had in mind was that of an economy without center firms, or conversely, an industrial base modeled on the economic structures of the pre-industrial age.

Given the continuities in political philosophy and personnel between Wilson's New Freedom and Roosevelt's New Deal, one might expect the newly elected president in 1933 to have instituted a strong antitrust campaign in the spirit of Brandeis. Yet, the New Deal started out with the opposite approach to industrial organization, with industrial planning, and only slowly came around to anti-trust action with the recession of 1937. "The New Deal began with government sponsorship of cartels and business planning; it ended with the anti-trust campaign" (Hawley 15).

When Roosevelt took office in 1933, recovery from the depression was everybody's concern and the new president's top priority. Based on the suggestions of influential industrialists the NIRA (National Industrial Recovery Act) was drafted and passed in June 1933. The aim of the industrial leaders "was not so much to expand the economy as to ration the nation's business among the surviving corporations consistently with Roosevelt's goal of stabilization 'for all time'" (Hofstadter 447). The NIRA in effect meant the suspension of antitrust laws "to permit trade associations to engage in industrywide planning" (Leuchtenberg 56). In 1935, however, the NIRA was found to be unconstitutional.

Partly as a result of the Supreme Court ruling, Roosevelt reversed his approach to big business and instead of cooperation, the New Deal now began to favor an "anti-business, pro-labour policy aimed at redistributing wealth and power to the less privileged" (Badger 94). Moreover, put on the defensive politically by the recession of 1937, Roosevelt began to think about an antitrust campaign. Clearly, in times of crisis, what Arnold had called the "folklore of capitalism" would help to deflect some of the criticism from his administration. The champions of the antitrust cause went on the offensive again, and the head of the antitrust division of the Justice Department publicly complained about "the sizable profits large corporations had made under the New Deal and concluded: 'The only just criticism that can be made of the economic operations of the New Deal is that it set out a breakfast for the canary and let the cat steal it" (Leuchtenberg 247). Another trustbusting crusade underway, once again radical rhetoric took the place of sound economic analysis and "the retreat to nostalgic trust-busting was accompanied by easy attacks on business that were in fact a substitute for realistic organization of the modern economy" (Badger 94).

A flurry of regulatory activity ensued. To everybody's surprise, quite understandable given his recent caustic criticism of trustbusting as empty rhetoric in The Folklore of Capitalism, Thurman Arnold was nominated as head of the Antitrust Division of the Justice Department in 1938 and promised to put the bite back into trustbusting. Like Brandeis,

Arnold saw "two economic worlds, one made up of organized industry, the other of small businessmen, farmers, and economic individualists" (Hawley 424), and the role of the state was to protect small business from the big concerns. Outdoing Brandeis in practice, even if not rhetorically, Arnold's tenure in the Justice Department resulted in "the most intensive antitrust campaign in American history" (Hawley 421), and until 1943, when he resigned, he had initiated "nearly half of all proceedings instigated under the Sherman act" (Hawley 441).[37]

Just as the recession of 1937 had meant a reversal of fortunes for the two warring New Deal parties, America's entry into the war meant another turnaround. The war effort required highly centralized and well-coordinated production. Arnold himself realized that "FDR recognizing that he could have only one war at a time was content to declare a truce in the fight against monopoly" (quoted in Badger 107). Predictably, as much as they had been sidelined when the National Industrial Recovery Act was repealed in 1935 and business-government coziness came to an end, with the beginning of the war "most of the old NRA gang moved back into power, this time under the banner of national defense" (Hawley 442). The administration granted immunity to practically all the major defendants in the antitrust cases in order to bolster the war effort. Beginning in 1941, Arnold's investigations of big companies encountered stiff opposition from the War and Navy departments "which argued that these antitrust actions impeded the war effort" (Taylor 27). Writing about the administration's approach to the oil industry, historian Daniel Yergin reports that Roosevelt himself joked

---

[37] Interestingly enough, Arnold depicted Nazi Germany as a kind of worst-case scenario in painting the dangers of economic concentration. Arnold was convinced that, left to their own devices, industrialists were capable of little beyond the pursuit of short term profits; yet, if controlled by the government as in the earlier New Deal experiment, high concentration would only lead to "statism" and "eventually, there would be a resort to fascism, to the German system, where the economy had become so rigid that it could not function without a head, a fuehrer to order the workers to work and the mills to produce" (Hawley 425). Obviously, Arnold saw Germany as a kind of object lesson in the dangers of cartels.

> "Old Dr. New Deal" had to call in his partner "Dr. Win-the-War." And what Dr. New Deal had found unpalatable and unhealthy about Big Oil -- its size and scale, its integrated operations, its self-reliance, its ability to mobilize capital and technology -- was exactly what Dr. Win-the-War would prescribe as the urgent medicine for wartime mobilization. (Yergin, Prize 372)

Thus faced with the prospect of having to abandon his successful antitrust campaign half-way through its completion, Arnold tried to save it by making it relevant to the changed political situation. He quickly recognized the possibilities for the Antitrust Division in the war effort and strategically shifted the justification of regulatory action from protection of consumers to efficiency in the war effort, and redefined trustbusting as a way to ensure higher wartime productivity. Even before the onset of the war, Arnold had approached the problem of trusts as one of artificially imposed productive bottlenecks which kept prices high, and in 1940 he published his thoughts as The Bottlenecks of Business. Assuming that similar bottlenecks must also exist in Germany, and they would be especially worthwhile targets for Allied action, he established the Economic Warfare Section in 1942 to analyze the industrial infrastructure of the enemy.

Besides pinpointing bottlenecks in the enemy's wartime production, the Economic Warfare Section also soon discovered that German cartels had a strangle-hold on vital U.S. industries. The redefinition of trustbusting as part of the war effort would turn out to be even more successful than Arnold had anticipated. The later head of antitrust in Germany, James Martin, recalls that the Economic Warfare Section found a curious connection between industrial bottlenecks in the production of crucial war materials and international business arrangements. The team thus became convinced that international agreements and cartels dominated by German firms severely affected American national security, and it seemed that "many of the shortages and 'production bottlenecks' in [...] key industries [...] were due to an 'economic fifth column,' to the cartel agreements and patent arrangements between such German firms as Krupp and I.G. Farben and such American giants as Du Pont, General Electric, and Standard Oil" (Hawley 441). To counter the influence of international cartels, Attorney General Arnold tried to prevent suspension of antitrust laws in the name of the war effort, and argued that they were as important as ever. He pointed out that "the Antitrust Division could become a vital defense agency" (Hawley 441). While the Antitrust Division did their part in the struggle against Nazi Germany, this redefinition of the purpose of regulatory action had the added effect of rescuing Arnold's program for industrial reorganization from obsolescence. The New Dealers' antitrust plans for the defeated Germany had their roots in the Economic Warfare Section and are thus obviously as much inspired by genuine concern about the German military-industrial machine, as by the wish to guarantee the continuation of their trustbusting efforts.

Overall, New Deal trustbusters clearly conceived of Nazi Germany as a warning for America. As they somewhat simplistically saw it, big business had successfully challenged democracy in Germany in the wake of World War I and installed a totalitarian government.[38] "As governments are now set up," James Martin, the head of the Decartelization Branch of Military Government in Germany argued, "they unleash powers which they cannot control. The State of Delaware, by virtue of its powers as a sovereign state, may charter E.I. du Pont de Nemours and Company, and so give it a legal existence. Or New Jersey may create a Standard Oil Company. Such organizations can, and often do, follow private goals that clash with the public interest" (Martin, All Honorable 270). Although Martin also concedes that America is not in any immediate danger of a German-style business counter-revolution yet, he also points out that in the U.S. after World War II "we do have economic power so concentrated that it would lie in the power of a group of not more that a hundred men -- if they could agree among themselves -- to throw the same kind of combined economic weight behind a single program [as German industrialists put behind the Nazis]"

---

[38] For a historically accurate account of the interaction between big business and the Nazis see Peter Hayes' Industry and Ideology (Cambridge: Cambridge University Press. 1987).

(295).[39]

Consequently, as Martin described his reform program, "we have to reassert public goals in the United States which will prevent the already apparent concentration of economic power in our own country from reaching the end it did in Germany" (299). Martin and many New Dealers like him thus saw their trustbusting efforts in Germany as part of a by now global fight for an American-style constitutional government and against the threat of a new feudalism through the domination of politics by the private interests of a few powerful businessmen. Another New Dealer concerned with the problem of Germany put the curious projection of the American tradition industrial discontent on Germany even more succinctly when he claimed that "the old fight of the American people against the monopolies at home must apparently be waged overseas, too" (Kahn 222). In both formulations, defeated Germany becomes an extension of America and the new battleground for the peculiarly American conflict between big business to the democratic ideals of the American Revolution of 1776, smouldering since the Populist campaigns of the 1880's. Obviously, like American authors and film makers at the same time, these New Deal reformers construct Germany as negative counter-image of an potent warning to America.

To New Deal reformers, defeated Germany seemed to be particularly well-suited as laboratory for the experiment of industrial reorganization and test run for the reform of American business structures. The country's economic structure at least in some aspects resembled that of the U.S economy. Business historian Jürgen Kocka has pointed out that the "similarities between the development of the modern corporation in Germany and its evolution in the United States are striking. [...] In both cases, the large firms clustered in capital-intensive, technologically advanced industries" (Kocka 99). Moreover, Germany seemed to be farther along on the road towards concentration, not only because she had perfected the cartelization of her economy, but also because her industries were distributed somewhat differently. "Firms in

---

[39] Well within the tradition of Populist paranoia about the dangerous power of big business, independent presidential candidate in 1948 Henry Wallace believed that the military-industrial complex was planning a coup (cf. Yergin, Shattered Peace 247).

the electrical-engineering and chemicals industries were more prominent in Germany, perhaps as a reflection of the extraordinary importance of scientific research and technology in German industrialization" (Kocka 99). The industrial reorganization of Germany could thus serve as a model for a reformed American economy and show the effectiveness of the New Dealers' program.

The decartelization of Germany by New Deal trustbusters in Military Government was conceived as a bold experiment in democratization, first and foremost of Germany, but by extension of the U.S. as well. Significantly, the New Dealers' reconstructed Germany is thus transformed into a positive counter-space, in contrast with and intended as inspiration to America. No longer an image of the totalitarian madness that could also happen in the U.S., decartelized Germany becomes an image of a better America, an experiment of what should happen at home. The occupied country was intended to reflect back on and influence the political and cultural landscape in post-New Deal America. The decartelization of the defeated country was to be the shining example of the efficacy of trustbusting action.

In their plans for the reconstruction of Germany, New Deal trustbusters followed a course laid out by Thurman Arnold for his campaign in 1937, which had in turn been based on the ideas of Louis Brandeis in 1912. The Antitrust Section in Military Government called for a return to the invisible hand of market forces instead of cartel planning. Martin quotes the then Attorney General, who realized in 1944 that "the German Government and the German people as a whole have never accepted the doctrines of economic liberalism which run through American history. [...] As long as [monopolistic firms] survive in their present form it will be exceedingly difficult to develop independent industry in Europe outside of Germany" (Martin, All Honorable 16). Although the focus has shifted from the national conflict between big business and individual entrepreneurs, the same old American trustbusting logic underlies this division into two economic worlds, into the good world of independent industry in Europe and the evil empire of German cartels. It should thus be clear that the trustbusters just essentially shifted their geographical focus, but still followed the same program.

Concerning the occupied country, Arnold proposed, in classic American trustbusting fashion, "that we break the power of the German monopolistic firms" (Martin, All Honorable 16). Anticipating to be lumped together with Morgenthau and his plans for Germany, Martin makes clear that he and his colleagues did not have the destruction, but the re-organization of German industry in mind. "The purpose of such a program would not be to destroy German economic life in its entirety, but to put its industries into a form where they will no longer constitute a menace to the civilized world" (16). The New Dealers thus did not call for an industrial counter-revolution for Germany and the country's return to an agrarian economy; rather, they favored a balanced economy without the domination of center industries. This balance they hoped to achieve by breaking up the German cartels, by reversing absentee ownership, by cutting back the influence of banks, by encouraging peripheral industries, and by an Americanization of the German economy through the introduction of economic liberalism, which, they hoped, would mean the return of the economic invisible hand.

The New Deal trustbusters' conception of postwar Germany as laboratory for democratic reform of the American economy was obviously a desperate attempt to continue in Germany their American antitrust campaign that had come to an end with the U.S.'s entry into World War II. Arnold's investigations of American big business between 1938 and 1943 provided the theoretical groundwork for prosecution of the big concerns in Germany after the war. Moreover, the antitrust Section of Military Government directly traced its roots to and was another incarnation of the Justice Department's Antitrust Division, which had earlier spawned the Economic Warfare Section. In addition, the very same personnel that had developed and administered the anti-trust program in 1938 descended on Germany in 1945. American policies for postwar Germany began where antitrusters had to leave off on the advent of America's entry into the war and the consequent need for the creation of centralized and cartel-like structures for the war effort. The Roosevelt administration's plans for the reconstruction of defeated Germany thus was a direct continuation of an earlier American campaign. Moreover, these plans were intended as the fulfillment and to some extent justification of the trustbusters' approach to business. When they proposed to reorganize German industry, the New Deal trustbusters had as much American industry in mind as that of the occupied country.

The New Deal looking abroad, finally, constructed an imagined American Germany that reveals more about the state of things at home than about the political and economic realities abroad. Both Morgenthau and the Decartelization Branch made similar mistakes in their economic analysis. Martin stresses that Morgenthau's "proposals were too drastic and showed too little concern for the economic needs of Europe as a whole" (156). Yet, like Morgenthau he failed to see that part of the peculiar shape of German industry, its disproportionate share of heavy industry, and the influence of banks, resulted from the particular shape of the markets they served. Germany had not yet developed by the 1920's a homogeneous mass consumer market comparable to that in the U.S.(cf. Chandler 36f.). This structural difference led to a higher concentration of heavy -- instead of consumer -- industries in Germany because they promised easier financial returns than light and consumer-goods industries which had to serve fragmented markets. Although American New Deal reformers may have found that it was possible to break up all German cartel structures by decree, it would have proven much harder to change the underlying market structures that facilitated the formation of those cartels in the first place.

Like Morgenthau, the New Deal reformers proposed the return to the American ideal of a by-gone age as solution to the German problem. While Morgenthau had in mind the pastoralization of the occupied country and proposed to remake Germany in the image of Jefferson's America, the pundits in the Justice department saw a Brandeisian balancing of small and big producers -- which successive generations of trustbusters had failed to bring about in America -- as the solution to the German problem. Both Morgenthau and people like Martin tended to lump all political (Nazism) and economic problems (cartelization) together and see their main cause in what has to be described as managerial capitalism, big economic structures with absentee ownership. In addition to this reductionist mono-causal analysis, both also failed to see that bigness per se was not the problem, but that industrialization was.[40]

In the final analysis, the "New Deal for Germany" must be seen as a polemic against the realities of managerial capitalism and as an expression of discontent with the industrial revolution in America or even industrial society in general, instead of a level-headed evaluation of the German problem as such. The solution of the political problem thus took the form of a familiar and traditional American complaint about industrialization. For both Morgenthau and the New Deal trustbusters the former Nazi state was a welcome screen, as it were, on which to project their economic critique and visions for change.

"The Hand in the German Glove": America Through a Glass Darkly

The attempted continuation of American antitrust in occupied Germany was a total failure. Of a hundred industrial combines initially earmarked by the OSS (the forerunner of today's CIA) for anti-trust action, the Decartelization Branch of Military Government took up sixty-nine, but undertook no measures until February 1947 since the Four Powers could not agree on a unified approach to German industry and differed in their views on reparations and industrial dismantling (cf. Taylor). Evidently, the Truman administration had other priorities and did not press the trustbusting case against the resistance of the other occupation powers. Under pressure from the British, who held most of the heavy industries in the Ruhr area, the number of cases was reduced to twenty-one; the Decartelization Branch finally prepared eight cases, amongst them the

---

[40] It is interesting to note that liberal critics in the Populist tradition finally seem to have realized the inevitability of productive concentration during industrialization. A reviewer of Martin J. Sklar's The Corporate Reconstruction of American Capitalism in the Radical History Review (No. 50, Spring 1991) thus claimed that "as attractive a a decentralist vision of economic organization is, the unhappy truth appears to be that large-scale production in such core industries as steel, autos, and chemicals is unavoidable, especially if the United States is to remain competitive in the global economy" (219).

breakup of the giant I.G. Farben concern.

With the change in political mood in the U.S. after Roosevelt's death and the end of the war, the trustbusters had increasingly lost influence both in Washington and in MG in Germany. In late March 1948, the Decartelization Branch practically ceased to exist after most of the staff left in protest. A congressional investigation ensued, and Martin claims that the resulting (Ferguson-) report sped up the retirement of the Military Governor, General Clay, and brought about the resignation of then Undersecretary of the Army General Draper, the former head of the Economics Division and major antagonist of the trustbusters in Military Government. But the fact that the commission only went into action after the 1948 elections implies that the issue was being soft-pedaled. It seems fair to assume that the sympathy the mass resignation of Decartelization staff had earlier caused in Washington had had its origins in election year politics rather than in widespread programmatic support for the trustbusters.

As James Martin describes in All Honorable Men, the eventual demise of New Deal antitrust in Germany was preceded by intensive internecine wrangling in Washington and within Military Government. Both Morgenthau and his Treasury Department and the old trustbusters-turned-military-administrators in the Justice Department had formulated their respective German policies against the resistance of the War and State Departments, the latter two ideologically in the clutches of what Daniel Yergin has called the "Riga axioms" which hypothesized revolutionary intentions a motive behind Soviet foreign policy moves. Unlike Treasury and Justice, both War and State favored a soft peace for Germany in order to contain Soviet influence and guarantee a stable Europe after the war. During Roosevelt's tenure, Treasury and Justice had prevailed; after the president's death, the intra-government feud over Germany flared up again and the two factions fought over the interpretation and execution of occupation policies. Truman "relied more than Roosevelt had on the State Department and was more readily influenced by the moderate views concerning the treatment of Germany which prevailed there" (Jonas 277f.). Everybody agreed that highly cartelized industries had been instrumental to the Nazi war effort, and especially now, under the changing political circumstances, nobody doubted that "a restored German industry [was] essential to reconstruction in Western Europe" (Jonas 278). The only question was, what shape restored German industry should take. More conservative administrators believed that radical decartelization policies in Germany would only prevent the reconstruction of Germany as centerpiece of European stability and thus make the old world easy prey for Soviet expansionism. New Deal reformers felt that radical industrial reform was necessary in order to solve the German problem once and for all; they also took the conservative point-of-view as a rationalization for big business interests intent on keeping the economic status quo.

In any case, the fight over the American approach to Germany constituted a kind of rearguard action by the New Deal trustbusters, who consequently reduced the German problem and Germany as the cultural "other" to the familiar and traditional terms of American trustbusting. To the New Deal trustbusters in Germany it was thus clear that "whatever it was that had stopped us was not 'the [American] government,'" that they "had been stopped in Germany by American business" (Martin, All Honorable 264). Interestingly enough, to them it thus seemed as if a conflict between two American parties was fought out in Germany. The shape of reconstructed Germany was predominantly determined by ideological differences between proponents of business interests and champions of antitrust. Earlier, during the war, the Attorney General had been concerned that many big firms only saw the war as an interlude between, and minor inconvenience for, their own campaigns for international economic domination. In 1942 he warned that a "small group of American business ... still think of the war as a temporary recess from business-as-usual with a strong Germany. They expect to begin the game all over again" (quoted in Kahn 108). As things went in occupied Germany, American big business indeed seemed to continue "the game" and successfully blunted the trustbusters' attempts at industrial reorganization.

Reformer James Martin had run into trouble even before he actually assumed his duties as head of the decartelization program in Germany by Christmas 1945. Still on his way to Germany, he learned that the Cartels Division had been discontinued and that its responsibilities had been relegated to a newly-formed Decartelization Branch, which was to be part of the Economics Division of MG. The trustbusters felt that the protection of virginity had been entrusted to the rapist, so to speak. The Economics division and its head, General Draper, were even more opposed to trustbusting than the War Department in general, which meant that Martin's efforts would be inhibited at every turn. To the same degree that frustrated trustbusters left, defenders of business interests seemed to move into Germany. Not only had most of the staff of the Economics Division, which increasingly dominated Military Government from 1945 on, been recruited "from the New York business community" (Taylor 36), but starting in the summer of 1945 "a large number of American businessmen with international cartel ties to German companies were traveling to that country" (Taylor 37). According to Martin,

> as the occupation went on, we saw more than a scattering of plants revived and put into full production, not because their product proved necessary to the orderly development of the economy and the best use of the scarce materials, but because the plants happened to belong to the Singer Sewing Machine Company, the International Harvester Company, the Chicago Pneumatic Tool Company, or General Motors; or because Swedish SKF, or Dutch AKU, or British Unilever, or American Bosch, claimed an interest in the German company; or because an American, Belgian or British company had had a prewar arrangement that made it desirable to get military government to reopen a particular line of German production. (219)

To Martin and others, it looked like the reformers were superseded by the carpet-baggers, which only seemed to underscore Martin's more general observation that "with World War II 'business' moved into 'government.' Men from high positions in investment banking and in the management of the top industrial holding companies came to Washington to guide the war production program. Later they moved up to high policy-making positions" (Martin, All Honorable 265). Mired in the traditional categories and concepts of American trustbusting, the reformers could not but assume that their attempts were being foiled by big business. That the reformulation of American policies for Germany might have had something to do with the changed geo-political situation or the course of events in the occupied country, hardly seemed to occur to the trustbusters in Military Government.

Martin's accusation that many of the people directly responsible for the failure of occupation policies all came from important and influential American firms bears out the point. The head of the Economics Division and thus Martin's boss, General Draper, as well as the Secretary of Defense, James V. Forrestal, came out of the investment banking house Dillon, Read&Co., the bank that had floated bonds for the highly cartelized German Vereinigte Stahlwerke (United Steel Works). Sasuly noted with indignant rage:

> An American investigator probing into the affairs of the great German steel trust, Vereinigte Stahlwerke, came upon a letter to a Vereinigte Stahlwerke executive dated in the 1930's -- and signed by William Draper of Dillon, Reed [sic!]. It was a quite normal, friendly, business letter. Certainly there was nothing illegal in the writing of such a letter in a normal, peace-time year. But certainly also it was expecting a great deal to suppose that men whose entire careers had been spent in friendly dealings with German businessmen could suddenly turn about and destroy their former associates. (Sasuly 197)

To the antitrusters this was an obvious case of conflict of interest. Similarly, Assistant Secretary of War until the end of 1945, John J. McCloy, prior to his employment in the War Department, had been a member of the law firm that had represented I.G. Farben and its affiliates in the U.S. before the war. Ambruster reports that when McCloy came to the War Department in 1941, he was put in a position where "he could speak with authority on such matters as handling the destruction of that mainstay of Germany's war potential -- I.G. Farben" (Ambruster 386). Moreover, after he resigned in late 1945, Ambruster recalls, McCloy argued in a public lecture that "Germany could never be made into an exclusively agricultural or pastoral society [... and] belittled the capacity of the enemy's remaining industrial plants" (Ambruster 386), theses directly contradicting official policies and reflecting the evaluation of the business community.

In addition to Draper and McCloy, there were numerous other administrators with similar backgrounds who were instrumental in the formulation and execution of occupation policies. Thus, for instance, the ambassador to the Soviet Union and England and later Secretary of Commerce and ambassador for the Marshall Plan (for the industrial reconstruction of Europe in general and Germany in particular), W. Averell Harriman, was a partner in the investment bank Brown Brothers, Harriman & Company, which had considerable interests in Europe. For Martin it was clear that "these men, with all their 'past experiences and convictions' found a ready-made kit of tools left over from the cartel era of the twenties and thirties. [... The] 'subconscious tendency' of these like-minded men could find a ready expression in all the machinery of collaboration which was waiting to be revived between German and foreign business groups" (266). To Martin, then, it appeared that American businessmen were the "hand in the German glove" (cf. 264ff.).

New Deal antitrusters were thus convinced that their efforts had been sabotaged by big business. Consequently, they clamored for attention in Washington by pointing out that America had won the war but lost the peace. They claimed that Military Government in Germany had failed to implement official policy, which was formulated in the Joint Chiefs of Staff directive 1067, issued in April 1945, and thus for all practical matters still a Rooseveltian document. This directive among other things also regulated the deconcentration of economic control and was the basis for the work of the Decartelization Branch. Addressed to the military governor of Germany it stipulated that "You will prohibit all cartels or other private business arrangements and cartel-like organizations [... and] effect a dispersion of the ownership and control of German industry" (Martin, All Honorable 158). According to Martin, Military Government failed miserably in this classical New Deal trustbusting program and did not bring about the desired balancing of the German economy, a balancing "between heavy and light industries, between industry and agriculture, and between production and consumption" (299). The occupation administration had thus failed to transform Germany in the image of an ideal in the tradition of American trustbusting. To charge that because their antitrust program failed, the occupation of Germany as a whole had failed, moreover, bespeaks the New Deal reformers' cultural myopia and bears out the point that they could but conceive of the occupied country's economic and cultural alterity in the familiar terms of the trustbusting tradition.

The New Dealers had come to Germany to save the trustbusting faith; having failed, the only explanation they could come up with was that they had been undone by their traditional enemies in the (American) business community. The New Dealers' thinking was so much rooted in the categories and preconceptions of the American trustbusting tradition that they failed to realize that as soon as there was no longer a need for a substantial weakening of Germany's industrial base, policy-makers who had earlier supported the New Deal industrial reformers no longer had any interest in their program. The successful demonstration of the atomic bomb, which exemplified the United States' new role as dominant and almost unchallengeable world power, made unnecessary the Morgenthau plan and foiled the New Dealer's plans for Germany. While Roosevelt had considered the de-industrialization of Germany as the only safeguard against a renewed German threat to world peace, the atomic bomb as diplomatic and military stick, in conjunction with the carrot of economic aid, would provide an alternative to a hard peace for Germany.

If the New Dealers had had the containment of Germany in mind when they devised plans for that country's industrial reorganization, they should have rested content, as their conservative colleagues did, once the United States had shown the world the awesome power of the atomic bomb. That instead their campaign for industrial reform and its failure became such an emotionally charged topic shows that they had other things in mind. It is clear that Martin and others were mainly interested in re-organizing German industry and thus conceived too narrowly of the German problem. Because of that fixation they failed to see that the atom bomb pretty much took care of the problem.

Yet, the New Dealers refused to acknowledge that their project had failed because of historical circumstance and not because of the devious machinations of big business. If earlier they had come to Germany in order to breathe new life into American trustbusting, thus conceiving of the reconstruction of Germany as the continuation of and momentary diversion from a course of action intended for American society, they now interpreted the failure of their project as an ominous sign of the decline of democracy in America. While imagining Germany within the framework of the trustbusting tradition, the New Dealers also claimed to recognize the power of German big business as a mirror image of American industrial giants. The New Dealers thus claimed that the defeat of trustbusting in Germany only complemented in a devious way the increasing power of business in America: "Though many of the events [that led to the defeat of trustbusting] occurred in Germany, before, and during the military occupation, they seemed in an increasing degree to be echoes of something more fundamental that was happening in the United States" (Martin, <u>All Honorable</u> vii). The New Dealers' industrial utopia of decartelized Germany had turned into the nightmarish dystopia of neo-feudal control of American politics. In contrast to Morgenthau's and their own earlier conception of a reconstructed Germany as a kind of trustbuster's utopia and potentially inspiring example of industrial regulation, that country had finally again become a parallel and negative counterspace, a kind of dark looking glass future America.

Still, Germany was conceived as a mirror image nevertheless. Obviously, the New Dealers' depiction of the conquered country tries to accommodate the cultural "other" to the familiar terms of the tradition of American trustbusting and the poetics of industrial discontent. Their image of Germany is thus identical to that of the other groups who chose to construct their American Germanies by projecting their own concerns onto the foreign surface.

Chapter Five - In the Land of Evil II: Thomas Pynchon's Parabolic Germany

As we have seen, American self-critiques after World War II repeatedly turned to (Nazi–) Germany for polemical purposes. Among these American cultural productions that invoked Germany as a parallel space to America, Thomas Pynchon's <u>Gravity's Rainbow</u> (1973) stands out for its detail and consistency. Pynchon's depiction of Germany conforms as much to the by now familiar American response to Germany -- seeing it as a mirror image of the U.S. -- as it is rooted in the peculiar politico-economic perceptions of the New Deal reformers who governed the occupied country, trying to implement their economic reforms. As various critics have noted, the details of Pynchon's depiction of German industry in <u>Gravity's Rainbow</u> are sometimes even verbatim transcriptions from Richard Sasuly's <u>IG Farben</u>, a book that can be considered the industrial reformers' official account of German cartelization (cf. Weisenburger). <u>Gravity's Rainbow</u>, then, brings together the general popular perceptions of Germany variously seen in earlier chapters and the specific politico-economic evaluation of the Nazi state advanced by New Deal reformers analyzed in the previous chapter.

   <u>Gravity's Rainbow</u> projects a particularly American demonology centered on Germany. In the earlier <u>V.</u> (1963), Pynchon had devoted a whole chapter to the exploits of fictional German scientist Kurt Mondaugen in Southwest Africa in the inter-war period, and thus reconstructed one of the darkest chapters of German colonial history, the attempted extermination of the Herero tribe in 1904. In that novel Pynchon already describes German national character as exemplary of the perversions of the West and uses the depiction of the foreign country as a critique of his own. In <u>Gravity's Rainbow</u>, Pynchon makes Germany and German culture the thematic focus as he criticizes and traces the origins of the postwar period and the age of the rocket.

   In a rare interpretive statement on <u>Gravity's Rainbow</u>, Pynchon explains what he sees in German culture, pointing out that "German

Christianity [is] perhaps the most perfect expression of the whole Western/ analytic/ 'linear'/ alienated shtick" (Seed 242). Obviously , Pynchon's quarrel with Germany is not so much a quarrel with the foreign country or even the culture per se; instead he takes Germany as illustrative example for a more sweeping indictment of Western -- and specifically American -- culture, pointing out that he takes of the German attempt to exterminate the African Herero as historical precedent of and illustration of American problems:

> I feel personally that the number done on the Herero head by the Germans is the same number done on the American Indian head by our own colonists and what is now being done on the Buddhist head in Vietnam by the Christianity [sic!] minority in Saigon and their advisors. [...] I don't like to use the word but I think what went on back in Südwest is archtypical [sic!] of every clash between the west and non-west, clashes that are still going on right now in South East Asia. (Seed 241)

Pynchon here seems to describe his historical poetics in Gravity's Rainbow, namely the analysis of contemporary problems with reference to historically and culturally remote conflicts. Because of the historical and cultural distance of German imperial behavior in Africa, it is much easier to criticize the American self with reference to the cultural other. Although this critical move has its dangers -- if one sees current events only as a repetition of historical precedents, history threatens to lose its historicity and gravitates towards myth -- it is characteristic of Pynchon's methodology, which must partly be understood in the context of 1960's political upheaval.

Even if too old to be fully part of the generation that came of age politically in the "Free Speech" movement in the early 1960's, Pynchon's political and historical vision seems influenced by Herbert Marcuse's popular but often oversimplified critiques of Western rationality that informed so much of student activism at the time. In addition, Pynchon's sympathies were squarely with the Civil Rights movement (in "Journey into the Mind of Watts" [1966] he reported on racial tensions a year after the eruption of violence in that section of L.A.), and he probably followed at close quarters the descriptive devaluation of terms like "fascism" in the wake of an increasing simplification of the political struggle into a contest between a state of "fascist pigs" and a righteous "protest generation." In the process, the political analysis implied by comparing a capitalist government with the Nazis was often also absurdly shortened and reduced to enraged cries of "Sieg Heil" in protest to admittedly brutal police action during the Oakland "Vietnam Day Committee" marches. Similarly, although Governor Ronald Reagan had ordered the National Guard to use helicopters and teargas in breaking up the People's Park experiment in San Francisco, student leaders could not resist rhetorical overkill, invoking the gassing of Jews at the hands of the Nazis and styling themselves the victims of yet another supposedly genocidal system.[41] Given such excesses, and further keeping in mind that the genesis of of Pynchon's novel coincides with the period of student unrest on the West Coast in the 1960's and early 70's, Gravity's Rainbow seems to provide a comparatively multi-faceted historical analysis.

While obviously a child of the sixties, Pynchon's historical methodology is also influenced by Henry Adams and his Education.[42] Adams' method in trying to understand history was to trace, as he put it,

---

[41] Todd Gitlin reports in his fascinating account of the 1960's that "much of the [SDS] movement thought Chicago was Mississippi -- or the early days of Nazi Germany. Hayden [...] was obsessed by a passion not to be like 'the good Germans,'" who had failed to stem the Nazi tide because they were afraid to go outside the limits of legality. Gitlin also describes habitual denunciations of "death-directed Amerika" which might be taken as the real-world complements and origins of Pynchon's critique of rationality and the depiction of Blicero's corporate-style death kingdom in Gravity's Rainbow. See Todd Gitlin, The Sixties. Years of Hope, Days of Rage. (New York: Bantam Books. 1989). 290, 402.

[42] Clearly adapting Adams' stylistic quirk in his autobiography, Herbert Stencil in Pynchon's novel V. uses the third person to talk about himself. Moreover, both Henry Adams and Pynchon's fictional Stencil frantically search for meaning in the nightmare of history.

the invisible power lines of his age. Adams took the dynamo as perfect symbol for and reigning spirit of the industrial age and saw it as equivalent to the medieval virgin as the icon of an earlier period. Both dynamo and virgin exude cultural energy, and just as the natural scientist might use metal shavings to visualize the distribution of invisible magnetic energy, Adams speculated that "the historian's business was" to make visible the power of ideas and "to follow the track of the energy; to find where it came from and where it went to" (389). In all his novels Pynchon also takes upon himself the historian's task as described by Adams, and V., The Crying of Lot 49 and Gravity's Rainbow have to be read as commentaries on and interpretations of recent history, as a tracking of cultural energies. But more importantly, if Adams saw contemporary America as culture of the dynamo, Pynchon sees America in the 1960's as a culture of the rocket.[43]

In Gravity's Rainbow, the rocket becomes the symbolical center of Pynchon's general critique of industrialized Western societies, another image for what Max Weber has called "iron cages," the containment of individual freedom in the rationalized state. But the depiction of the rocket also constitutes a specific critique of the American space program and a direct engagement with the particular historical moment of the novel's genesis. Indeed, it almost seems obvious that Pynchon intended the novel as a commentary on contemporary America, since a thinly disguised Richard M. Nixon appears in its closing pages as the night manager of the allegorical "Orpheus theater," about to be destroyed by the descending rocket.

Over the last decade, Pynchon criticism has been moving toward a recognition of the specificity and importance of the social, cultural and historical themes in his fiction, but, as John Krafft has pointed out, "few critics have directly engaged Pynchon's passionate engagement with the 60's" (283). The same holds true for Pynchon's preoccupation with Germany and German culture. In spite of numerous detail studies of Pynchon's reception of German culture and history,

---

[43] Khachig Tölölyan compares the rocket to the canonical texts of other cultures; thus just as the Jews conceived of themselves as the People of the Book, and the Greeks saw themselves in Homer's texts, "we are instead the people of the Rocket" (52).

many of which note with one critic "the uncanny overall exactness (apart from a few warped details) of Pynchon's picture of [...] Germany during and shortly after World War II" (Friedman and Puetz 77), Pynchon scholars have hardly ventured beyond the kind of general conclusion exemplified by one critic who sums up his analysis of war as background of Gravity's Rainbow that "Pynchon wants us to see Germany as an embodiment of the most extreme tendencies of technological society" (Tölölyan 52).[44] Moreover, many critics still see Pynchon's "Zone" either exclusively as a linguistic battlefield for postmodern aporias or as a metaphysical playground for the forces of good and evil. Both themes are of enduring importance, but they have been overemphasized by critical approaches to literature which sideline social and historical contexts. The important point is that these readings do not have to be rejected, but that a Gravity's Rainbow different from those standard interpretations can be perceived. In this more historically and culturally situated reading, German rocketry becomes a metaphor for the American effort to put a man on the moon; Germany as the Zone in Gravity's Rainbow becomes a distorted but recognizable postwar America.

In the following, I first analyze the way in which Pynchon describes and comments on his age by examining its origins in the immediate postwar period. Next, I analyze in detail three areas of cultural and historical figuration in Gravity's Rainbow in which Germany is taken as mirror image of America: the projection of Southern California in the 1960's onto Berlin during the Weimar period; Pynchon's utilization of a specific interpretation of German culture in a generalized critique of

---

[44] Some of the best contextualizations are provided by David Cowart in Thomas Pynchon: The Art of Allusion (Carbondale: Southern Illinois University Press. 1980) and in "Germany and German Culture in the Works of Thomas Pynchon" (in Peter Freese [ed.], Germany and German Thought... Essen: Verlag die blaue Eule. 1990. 305-18). Khachig Tölölyan has pieced together part of the novel's historical context in "War as Background in Gravity's Rainbow" (in Charles Clerc [ed.], Approaches to Gravity's Rainbow Columbus: Ohio State University Press. 1983. 31-67). -- For Pynchon scholarship in general see Clifford Mead, Thomas Pynchon: A Bibliography of Primary and Secondary Materials (Elmwood Park: Dalkey Archive. 1989).

Western rationality; and finally, the particular critique of the American space program Pynchon implies through his depiction of the German V-2 rocket program.

"His time's assembly": Gravity's Rainbow as Cold War parable

On the anniversary, as it were, of Orwell's dystopian novel in 1984, Pynchon in a New York Times Book Review essay pondered the question "Is It O.K. to Be a Luddite?" In the piece, Pynchon traces the history and significance of what he calls the figure of the "badass," and explains it as a wish-fulfilling projection under the pressure of technological advances. The significance of the "badass," Pynchon points out, is that he is "able to work mischief on a large scale" ("Luddite" 40), can cause the breakdown of and chaos in the daily routines of our rationalized and mechanized lives. Pynchon claims that from the mythical figure of King Ludd, destroying mechanical stocking frames, to King Kong, going all out against the modern world, the "badass" figure constitutes part of a broader "resistance to the Age of Reason, a front which included Radicalism and Freemasonry as well as Luddites and the Gothic novel" (Pynchon, "Luddite" 41). Pynchon makes clear that Luddite rage and "badassery" are never directed at particular technologies but at the technological principle itself; moreover, he suggests that the "badass" monster in some ways also must be taken as a displaced image of the technological spirit it attacks. King Ludd and King Kong thus become impersonations of the rational spirit they try to destroy. And not surprisingly, Pynchon sees Mary Shelly's Frankenstein as the quintessential Luddite novel, and reads it as a "warning of what can happen when technology, and those who practice it, get out of hand" (Pynchon, "Luddite" 40). Frankenstein's monster is both an expression of modern science -- and its antidote, the evil spirit that will destroy its master.

In many ways, Gravity's Rainbow is a postmodern version of Shelley's Frankenstein, or the Modern Prometheus. Similar to Shelley's Frankenstein, Pynchon's Professor Laszlo Jamf, the inventor of the Imipolex G plastic, is another mad scientist who has a hand in the creation of several monsters, among them the rocket and the I.G. Farben cartel. And similar to Frankenstein's monster who eventually turns against his creator, Tyrone Slothrop -- experimentally conditioned as a baby by Jamf and thus his creature -- eventually turns against his maker, hurling various wrenches into the military-industrial social laboratory that brought him forth.

Structurally almost identical to the eventual enquiry into his origins that Frankenstein's monster eventually undertakes, Slothrop's quest for the rocket and the mysterious "Schwarzgerät" is also a journey back to his origins, the attempt to find out what happened to him as a baby. "Signs will find him here in the Zone, and ancestors will reassert themselves" (Pynchon, Gravity's Rainbow 281; henceforth abbreviated as GR), comments the narrative voice of Pynchon's novel in describing the quality of Slothrop's journey in postwar Germany. Like Frankenstein's monster, who discovers his creator-scientist's diary and reads about his own conception, Slothrop finally comes very close to discovering his personal origins by deciphering the paper trail left by Jamf. That this section of Gravity's Rainbow is especially influenced by Frankenstein is seen in the fact that Slothrop finally receives the pertinent files at Jamf's grave in the mountains above Zürich (cf. GR 269), a topography that combines the geographical location both of the genesis of Shelley's novel in the mountains around Geneva, and the setting of the final showdown between Frankenstein and his monster in the Mont Blanc range at the end of her text. But unlike the final showdown between the modern Prometheus and his creature in Frankenstein, Slothrop neither meets his maker nor even finally understands all the implications of his existence.

Although in the same "Luddite" genre as Frankenstein, or the Modern Prometheus, Gravity's Rainbow by contrast is the tale of the postmodern Orpheus, Slothrop, who descends into both the underworld of his past and the hell of postwar Europe.[45] In Gravity's Rainbow, this journey into hell is staged as the descent into various forms of profanity and dissipation (Pynchon's working title for the novel was "Mindless Pleasures"), perhaps most graphically dramatized as a hallucinated escape down a toilet during one of Slothrop's drug-induced fantasies. But

---

[45] The analogy was first suggested by Joel D. Black in "Pynchon's Eve of De-struction." Pynchon Notes. 14 (Feb. 1989). 31.

Slothrop's sojourn in the hellish regions remains unrewarded, and, like Orpheus' journey, Slothrop's quest results in dispersal and (postmodern) dismemberment instead of self-knowledge:

> There is also the story about Tyrone Slothrop, who was sent into the Zone to be present at his own assembly -- perhaps, heavily paranoid voices have whispered, his time's assembly -- and there ought to be a punch line to it, but there isn't. The plan went wrong. He is being broken down instead, and scattered. (GR 738)

Indeed, Slothrop's dispersal takes such radical form that even his dreams, as part of his scattered remains, are picked up by others, and when Gottfried is launched towards his sacrificial death in the final pages of the novel, he dreams Baby Tyrone's primal dream of being conditioned for a sexual response with Imipolex G, the material that now also envelops Gottfried: "The soft smell of Imipolex, wrapping him absolutely, is a smell he knows. It doesn't frighten him. It was in the room when he fell asleep so long ago, so deep in sweet paralyzed childhood ... it was there as he began to dream" (GR 754).

But although Slothrop as character has more or less evaporated by the end of Gravity's Rainbow, "has become one plucked albatross. Plucked, hell -- stripped" (GR 712), as Pynchon's narrative voice puts it, the novel itself does not disintegrate, contrary to the claim of some critics. And indeed, "his time's assembly" (GR 738) not only takes place in the narrated Zone (the various zones of influence in wartime Europe), but also in a narrative Zone (the imaginary space created in the book): Gravity's Rainbow aims to be just that, tries to provide not just an assemblage of disjointed facts but the assembly, the piecing together into a coherent whole, of the post-World War II world, in a parable of the contemporary situation. Writing about the significance of the year 1945 in his defense of the Luddite persuasion, Pynchon indirectly explains the motivation for the historical setting of Gravity's Rainbow:

> By 1945, the factory system -- which, more than any

piece of machinery, was the real and major result of the
Industrial Revolution -- had been extended to include the
Manhattan Project, the German long-range rocket
program and the death camps, such as Auschwitz. It has
taken no major gift of prophecy to see how these three
curves of development might plausibly converge, and
before too long. (Pynchon, "Luddite" 41)

The industrial revolution, itself only one result of an enlightenment
revolution that had intended to free the individual from the fetters of
material and intellectual domination, had begun its final assault on
humanity by the end of World War II and was about to devour its
children. And just as every other Luddite attack would be directed
against one symbol but really be aimed at technology as such, Gravity's
Rainbow takes the rocket as its reigning metaphor for an organizational
revolution much more threatening to individual freedom than any single
technology.

Consequently, Pynchon constructs the Zone in Gravity's
Rainbow, Europe shortly before and after the collapse of Nazi Germany,
as the symbolic equivalent of the Cold War world, which he sees
adumbrated in the period covered by the framing narrative of Gravity's
Rainbow. The twelve months from September 1944, when the first V2
fell on London, and August 1945, which saw both the Potsdam
conference (which marked the breakdown of U.S.-Soviet cooperation)
and the bombing of Hiroshima and Nagasaki, foreshadow the apocalyptic
possibilities of the Cold War. Just as different historical "dates" converge
in the narrated time of Gravity's Rainbow, a plethora of themes and
forces heralding the emerging postwar order -- on both a global and an
American national scale -- come together in the "zone" that makes up
the narrated space of the novel. In that sense, Pynchon's Germany is not
to be taken as a historically accurate depiction of the foreign country,
but as a particularly obvious example of generally Western -- or more
particularly -- American cultural tendencies.[46] And just as the Luddite

---

[46] Critics have noted the non-realistic character of Germany in Gravity's Rainbow. Thus
Khachig Tölölyan argues that "Pynchon wants us to see Germany as an embodiment

imagination has come up with various unnatural monsters to express the horror of the Age of Reason, Pynchon tries to approximate the terror of the Cold War world in his novel. But instead of making one of his novel's characters a monstrous "badass," Pynchon assembles his novel into a narrative "countercritter Bad and Big enough" (GR 41) to parallel -- or maybe parabolically approximate -- the rise of the military-industrial complex.[47]

      Historical and geographical cross-mapping is one of Pynchon's characteristic narrative techniques, and in Gravity's Rainbow he not only sees the Cold War decades encapsulated in the immediate postwar period, but also depicts Berlin during the turmoil of the Weimar years as an adumbration of Southern California in the 1950's and 60's. Parallel to California, Pynchon describes Berlin with its confluence of the film industry, occultism, radical politics, sexual experimentation, drugs and rocketry as a "state of mind" rather than just a geographical place.[48]

---

of the most extreme tendencies of technological society," and that "that is why the V-2 must not be seen as a specifically German object" (52). Similarly, Richard Martin claims that "immediate post-war Germany supplies Pynchon with the perfect metaphor for out-of-time displacement that he needs, but is almost deliberately not Germany" (18). Although Martin is right to point out the symbolic import of Pynchon's Germany, he fails to appreciate (although he teaches at Aachen university in Germany!) the historical, geographical and cultural accuracy of Gravity's Rainbow. Pynchon's postwar Germany "is" Germany, as much as any piece of fiction can aspire to that status; but it is also more in the same sense that any symbol is itself and something else.

[47] Pynchon sees Eisenhower as an unwitting Luddite (cf. Pynchon, Luddite 41).

[48] The description is Richard C. Carpenter's in "State of Mind: The California Setting of The Crying of Lot 49." Carpenter, however, mainly concludes that "the setting of The Crying of Lot 49 is, then, an arena of the mind, and the mind is that of the reader" (113), but does not investigate the relation between the factual historical context and Pynchon's fictional rendition of California.

From philosopher Theodor W. Adorno to playwright Carl Zuckmayer, the progressive intelligentsia emigrated from Weimar Germany to Southern California to escape persecution by the Nazis. In and around Los Angeles they not only tried to recreate some of the feel of Weimar culture, but as the example of Adorno and Horkheimer's critique of the "culture industry" in Dialectic of Enlightenment shows, they also conceived of their American surroundings in terms of their German origins. In Gravity's Rainbow, Pynchon takes a similar approach and recreates a particularly American cultural geography in a German setting. Pynchon's fictional inter-war Berlin in fact bears an uncanny resemblance to the actual California described in the first chapter of Mike Davis' cultural history of Los Angeles, City of Quartz (1990). Indeed Pynchon's narrative recreation of Berlin during the depression contains a proto-Hollywood and proto-Disneyland, as well as a drug scene and what I.G. Farben Verbindungsmann Wimpe calls "German dope" (GR 345). Weimar Berlin also joins phony spiritualism in the séances staged by the fictional Peter Sachsa with and the realization of a cartelized war economy envisioned by the historical Walter Rathenau, who is consulted by industrialists and politicians in Sachsa's table-rapping sessions. At the same time, Pynchon's Berlin links political unrest with rocket experimentation as Leni Pökler and her Communist friends battle the Nazis while her husband Franz joins the team of rocket enthusiasts in Berlin-Reinickendorf. The confluence of disparate sub-cultures in Gravity's Rainbow doubles the cultural cauldron of post-World War II Southern California, which according to Davis engendered such monstrosities as the "bizarre liaison [that] directly connected the oldest metaphysic, the Luciferian Magick or Black Art, to Cal Tech and the founders of the American Rocket State, and then, through an extraordinary ménage à trois, to the first world religion created by a science-fiction writer" (59), L. Ron Hubbard's "Scientology."

Weimar Berlin in Gravity's Rainbow is depicted as a kind of proto-Southern California in the 1960's. The two are parabolically linked in the narrative through the flight-path of the rocket that first ascends in depression-time Berlin (GR 160) and eventually allegorically hovers as apocalyptic messenger over the Orpheus theater in Nixon-era Los Angeles on the final pages of Gravity's Rainbow. On a very literal level, the socio-cultural trajectory of the V2 is defined by the westward march of rocket technology after World War II from Germany to America. In Pynchon's work that migration is expressed by the arc of the rocket from its experimental origins on the "Raketenflugplatz" in Berlin Reinickendorf, retold in Gravity's Rainbow, to its mass-manufactured destination in the Southern Californian aerospace industry, depicted earlier in the fictional Galatronics Division of the Yoyodyne corporation in The Crying of Lot 49 and anticipated by the character Clayton "Bloody" Chiclitz. Chiclitz first appears as Yoyodyne's CEO in The Crying of Lot 49, and shows up again as member of the Army's T-force "scouting German engineering, secret weaponry in particular" (GR 558) in Gravity's Rainbow.[49] His transformation from prewar toy manufacturer to postwar defense contractor illustrates that in California the dragon's seed of the German rocket program has exploded into a whole industrial sector, an observation borne out by Yoyodyne's corporate hymn:

> Bendix guides the warheads in,/ Avco builds them nice./ Douglas, North American,/ Grumman get their slice./ Martin launches off a pad,/ Lockheed from a sub;/ We can't get the R&D/ On a Piper Cub./ Convair boosts the satellite/ Into orbits round;/ Boeing builds the Minuteman,/ We stay on the ground. (Pynchon, Lot 49 83)

The lyrics of the hymn read not only like a who's who in space age military hardware, but also list some of the major West coast employers,

---

[49] One of the few characters to appear in all three of Pynchon's earlier novels, industrial tycoon Chiclitz runs his company as a kind of clearinghouse for German technology and scientists: in V., ex-rocket scientist Kurt Mondaugen is ferreted out by Stencil in on of Chiclitz' numerous factories; their meeting provides the motivation for Pynchon's detour into African and German imperial history in chapter nine of V.. -- On the history of the migration to America of Nazi scientists see Clarence Lasby, Project Paperclip and John Gimbel, Science, Technology, and Reparations.

who, through their involvement with rockets, all in some way or other trace part of their lineage to the German rocket program.

Weimar Berlin and Southern California in the 1960's are more than just the origin and destination of the rocket's developmental trajectory, however; they are also both characterized by a confluence of the military industrial complex, rocket physics, occult metaphysics, drugs, and radical politics, and as the home to the movie dream industry of their respective countries. In a sense the Ufa studios in Berlin Neubabelsberg, site of production of many "vaguely pornographic horror movies" (GR 393) both in reality and in Gravity's Rainbow,[50] become a precursor to postwar America's "Hollywood, Babylon," to use the title of a popular chronique scandaleuse (1975). Moreover, the Nazi rocket state in Gravity's Rainbow also anticipates the invention of the two Disney theme parks in the fictional Zwölfkinder resort. As the narrative voice of Gravity's Rainbow muses, such places are necessary because "in a corporate state, a place must be made for innocence, and its many uses. In developing an official version of innocence, the culture of childhood has proven invaluable" (Gravity's Rainbow 419). But unlike the real Disneyland, which re-institutes adults' sentimental fantasies about a simpler, smaller and more manageable childhood world, Pynchon's fictional Zwölfkinder stages the realization of adult sexual fantasies, as is made clear by Franz Pökler's string of incestuous holidays at the resort with his nubile daughter. Both the fictional Zwölfkinder-resort and the Neubabelsberg film studios in Gravity's Rainbow as prototypes of the entertainment industry clearly prefigure the American West Coast after the war.

Just as Weimar Berlin Gravity's Rainbow prefigures Southern California in the 1960's, Germany as "the zone" in Pynchon's novel contains the seeds of subsequent Western history. But the German zone also figures as a kind of historical and geo-political singularity ideally suited to Pynchon's imaginative confrontation with his age. When

---

[50] For his account of the Weimar republic film industry and his depiction of fictional director Gerhardt von Göll, his pornographic film Alpdrücken, and actress Margherita Erdman, as well as for numerous little details, Pynchon drew heavily on Siegfried Kracauer's From Caligari to Hitler (cf. Weisenburger).

Thanatz at one point in the novel reminisces about Blicero that "it was not Germany he moved through. It was his own space" (GR 486), he might have described the author's intentions in <u>Gravity's Rainbow</u>, constructing an image of Germany for his own purposes.

"Zonal Shapes": German Culture as Parable of Western Rationality

Pynchon has Cold War America in mind when he writes about "the zone" in <u>Gravity's Rainbow</u>, and intends to criticize more than just the postwar order emerging after the fall of Nazi Germany. Pynchon's cultural and historical critique in <u>Gravity's Rainbow</u> is aimed even at rationality itself, at a tradition of death-inducing analysis that he sees exemplified in German culture. And thus not surprisingly, it is on a German toilet ship, the "Anubis" (named for the Egyptian god leading the dead to judgement), that Slothrop encounters the lowest forms of depravity on his parabolic pilgrim's progress through the hellish Zone. The ship links the aspects of excrement (toilet ship) and death (Anubis) with the kind of specialization that Pynchon sees as typically German, as he makes clear on introducing the vessel as "a triumph of the German mania for subdividing" (GR 448). Pynchon intends his depiction of German culture and the German death wish to be read as a parable of the West in general and contemporary America in particular. As a result, German geography, history, science and even (Lutheran) protestantism become

> the most perfect expression of the whole Western/ analytic/ "linear"/ alienated shtick. It is no accident that Leibniz was co-inventor of calculus, trying to cope with change by stopping it dead, chopping it up into infinitesimals, going in to look at it, the cannonball frozen in midflight, little piece by little piece –– no accident that Gauss, who contributed most heavily to Modern analysis, spent his time moonlighting as a diplomatic trouble-shooter travelling from little state to little state, trying to cool off hassles among the hundred princes of the period. (Seed 242)

In spite of its sophomoric character, the importance of this passage lies in the fact that Pynchon turns to Germany to illustrate his indictment of "Western rationality." Clearly, Pynchon is not primarily interested in a critique of German culture, but rather takes Germany as an exemplary case highlighting the direction taken by Western history in general. In Gravity's Rainbow, he thus takes up the example of mathematician and philosopher Leibniz to comment on the "strange connection between the German mind and the rapid flashing of successive stills to counterfeit movement" (407). Like Pynchon, seemingly haunted by the specter of German culture, Slothrop is flooded by recurring "zonal shapes" (GR 567) such as the peculiarities of German architecture, stairstep gables, which become "monuments to Analysis" that stand as "reminders of impotence and abstraction" (567), figuring as yet another form of the Western and German preoccupation with subdividing. What Pynchon sees as the general tendency in the West, the analytical spirit that transforms the living into the dead, he finds most poignantly expressed in German culture.

Informed by the metaphysics of Gravity's Rainbow, which sees analysis as the ultimate evil, German scientists become Nietzschean demonic figures who justify the dismantling of morality by proposing to move beyond the categories of good and evil, as does Laszlo Jamf with his conception of a National Socialist chemistry. Lecturing to future rocket engineer Pökler and his fellow students at the T.H. Munich in the 1920's, fictional Jamf exalts the ionic over the covalent chemical bond, the capturing of electrons over the sharing of them in a chemical reaction. His call to break out of the limitations of their discipline, as Pökler is later to remember, would come to a conclusion with the dramatic battle cry to leave behind organic chemistry and the exhortation to "move beyond life, toward the inorganic. Here is no frailty, no mortality -- here is Strength, and the Timelessness." Beyond words now, as Pökler remembers, Jamf would end with "his well-known finale, as he wiped away the scrawled C-H on his chalkboard and wrote, in enormous letters, Si–N" (580). Obviously, Jamf here has in mind more than just the professional reorientation of a new generation of scientists; the shift in chemical symbols from hydro-carbon to nitro-silicate also marks a metaphysical shift from life to -- SIN, to death. In this respect, Jamf's Nietzschean chemistry is similar to Blicero/Weissmann's neo-Romantic quest for transcendence of Western morality in rituals of pain and death.

Similar to Jamf as Pynchon's German allegory of Western science, Western culture finds its allegorical representation as death in the the archfiend of Gravity's Rainbow, SS-Colonel Weissmann a.k.a. Dominus Blicero. Tracing his etymological roots to the German equivalent of "old Nick" ("bleichen"/"blecken"= to bleach/bare teeth; cf. Weisenburger 31), Blicero embodies the different strands that Pynchon deems characteristic of German culture in particular and Western thought in general. He combines a romantic sense of destiny with a death wish and a yearning for transcendence, which find expression in a kind of rocket mysticism. He also personifies the Nietzschean celebration of power and abandonment of morality and combines it with the analytical tradition of scientific thought, which according to Pynchon aims for various forms of fragmentation and control.

Monomaniacal and torn like Melville's Captain Ahab, Weissmann's (German) personality brackets contradictory impulses, a yearning for romantic transcendence and the need for social and technical control. The same elements also go into the metaphysical makeup of the rocket, which is a vehicle both for death and for escape into space. And thus, while Leni Pökler, the rocket engineer's wife, believes that "they're using it [the rocket] to kill people," her husband maintains that "we'll all use it, someday, to leave the earth. To transcend" (Gravity's Rainbow 400). Just as the rocket has a good and a bad use, Blicero is both an oppositional character and one of "them" in Gravity's Rainbow. While his sadomasochistic antics and the diversion of the rocket for the realization of his sexual fantasies seem to throw a wrench into the mechanics of the war-machine, Blicero also displays a mania for control, most obviously in his manipulation of Pökler. Fictional Weissmann's structure of scientists, engineers, manufacturers and the military that he creates for the special assembly of the 00000 rocket, only seems to imitate the historical rocket cartel involved in the development of the rocket in general. In spite of his oppositional gestures, Blicero thus participates in the creation of a rationalized cartel-like structure encompassing all aspects of the private and public spheres, a kind of Hobbes-inspired (Leviathan) monster state that controls all aspects of reality from individual desire to industrial production.

Blicero not only commands "the rocket," in itself a symbol of death, he also personifies the spirit of the rocket program in Gravity's Rainbow as a sadomasochistic ritual. Although Pynchon's narrator argues that "Christian Europe was always death [...], death and repression" (317), he also repeatedly makes clear that yearning for death is a particularly German feature. Thus, for instance, fictional Nazi architect Etzel Ölsch's "New German" designs "all were visually in the groove [...] except that none of the buildings will stay up. They look normal enough, but they were designed to fall down" (300). Like those buildings, it sometimes seems as if the whole Nazi apparatus had been conceived as an infernal self-consuming construct, and Ölsch's architecture thus expresses the almost suicidal character of Nazi challenge thrown out to the world, which in turn only exemplifies a deeper German death wish. Similarly, German composers and their supposed predilection for "the simple-minded German symphonic arc, tonic to dominant, back again to tonic [teutonic!]" (443) only bear witness to the singular German obsession with violent death. And thus not surprisingly, according to Pynchon, while "a person feels good listening to Rossini. All you feel like listening to Beethoven is going out and invading Poland" (GR 440). According to Pynchon, German idealist poetry has a similar effect on people. His archfiend Blicero is inspired by Rilke's poetry, and reads one of the Duino Elegies' lines -- "Want the Change" (97) -- as a celebration of transcendence in death.

Rilke-reading Blicero is the personification of a German techno-Romanticism, which, as rocket engineer Pökler describes it, embraces "power not for its social uses but for just those chances of surrender, personal and dark surrender, to the Void, to delicious and screaming collapse" (Gravity's Rainbow 578). The one dreamlike, the other nightmarishly obsessed, engineer Pökler and Blicero both project their (German) death wish on the rocket, which becomes a kind of sadomasochistic symbol promising power and chastisement. Blicero, "a Wandervogel in the mountains of Pain" (99), is helplessly in love with "the last explosion -- the lifting and the scream that peaks past fear"

(324), which he will find in the parabolic arc of the rocket hurtling towards its target. It is triple agent and one-time Blicero sex-object Katje who describes the rocket's dark power and understands "the great airless arc as a clear allusion to certain secret lusts that drive the planet and herself, and Those who use her -- over its peak and down, plunging, burning, toward a terminal orgasm" (223).[51] Transformed from merely a piece of technology into a fetish by a culture in love with its own death, the rocket promises both escape from domination and lustful surrender to it.[52] Consequently, Blicero sends Gottfried screaming across the sky inside the Rocket to satisfy his yearning for transcendence and transformative change. The sacrificial murder of Gottfried fulfills the rocket's "prophecy of Escape" (758), which is death in the sadomasochistic wedding of the living with the dead, transcendence in the union of the animate and the inanimate. The "screaming [that] comes across the sky" (3), the rocket with Gottfried inside, speeding towards annihilation, is at once the victorious shout in the ultimate battle for transcendence and the orgiastic cry that announces the fetishized lovers' mystical union in death.

Gottfried's transformation into part of the Rocket, the "Schwarzgerät," is probably the most haunting version of Pynchon's critique of the instrumental character of Western rationality, which strives to transform life into death. Blicero/Weissmann's theatricals of sadomasochism ultimately lead to the fetishization of Gottfried when he ends up as inanimate object of desire in a S-M fantasy pushed to its

---

[51] In a perverse sense Blicero is a literalization of the non-conformist psychopath exalted by Norman Mailer in "The White Negro," as much as Slothrop anticipates the beat generation on a sexual rampage. Like Mailer's psychopath, Blicero quests for "the apocalyptic orgasm" (Mailer, "White Negro" 352).

[52] The strain of sex-cum-apocalypse in Gravity's Rainbow aligns the novel with the tradition of depicting (Southern) California in millenial terms and particularly Nathanael West's The Day of the Locust (1933). Leslie Fiedler singled out the predominant theme of West's novel in his famous study of American literature and characterized it as "the dream dreamed by all of America, the dream of a love which is death" (Fiedler 327). Pynchon seems to have come to the same conclusion.

extreme. Gottfried approaches the inanimate state in his union with the Rocket, and his transformation into the "Schwarzgerät"-fetish yet again expresses the death drive of German/Western culture. Pynchon characterized the fetishistic implications of that death-mysticism in V. as

> the single melody, banal and exasperating, of all Romanticism since the Middle Ages: "The act of love and the act of death are one." Dead at last, they [the lovers turned into fetishes] would be one with the inanimate universe and with each other. Love-play until then thus becomes an impersonation of the inanimate, a transvestism not between sexes but between quick and dead; human and fetish. (Pynchon, V 410)

For Pynchon, the technological transvestism is the twentieth century rewriting of the Romantic love-death myth and the shooting of rocket 00000 with Gottfried as sacrificial offering inside is the love-play between the living and the dead, between living Gottfried, approaching the inanimate state as "Schwarzgerät," and his lover, the Rocket.

Gottfried's transformation into part of the rocket, however, not only rewrites the Romantic love-death myth but also allegorically expresses the subordination of the individual to the needs of technology:

> Stuff him in. Not a Procrustean bed, but modified to take him. The two, boy and Rocket, concurrently designed. Its steel hindquarters bent so beautifully ... He fits well. They are mated to each other, Schwarzgerät and next higher assembly. His bare limbs in their metal bondage writhe among the fuel, oxidizer, live-steam lines, thrust frame, compressed air battery, exhaust elbow, decomposer, tanks, vents , valves ... (GR 751; Pynchon's ellipses)

Gottfried is symbolically fitted into the rocket as updated version of what Max Weber has called the "iron cages" of the modern age, "the technical and economic conditions of machine production which to-day determine the lives of all the individuals who are born into this mechanism, not only those directly concerned with economic acquisition, with irresistible force" (Weber 181). Other characters in Gravity's Rainbow are similarly victimized and integrated into the (military-)industrial machine and restrained by the iron cages of the Cold War world, allegorically depicted in the rocket.

In particular, Gravity's Rainbow traces the construction of the internalized iron cage as a process of social conditioning in action with rocket engineer Franz Pökler, who is consistently groomed by Blicero for his role in the development of the special 00000 rocket. Blicero seems to understand Pökler's psychology only too well and plays on his incestuous yearnings for his daughter, Ilse, as well as Pökler's fears of losing her. Through the implicit threats of taking away Ilse permanently, and by keeping him focused on his job as engineer, Blicero conditions away Pökler's rage and breaks his will. In their regular meetings "Pökler understood that he had been negotiating for his child and for [his wife] Leni: that the questions and answers were not exactly code for something else, but in the way of an evaluation of Pökler personally. He was expected to behave a certain way -- not just play a role, but to live it" (417). Pökler thus effectively internalizes Blicero's demands, lives in voluntary slavery and becomes Blicero's creature as well as that of the rocket. In the end, Pökler -- as much as Gottfried -- becomes a victim of the rocket, and is metaphorically put into the rocket as "iron cage," just as Gottfried quite literally ends up as part of it. Pökler internalizes Blicero's strictures, becomes "an extension of the Rocket" (402). He is controlled in the "iron cage" of the Rocket-cartel's productive order. In Pökler, Pynchon describes what he sees as the postwar industrial order, the rocket state which controls every aspect of the private and the public spheres, has cartelized reality so to speak.

"The Romance of the Moon": The Apocryphal Origins of Manned Spaceflight

We have seen how German culture and the rocket figure emblematically in Pynchon's general critique of modernity. However, the depiction of the German V-2 program in Gravity's Rainbow can also more narrowly be read as a literal commentary on the American space program of the 1960's. Pynchon's particular enquiry into and critique of the motivations behind the moonshot will occupy our interest for the rest of this chapter.

There are only two seemingly incidental direct references to the American space program in the manifest content of Gravity's Rainbow. The opening section of the novel has as epigraph a quotation from Wernher von Braun. The second reference is less obvious and comes when at one point Pökler's daughter, Ilse, looking at a map of the moon on the wall of her father's bunk, dreams herself into "a small pretty crater in the Sea of Tranquility called Maskelyne B" (Gravity's Rainbow 410), the landing spot of the historic Apollo 11 flight. Yet, it seems that in the depiction of the rocket and especially in the sadomasochistic and spectacular circumstances of Gottfried's first and final flight, Pynchon's novel both constructs an apocryphal origin for manned spaceflight and indirectly criticizes the American space program. Just as Pynchon's wholesale indictment of Western rationality is articulated through his depiction of German culture, his more specific critique of America in the 1960's is similarly projected onto Germany in the first half of this century: like so many other American authors in the twentieth century, Pynchon is looking at (Nazi) Germany in order to criticize America.

Radical sociology in the 1960's held with Herbert Marcuse that America had become "a society organized along increasingly rational lines to serve increasingly irrational ends" (quoted in Sanders 190). If Pynchon was looking for a historical precedent for that observation, he could not have found a more perfect example than the German long range rocket program. War historian David Irving noted that "the vast A-4 project had been conceived not out of military expediency but to quench the innate German thirst for Romanticism" (304). Critics have made the same observation about the American space effort, noting that the program produced only meagre results considering the time and effort invested in them and mainly resulted in the creation of a vast rationalized apparatus used to pursue irrational ends (cf. Young 18). In fact, the actual history of the American space program, from Project Mercury to the Apollo moon landings, point for point bears out Pynchon's implicit critique of spaceflight as both irrational quest and yet another step towards a corporate state.

Summing up their historical account of American manned spaceflight, the authors of Journey to Tranquility conclude that the program was "an exercise not in logic but in something close to mysticism: a ritual, supposedly lying deep among man's primitive aspirations" (Young 294). Echoing Henry Adams' description of his age as a culture of the dynamo, they proceed to characterize America in the 1960's as the culture of the rocket, and quote physicist Harold Urey, who compared Apollo to such activities "as building the Parthenon and the temples of the ancient world, the building of St. Peter's with its marvelous decorations at a time when it represented real sacrifice on the part of people ... The space program in a way is our cathedral which we are building" (Young 295; author's ellipsis, my emphasis). Pynchon literalizes the idea of sacrifice to technology in Gravity's Rainbow in Gottfried's death inside the rocket. In Gravity's Rainbow he also comments on manned spaceflight as spectacle that diverts attention from underlying political, military, and economic interests. Just as Blicero not only shoots his special 00000 rocket in pursuing his monomaniacal quest, but also leads a regular rocket battery that is part of the military-industrial war machinery, the Apollo program was fueled by substantial political, military and economical interests.

Like the industrial revolution, which resulted primarily in the creation of a factory system and was thus more an organizational than a technological breakthrough, as Pynchon claims in "Is It O.K. to Be a Luddite?", the Apollo program as a Cold War version of the "Manhattan project" firmly established the power of the military-industrial complex and advanced the cartelization of state and economy. Early in the American space program, a critical senator noted that it "is probably the most centralized government spending program in the United States. It concentrates in the hands of a single agency full authority over an important sector of the American economy. The economic situation created by the space program could well be described as corporate socialism" (quoted in Young 167). Indeed, the space program, with its boost to the economy in general (cf. Young 116) and the Southern economy in particular (including the Kennedy Space Center in Florida, Alabama rocket town Huntsville, and the flight control center in Houston), can be seen as a perverse and selective return of the abortive national industrial recovery act of the early New Deal. Apollo was thus primarily neither a technological breakthrough nor a historical engineering feat, but rather a major step towards the integration of government and industry.

In particular, the manned spaceflight program saved the aerospace industry from a major downturn and artificially continued the boom it had experienced throughout the 1950's, which had seen the creation of America's strategic missile capability (cf. Young 93f.). Chagrined about the monster he had helped to create and critical of the already formidable power of the armaments industry, President Eisenhower developed major reservations about manned spaceflight mainly for budgetary reasons. America, he thought, could very well do without a space race and without further growth of what he called the "military-industrial complex" in his Presidential farewell address in 1961. "The potential for the disastrous rise of misplaced power exists and will persist," Eisenhower claimed, and America should be wary lest this newly-created cartelized state "endanger our liberties or democratic processes. We should take nothing for granted" (Ambrose 612).

The "Sputnik" scare put an end to fiscal conservatism and severely hampered the Republican presidential campaign. Eisenhower tried to play down the importance of the Soviet satellite orbiting earth and attempted to allay fears about national security by pointing out that American rockets were superior as weapons, even if they were not as powerful as Soviet boosters (cf. Carter, Final Frontier 155). Unlike their Soviet counterparts, American engineers had succeeded in miniaturizing nuclear warheads, and the American military thus had no need for gigantic launch vehicles. The Russian handicap in miniaturization proved to be an advantage for spaceflight, making it possible to use existing launchers to propel a human payload into space. However, the relationship between technological sophistication, military expediency and spaceflight either escaped most politicians and many experts, or was obfuscated in the ensuing national hysteria over the "missile gap." Bigger meant better and the Soviets unarguably had more powerful rockets. Thus, although there were no rational political and military reasons for an entry into a space race with the Soviets, the potential emotional appeal on the electorate could not be discounted nor the vested interests of the aerospace industry disregarded. The military-industrial complex and the democratic opposition began to attack

Eisenhower for his seeming complacency about being overtaken technologically by the Soviets (Young 49). Capitalizing on the national mood, Kennedy pandered to the cravings of both popular sentiment and the the military-industrial complex in his bid for the presidency, and projected the image of a leader with a vision who would try to bring America up to par again with the Soviets by putting a man on the moon by decade's end.

An expert manipulator of public opinion and the media, not least emerging television, Kennedy perfected the art of politics as spectacle. "Insatiable in his appetite for drama, unsceptical in his belief in prestige" (Young 73), he recognized the dramatic potential of the conquest of space, which could also easily be manipulated as a diversionary political tactic. So far, space exploration had mainly relied on unmanned probes and low key high-altitude flights by the military. But in order to keep the public's attention and to heighten the effect of the spectacle, the space lobby realized that it was necessary to send astronauts into space, to add an element of human interest in order to sell technology. "It is man, not merely machines, in space that captures the imagination of the world" (Carter, <u>Final Frontier</u> 151), Kennedy was told in a secret memorandum from his Secretary of Defense. Cultural historian Michael L. Smith concurs, stating that "sending men into space was preferable to unmanned projects for only one reason: It vastly enhanced the dramatic impression created by the nation's space exploits" (Smith, "Selling the Moon" 194). The astronaut "was what the romance of the moon, and hence its political value, was all about" (Young 136).

According to Smith the race to the moon was predominantly conceived and realized as a propaganda campaign, not unlike the Reagan administration's "Star Wars Initiative," in order to create a national sense of purpose and provide a "vision" for the 60's. Smith tries to show that "U.S. space policy did not emerge from the sudden 'compelling urge' among the country's political, military, and scientific elite to learn the origins of the solar system by 1969." Instead, he claims, the key concern of political, military and industrial decision-makers involved in the space program was "its propaganda value, abroad and at home," which was packaged in and sold to the public with the help of a "vertiginous 'outer shell' of curiosity and scientific wonders" (Smith, "Selling the Moon" 194). Whether one believes in this kind of giant conspiracy, or holds that these groups acted independently of each other and their interests happened to converge, is finally irrelevant; they all gained by the space program, which could easiest be sold to the public as scientifically important.

The defense industry was mainly interested in the profits to be made going for the moon. The Pentagon would get more and new weapons systems as a convenient by-product, and space-crazy politicians could count on the moon shot for projecting a renewed sense of national mission that would divert attention from more complicated questions and problems abroad and at home. Kennedy's announcement, for instance, that the U.S. would try to put a man on the moon before the end of the decade, came only a week after the Bay of Pigs debacle. Although nobody probably fully believed that the prospect of conquering the moon would undo the embarrassing fact of the Bay of Pigs, it would certainly focus public interest on something different, causing the nation to forget America's questionable behavior around the world and concentrate on its role in space instead. The moon shot, first step in the conquest of space, can thus be seen as a compensation for the pathetic failure of the Cuban invasion.

Similarly, the Apollo program also coincided with deepening American involvement in Southeast Asia. Even if in the eyes of the world, national strength projected by the American conquest of the moon hardly balanced "Vietnam, assassination, ghetto violence and economic injustice" (Young 290), there was "one part of the world where American prestige has incontrovertibly been lifted by Apollo, and that is in America" (Young 291). Smith sums up his evaluation of the space program by pointing out that finally "the Apollo space capsule was also a time capsule, allowing the nation's Space van Winkles to carry a vision of the fifties intact through My Lai and Watts, assassinations and campus riots, and the Tet offensive. For many commentators, both friend and foe, the social function of Apollo was to sustain a pre-Vietnam dream of conquest" (Smith, "Selling the Moon" 205).

At the same time that Apollo diverted the attention of middle America from problems at home and abroad, the space program also provided progressive critics with a convenient symbol for their political critique. Just as early modern Luddite wrath had been directed against the mechanical loom as symbol of the dawning machine age, and just as populist critics saw the political and economic might of industrial capitalism exemplified in the railroad steam-engine, these critics saw the usurpation of political power by the military-industrial complex represented in the rocket. Thus surprisingly, Apollo was as much a time capsule for liberal critics as for mainstream America, allowing them to continue the tradition of populist (or even Luddite) discontent with industrial capitalism.

Like the New Deal reformers who saw the hand of American business in the German glove, as we saw in the last chapter, Pynchon makes out international cartels as the driving force behind the ascendancy of the rocket. Moreover, in his specific critique of the American space program, Pynchon goes a step further than Smith, who points out the internal contradictions of Apollo. Instead, Pynchon connects Apollo to the German rocket program, seeing the same military and economic impulses informing the American space program at work in the German V-2 effort. In Gravity's Rainbow he is thus able to criticize contemporary America by looking backwards to Nazi Germany. Interestingly enough, the real antagonist in Gravity's Rainbow is not Blicero, in spite of his fiendish antics, but a multi-national industrial complex led by or grouped around the German I.G. Farben cartel. Indeed, parallel to Slothrop's unfolding quest for the elusive "Schwarzgerät" and the fabulous Imipolex G synthetic, it becomes clear that a kind of monster consortium made up of industrial giants such as British ICI, Dutch Shell, Swiss Sandoz, Ciba Geigy and Grössli, American DuPont and General Electric, German Siemens, Stinnes, AEG and I.G. Farben all contributed to its creation. The list could have been dreamed up by one of the New Deal reformers!

At some point Slothrop's Soviet counterpart, the agent Tchitcherine, realizes the true import of the rocket when he undergoes a mock religious revelatory experience and hallucinates a finger in the sky that calls his attention to:

A Rocket-cartel. A structure cutting across every agency

human and paper that ever touched it. Even to Russia ...
Russia bought from Krupp, didn't she, from Siemens, the
IG ...
Are there arrangements Stalin won't admit ... doesn't
even <u>know</u> <u>about?</u> Oh, a State begins to take form in the
stateless German night, a State that spans oceans and
surface politics, sovereign as the International or the
Church of Rome, and the Rocket is its soul. IG Raketen.
(GR 566; Pynchon's ellipses)

Clearly, that IG Raketen, intended as parallel to the IG Farben and to be translated as "Rocket Community of Interests," cuts across national boundaries and forms a kind of unelected world government outside and above the control of individual states. As we have seen in the previous chapter, this is the very nightmare scenario that trustbusters had painted for almost a century, a kind of corporate neo-feudalism without limits and cutting across nations. Pynchon's rocket screaming across the sky thus has the same symbolic function as the colossal steam engine wreaking havoc in Frank Norris' <u>The Octopus</u>, with octopus, steam engine and rocket all expressing the concentration of economic and political power. And as Pynchon's critical program remains a virtual rehashing of the populist and New Deal agenda, the muckraker's octopus as image of the tentacled corporation undergoes a parodistic transformation in <u>Gravity's Rainbow</u> and appears as a prop in Pointsman's elaborate plan to match Katje and Slothrop on the Riviera (cf. <u>Gravity's Rainbow</u> 186ff.). The rocket cartel thus employs the symbol of its own power in Pynchon's novel.

Like the populist critics and New Deal reformers before him, Pynchon is seduced by the simplicity of a mono-causal explanation for complex historical developments, seeing a conspiracy of big business behind the war. So great is the power to control reality of the cartels and the IG Farben concern that they approach metaphysical dimensions in <u>Gravity's Rainbow</u>. As Pynchon's narrator puts it:

Don't forget the real business of the War is buying and
selling. The murdering and the violence are self-policing,

and can be entrusted to non-professionals. The mass
nature of wartime death is useful in many ways. It serves
as spectacle, as diversion from the real movements of the
War. It provides raw material to be recorded into History,
so that children may be taught History as sequences of
violence, battle after battle, and be more prepared for
the adult world. [...] The true war is a celebration of
markets. (105)

In his economic critique, Pynchon essentially follows the New Deal
reformers who also saw German big business and the dealings of the
German I.G. Farben octopus behind the war (cf. Morgenthau's description
mentioned in the previous chapter). But Pynchon's world in Gravity's
Rainbow is not only informed by the conspiracy theories of the New Deal
reformers, it also has a decidedly Luddite bent. As a result, it finally
seems as if not even the cartels and the military-industrial complex, but
rather technology itself is the villain in Pynchon's political morality play.
And consequently, technology dominates the individual as much as
reality, and becomes vampire-like, as the fictional Enzian realizes at one
point in Gravity's Rainbow:

This War was never political at all, the politics was all
theatre, all just to keep the people distracted ... secretly,
it was being dictated instead by the needs of technology
... by a conspiracy between human beings and techniques,
by something that needed the energyburst of war, crying,
"Money be damned, the very life of (insert name of
Nation) is at stake," but meaning, most likely, dawn is
nearly here, I need my night's blood, my funding, funding,
ahh more, more. (521; Pynchon's ellipses and emphases)

The description of technology, and by extension: the Rocket, as vampire
in Gravity's Rainbow is Pynchon's neo-gothic extension of a populist
critique of cartels and their threat to liberty and democracy, familiar from
our discussion of the New Deal reform program. As IG Farben
representative Wimpe points out, "our little chemical cartel is the model

for the very structure of nations" (349), a rationalized construct controlling economic or political exchange. Like Norman Mailer, who describes the totalitarian trends in emerging Cold War society in The Naked and the Dead by having his fictional General Cummings declare the army as the model for a future society, Pynchon takes the rocket cartel and rocket technology as the emblems of the postwar order.

It could be objected that Pynchon simplistically blames technology for all the ills besetting Western culture. Indeed, critic Scott Sanders has found fault with the reification of technology in Gravity's Rainbow, claiming that "instead of treating it as a body of knowledge which men have developed for satisfying their needs and for dealing with the material world, instead of presenting it as a complex of relations among men, Pynchon has elevated technology into a metaphysical principle standing outside human control" (Sanders 191). It is not quite clear whether Sanders has simply misunderstood the thrust of Pynchon's argument, or whether, for reasons of his own, he chooses to disapprove of Pynchon's poetical transformation of technology. Like Shelley in Frankenstein, or even like Stanley Kubrick in Dr. Strangelove, Pynchon argues that technology acquires a dynamic of its own and begins to evade human control. Pynchon depicts technology as a reification of social relations. If he seems to reify technology that is the inevitable and necessary result of trying to comment on and depict contemporary social reality. Technology is not just a body of knowledge, technologique, but more precisely a way of structuring human interaction. In his essay on the Luddite imagination, Pynchon thus implies that the industrial revolution meant an organizational -- and not just a technological breakthrough. It entailed not primarily a mere change in the material basis of society with the creation of a factory system, but resulted in more profound institutional transformations with the concurrent evolution of a managerial and administrative apparatus. The industrial revolution meant the eventual transition of power from a feudal to a managerial, scientific and engineering elite. As a result, the organizational structure that created the rocket in Gravity's Rainbow is much more awe inspiring and monstrous than the product itself, the vengeance weapon.

As we have seen, Pynchon believes with his characters in Gravity's Rainbow that the war "was all theatre, all just to keep the people distracted" (521). Pynchon similarly describes the German rocket program, exemplified in Blicero's 00000 rocket, as sadomasochist theatricals that at least to Blicero is much more important than the war. Going beyond the critique advanced by liberal critics such as social historian Smith described earlier in this chapter, Pynchon seems to say that the American space program is not only a political distraction and "an extravagant feat of technological exhibitionism" (Smith, "Selling the Moon" 180), but that its appeal to the public must be seen in its character as sadomasochist spectacle of sacrifice.

Just as the name of science was invoked in the justification of spaceflight, manned spaceflight provided the necessary entertainment value in order to excite the public's imagination and keep public interest.[53] Thus, Tom Wolfe points out in his account of Project Mercury, The Right Stuff (1979), that "from a sheerly political or public relations standpoint, the astronaut was NASA's prize possession" (160). If the spectacle of manned spaceflight was the equivalent of the Roman circus, the astronauts became modern day gladiators, consecrated to death, as it were, actors and victims at once in the rocket age spectacle of human sacrifice. Pynchon takes up the cue, so to speak, and imaginatively transforms the first manned spaceflight, Gottfried in the 00000 rocket, into an act of sacrificial murder.

Wolfe in The Right Stuff tries to understand the fascination of manned spaceflight and explain the power it wields over the popular imagination. Although his thinly veiled admiration for the astronauts at once perpetuates the mystification and illustrates the power of marketing manned spaceflight as crusade for a new sense of mission, his account of the origins of the American space program also circumscribes the undercurrent in spaceflight as spectacle of sacrifice, both in the

---

[53] The lack of scientific and technological reasons for manned spaceflight became glaringly obvious, I think, when a few days after the "Challenger" space-shuttle exploded shortly after takeoff, the unmanned space probe "Voyager" sent back perfect pictures and other data while passing Jupiter. Most of the scientific data and technological advances resulting from manned spaceflight could have been had for a fraction of the cost if unmanned spacecraft had been used. The only exception is probably Neil Armstrong's walk on the moon.

sense of personal effort and constraint and as (sadomasochistic) ritual offering. Wolfe depicts the astronauts as a modern day version of the archetypal warrior in "single combat," as he puts it. In spite of Wolfe's explicit adulation of astro-power, his account also implies that the real fascination of manned spaceflight lies somewhere else, in the sadomasochistic spectacle of control and domination enacted with and on the astronaut placed on top of a huge Roman candle (the rocket consisting mainly of liquid hydrogen and oxygen). As Wolfe puts it, "from the beginning the reporters and broadcasters dealt with the subject [of manned spaceflight] in tones of awe. It was the awe that one has of an impending death-defying stunt" (71). The terms Wolfe uses to describe public sentiment on the eve of the first spaceflight are even more revealing:

> Now the sun was up, and all across the eastern half of the country people were doing the usual, turning on their radios and television sets, rolling the knobs in search of something to give the nerve endings a little tingle - - and what suspense awaited them! An astronaut sat on the tip of a rocket [in the small capsule on top of a launch vehicle], preparing to get himself blown to pieces. (Wolfe 200)

This description implies that Wolfe -- I think correctly -- identifies the fascination with manned spaceflight as the morbid fascination with the spectacle of ritualized death, expressing itself historically in the appeal of the Roman circus and in our contemporary culture in the mass appeal of Formula I racing.

Just as the rocket program expresses contradictory impulses, the rationalized realization of irrational ends, the spectacle of the astronaut contains elements of mastery and domination both, and the figure of the astronaut dramatizes both control and passivity, defiance and submission. On the one hand, the astronaut seems the epitome of virility and manly action. Groping towards a definition of the "right stuff," Wolfe rhapsodizes that "it seemed to be nothing less than manhood itself. [...] Manliness, manhood, manly courage ... there was something ancient, primordial, irresistible about the challenge of this stuff, no matter what a sophisticated and rational age one might think [the astronaut] lived in" (Wolfe 22). On the other hand, the astronaut also becomes the very personification of the individual constrained in the iron cage of the industrial economic and social order, passive, victimized, and part of the machine like Gottfried in Pynchon's novel. Wolfe at length and with typical gusto recreates the selection and training of the first astronauts, who had to be conditioned for their role as passengers, administrators soon realized that what was required was "a man whose main talent was for doing nothing under stress" (151). The chosen group thus was not spared any humiliation, a process that acquires a sadomasochistic look in Wolfe's account. From prostate examinations, daily enemas and various other probings of the bowels in particular, and every other bodily orifice in general, "Up yours! seemed to be the motto of the Lovelace Clinic -- and they even made you do it to yourself" (Wolfe 76). The total invasion even of bodily "privacy" prepares the astronauts for their role as victims in a public spectacle of sacrifice. Moreover, not even the astronauts' families are spared the positively sadistic scrutiny of the public gaze -- is the wife going to break down because she cannot take the tension any more? -- and in describing the "assembled rabble of reporters, radio stringers, tourists, lollygaggers, policemen, and freelance gawkers" on the front lawn of the Glenn house, Wolfe wryly notes that "a public execution wouldn't have drawn a crazier mob" (259).

The rocket signifies both the hope and doom of the late twentieth century, the hope of escape into space and the possibility of nuclear apocalypse, as manned spaceflight becomes a modern version of the mystery play. The astronaut in his capsule atop the rocket personifies American Cold War culture and society built on thermonuclear rockets -- and literally on top of the subterranean silos of the Strategic Air Command. And just as the astronaut's life is threatened by the possibility of something going wrong, we lead our daily lives under the shadow of the rocket. The spectacle of the astronaut is fascinating because it externalizes and symbolically heightens the precariousness of our own cultural situation. But at the same time, the paradoxical situation of the astronaut as pilot, presumably steering the ultimate vehicle yet completely helpless as passenger of a ballistic projectile controlled by an immense team effort, also describes the situation of the individual in the cartelized state as exchangeable and insignificant cog in the corporate wheel. In spite of its diversionary character, the spectacle of spaceflight thus also acquires aspects of symbolical truth as allegory of the corporate state's functioning. And this is precisely what Pynchon is trying to depict in Gravity's Rainbow, the American rocket state projected back onto and shown in its origins in (Nazi) Germany.

The elements that historical accounts of American manned spaceflight share with the account of its apocryphal origins provided by Pynchon, then, are first its character as diversion, staged to mask the real goals of and interests of the space program, goals and interests that were more political and economic than scientific; and second, its basic character as spectacle of ritual sacrifice inscribing the iron caging of the individual in the industrial corporate state. The V2 in Gravity's Rainbow becomes the metaphorical prototype of American manned spacecrafts. Blicero/Weissmann's ritual sacrifice of his lover is Pynchon's mytho-poetic account of the origins of American spaceflight in Nazi Germany. Pynchon implies that Blicero/ Weissmann's sadomasochist techno-mysticism is the ruling spirit of contemporary America, a rationality that is a celebration of death and that stages spaceflight as a diversion from the economic and political realities created by today's military-industrial complex; and Germany as the rocket-dominated zone in Gravity's Rainbow, finally, is an image and critique of America in the space age.

Chapter Six - How German Is It?

American representations of Germany have repeatedly been used as a self-reflexive historical and political commentary, as I have tried to show in the preceding chapters. We have now seen in a few specific cases how the example of Germany was variously taken as counterpoint to America, ranging from the articulation of political anxieties in literature from Gravity's Rainbow to The Last of the Conquerors, Hollywood films that deal with the problem of fraternization, and outright political discourse in the New Dealers' formulation of foreign policy in the trustbusting tradition. Yet, obviously, not every American depiction of Germany in the post-World War II period was either intended or can be understood as a specific political commentary on the American self. Thus it seems necessary, finally, to consider some limiting cases that self-reflexively comment on America by looking at Germany without specifically advancing historical or political self-critiques.

While both reflecting contemporary American conceptions of Germany and commenting on their own culture, John Hawkes's The Cannibal, Sylvia Plath's "Daddy," Joyce Carol Oates's "Master Race," "Ich Bin Ein Berliner" and "Our Wall," and Walter Abish's How German Is It remove Germany from history and political specificity, transposing it metaphysically into a realm of general otherness. Neither of the four authors turns to Germany for specific political allegories of America in these works; instead, their representations of the foreign country articulate more general existential concerns. Thus, Hawkes transforms occupied Germany into a nightmarish landscape and symbolical rendition of the human unconscious. In "Daddy," Plath both tries to circumscribe a poetic space apart from the patriarchal tradition by exorcizing the memory of her dead father, reinventing him as Nazi and casting herself in the role of persecuted Jew. Oates equates male chauvinism with the supposedly German ideology of racial supremacism in "Master Race." In "Ich Bin Ein Berliner" and "Our Wall" she allegorically rewrites the basic idea of Freud's Beyond the Pleasure Principle, dramatizing the dialectics between freedom and death through the image of the Berlin wall. And finally, in How German Is It Abish projects an invented Germany as a kind of Africa of the imagination, a fabled and fabulous locus for the projection of narrative desire.

Overall, these texts not only illustrate the obvious limits of my thesis about the historical and political specificity of self-reflexive accounts of alterity in the case of America's Germany, they also delineate in a compelling way the underlying assumption of that thesis, namely that the representation of the foreign country always also articulates a cultural alterity that provides a contrasting perception of the cultural self. This becomes most obvious in How German Is It, which can be taken as a meta-fictional exploration of the representational dynamics determining the American image of Germany. Limiting case and meta-fictional enquiry at the same time, Abish's novel thus not only constitutes a limiting case like the other texts considered in this final section, but also provides the most compelling example of self-reflexive American accounts of Germany.

Fascinating Fascism and Psychic Landscapes in Hawkes, Plath, and Oates

In her essay "Fascinating Fascism" (1974), Susan Sontag tries to account for the rise and popularity of what she calls a fascist aesthetics in the contemporary American art scene and the ascendancy of Nazi paraphernalia as centerpieces of "a particularly powerful and widespread sexual fantasy" (99). Sontag notes with some amazement that "Nazi Germany, which was a sexually repressive society, [has] become erotic" (102) and suggests that this fascination with fascism has not so much to do with the actual historical phenomenon as it manifested itself in Germany, but rather with a sadomasochist fantasy of domination and surrender. Sontag's specific analysis anticipates Saul Friedländer's more general remark (quoted before in an earlier chapter) that Germany has become the supreme metaphor of evil. Similarly, Sontag seems to say that (German) Fascism and its symbols have become the reigning metaphor for sadomasochist fantasies.

As examples of "fascinating fascism," Sontag singles out the American reception of ex-Nazi film maker Leni Riefenstahl and a widespread fascination with Nazi regalia like uniforms and medals, particularly noting the appropriation of Nazi symbols in pornography and far-out sexual experimentation. Although Sontag charts the sadomasochist undercurrents and implications of a fascination with a fascist aesthetics (of submission and control) very well, she only hints at an explanation for it by discerning a turn towards the irrational and exotic in contemporary America. "For those born after the early 1940's," Sontag claims, "bludgeoned by a lifetime's palaver, pro and con, about communism, it is fascism -- the great conversation piece of their parents' generation -- which represents the exotic, the unknown. Then there is a general fascination among the young with horror, with the irrational" (101). Sontag thus implies that the fascination with fascism she finds in the America of the 1970's is a turn towards the irrational in reaction to a previous excessive rationality. To escape the bright daylight of rational (politicized) discourse that leaves no room for mystery, the magnificent experience, or the dark night of the soul, the imagination turns to fascism as the exotic and the taboo. Of course such a fundamentally aesthetic fascination with fascism does not lead to an exploration of its historical realities; instead, it is only interested in the phenomenon as an idea and a focus for an anti-rational fantasy.

The perverse late 20th century turn to German fascism as exotic alternative to American rationality that Sontag analyzes in her essay, of course has its early 19th century precedent in Romanticism and its turn toward the German/Gothic. In both cases, significantly, the reception of German culture constitutes not an interest in the real country but the invention of an idea of Germany. In the introductory chapter we thus saw how Poe, the premier example of American Romanticism, gave the most fitting characterization of Germany as idea and not reality when he remarked that "terror is not of Germany, but of the soul" (Poe 129). Like Poe, novelist Hawkes, short story writer Oates, and poet Sylvia Plath are little interested in particular German realities, exploring instead the terror of the soul by talking about "fascinating fascism" and Germany.

In his experimental novel The Cannibal (1949) John Hawkes creates a neo-gothic and nightmarish geography of primal fears, exploring the dark and hidden reaches of the human psyche by projecting them onto a German locale. Although he saw the end of the war near Bremen, Germany as an ambulance driver for the American Field Service (like other American authors before him, most prominently Ernest Hemingway a generation earlier), Hawkes in The Cannibal neither analyzes the actual situation in the American-occupied country, nor comments directly on the realities of the post-war period. Instead, his narrative dramatizes the pre-Oedipal anxieties which beset the mind of the conqueror by transforming Germany in 1945 into an image of the long dark night of the soul. Hawkes explains in an interview that "the novel is a conscious effort to create a landscape that is a version of the unconscious" (Hawkes, "Life and Art" 119). Concerning its genesis, he recalls that "so, here I was reading about Hitler, thinking about a cannibal in Germany and thinking about a friend who had been hospitalized for emotional reasons, thinking about my own days of hospitalization, and suddenly [..] I knew I was going to create my own post-world-war Germany, a sort of reconstruction of a ruined Germany" (Hawkes, Interview 82). The result is a heavily fragmented collage of anxiety and decay, which has its origins in Hawkes's psychic needs rather than in German historical reality.

The novel is divided into three parts, the middle section consisting of a flashback to Germany on the eve of the Great War in 1914, the framing sections set in 1945. After its defeat, Germany has been divided into three sectors, each overseen by a lone administrator policing his sector on a motorcycle. The novel's imaginary locale, Spitzen-on-the-Dein, is not only located on the borders of fact and fantasy,[54]

---

[54] The town may even have been inspired by a Life report on a similarly imaginary place in Germany. In a letter to the editors of Life, a Time correspondent in 1945 reported on the spurious Unterstitzen on the Bleiweis: "Not only is Unterstitzen not on the Bleiweis river, but there is no such town and no such river. Both were invented by the war correspondents in Germany when they kept asking when our armies were going to get to Berlin and kept getting the answer that there was just one more river to cross" (Life 4 June 45, 2). Thus one day a Life correspondent asked the briefing general whether they had already taken Unterstitzen, and the general confidently replied they would in a few days.

the town also lies outside the boundaries of rationality, as is made clear even in the first paragraph, which establishes the drab existentialist stage for the novel by following a part Faulknerian (The Sound and the Fury) part Beckett-esque (Waiting for Godot) fool-figure, who imagines himself to be the son of the long-deceased Kaiser, on his way from the shattered insane asylum into town.

Although Hawkes dispenses with conventional ideas of sequentiality and causality in his novel and thus almost arrives at a kind of prose poem -- "totality of vision or structure was really all that remained" (Hawkes, Humors 68) he said of the text -- there exist a few narrative strands that provide minimal plot cohesion. Both the novel and the fictional town are dominated by two clusters of characters, the one centered on the household and person of the quasi-mythical Madame Snow, who becomes an allegory of Germany, the other coalescing around the leader of the neo-Nazi insurrection, the newspaper-editor Zizendorf, who plans to murder the American overseer of his part of the country, the officer Leevey on his motorcycle. In the framing sections of the narrative, set in 1945, Madame Snow runs a boarding house in which live her sister Jutta and her two children, and the "Duke." Throughout the story, the Duke is on a nightly hunt for Jutta's little boy, his "fox," whom he finally kills in order to prepare a cannibalistic meal for himself and the boy's grandmother, Madame Snow. Obviously, in its teutonic furor, the German colossus has eaten its children, dramatizing historical as well as infantile nightmares and anxieties.

The middle part of the novel charts the courtship and marriage of Madame Snow, while, parallel to the 1945 Madame Snow sections in the framing parts of The Cannibal, Zizendorf and his co-conspirators lie in ambush, waiting for the American occupier on his motorcycle; a flashback account also relates the initial occupation of Spitzen-on-the-Dein by an American platoon, and the symbolical war-crimes trial of the town's pastor for failing to speak out against the Nazis.[55] The conspirators

---

[55] Here The Cannibal comes closest to a direct historical commentary on contemporary Germany, and the novel's pastor Miller seems both in his title, name, and biography reminiscent of German Pastor Martin Niemöller, "the one German whom Christians everywhere have respected" (Time 18 June 45, 26), too outspoken about his beliefs

finally successfully ambush Leevey, the overseer, killing him and keeping his motorcycle. Zizendorf prints a proclamation of the country's liberation, a lengthy tirade that pits German national spirit against America's "masses of industry" and redefines the course of history: "From the ruins of Athens rise the spires of Berlin" (Hawkes, Cannibal 176f.).

The Cannibal most hauntingly dramatizes what contemporary observers saw as the threat of Nazi resurgence in Germany and the supposed deviltry of the civilian population. But the novel also inverts the resulting fear of Americans "going native," the dissolution of cultural and ethnic borderlines, in the construction of its narrator, Zizendorf. Although Hawkes does not dramatize the shift in perspective on the plot level by having one of his characters change sides, similar to Danny in The Big Lift or Phoebe Frost in A Foreign Affair discussed in an earlier chapter, he rather makes his narrator one of "them," effecting the changed perspective on a narrative level. Readers, so to speak, go native with the narrator of The Cannibal, who as a German is both an alien voice and an alien perspective in an American novel. But unlike in A Foreign Affair and The Big Lift, this crossing of cultural boundaries is not intended to evoke sympathy or problematize the encounter between Germans and Americans. Rather, Hawkes puts his readers in the position of having to perceive the action through he eyes of the "enemy," and uses this alien narrator to prevent easy readerly identification with the characters and

---

and consequently interned in the Dachau concentration camp by the Nazis. Yet, Time also reported on Niemöller's divided sympathies, noting that as late as 1939 he had offered to serve as submarine officer as he had done during WWI. Niemöller's own explanation for this obvious contradiction was that he "had nourished the hope that National Socialism, if it had gone the right way, might have developed into a system for creating good for the German people" (Time 18 June 45, 26). In Hawkes' novel, the town's teacher rises in defense of Miller along the same lines, pointing out that "Herr Colonel, I think perhaps you should take into account that there was, you know, a new gospel, the war made a change in what a man might want to preach to the dumb people" (Hawkes, Cannibal 136). But Miller has to face the firing squad nevertheless, and is killed by Zizendorf who is made to join the executioners.

to undermine realist expectations. For the same reasons, Hawkes also paradoxically makes Zizendorf an omniscient first person narrator, resulting in further defamiliarization.

While in the examples analyzed in earlier chapters Germany as the cultural "other" is often stripped of its specificity, presented as an idea and essentialized in several ways, in The Cannibal this representational distortion does not articulate specific political fears, constituting instead a narrative descent into the regions of childhood and nightmare fears as such. For instance, the political threat of a resurgence of Nazism and the security risk posed to American GIs exemplifies the threat of voracious and threatening female sexuality. In one of the rare glimpses that the novel provides of Leevey, the American overseer, he fights with a contagious "laughing slut who was covered with invisible red clap" (Hawkes, Cannibal 144). Here the fear of female sexuality and contagion is not a displaced political anxiety; instead the scene as travesty of fraternization dramatizes (Leevey's) childhood fears of a cannibalistic mother. Moreover, Leevey further embellishes the (sexual) threat and paranoically fantasizes the breakdown of authority and the dangers of crossing the "color line" when he muses that "he had heard the stories, stories of murder in the empty lot, the special deaths, the vaginae packed with deadly poison" (Hawkes, Cannibal 144). Like Hawkes's depiction of the anxieties about fraternization, which point to sexual anxieties, the presumably politically motivated ambush on Leevey is a rewriting of an Oedipal drama: as much as Mme. Snow as cannibalistic mother stands for Germany, the American Leevey represents the law of the father who stands in the way of a (sexual) union between mother (Mme. Snow) and son (Zizendorf). In The Cannibal, psycho-sexual drama is displaced into the political and historical conflict of the military occupation -- a reversal of the direction of the symbolical equation found in most other examples of America's Germany.

The political threat of a Nazi resurgence in the occupied country as well as the sexual threat of Madame Snow, the novel's surreal geography and mythicized history allegorically depict Hawkes's psychic landscape of primal fears. Zizendorf hails Madame Snow as another White Goddess, representing (self-) destructive Germany, when he pays tribute to her: "she was the very hangman, the eater, the greatest leader of us all" (Hawkes, Cannibal 131). Germany is thus again not only metonymically transformed into a threatening woman, but German history is essentialized and mythicized through the identification of Madame Snow with the White Goddess, "ancient power of fright and lust" (Graves 24), queen of the nightmare in the age-old mythical matrix. To Leevey and the occupation personnel in The Cannibal, Germany is "the evil zone" (Hawkes, Cannibal 133), a geography threatening like Madame Snow's radical otherness, which is sexual, moral (cannibalism), and metaphysical (personification of myth). Germany as an image for the unconscious in The Cannibal becomes dark, illogical and threatening. Moreover, Germany in Hawkes's novel is also uncharted and outside the boundaries of rational discourse like a colonial space. Theorist of colonialism JanMohamed explains that "colonialist literature is an exploration and a representation of a world at the boundaries of 'civilization," a world that has not (yet) been domesticated by European signification or codified in detail by its ideology. That world is therefore perceived as uncontrollable, chaotic, unattainable, and ultimately evil" (JanMohamed 64). JanMohamed, of course, has mainly Africa in mind in this definition, but his description also seems to apply fully to Hawkes's novel. In The Cannibal, then, the German geography is transformed into an Africa of the imagination, a dark continent onto which the West's unspeakable and infantile anxieties are projected. Clearly, while Hawkes's novel transforms Germany into a self-reflexive space, The Cannibal seems to depict general Western psychological fears rather than specifically American political anxieties.

Like Hawkes, Sylvia Plath and Joyce Carol Oates make Germany a foil for their explorations of the human psyche and their articulation of female rebellion against patriarchy rather than for a critique of the United States. In "Daddy" (1962) Plath displaces a biographical conflict with her father and her husband into the Freudian struggle between a Nazi father figure and a Jewish daughter. At the same time the historical subtext of the Holocaust also structures her poetic rendition of the conflict between the woman-poet and a predominantly male tradition. Like Hawkes, Plath departs in her use of the symbolical equation involving Germany from the examples analyzed in earlier chapters, transforming that country and its history into an objective correlative (to use T.S. Eliot's famous term) of her highly personal <u>psychic</u> needs, instead of commenting self-reflexively on American history or politics by talking about Germany.

Critics agree that "Daddy" is Plath's attempt both to exorcize the memory of her recently departed husband and the "imago" of her father who died when she was a child.[56] The poem constructs a nightmarish complex of a daughter's guilt-ridden love-hate relationship with her father, summarized in the opening lines of the second stanza: "Daddy, I have had to kill you./ You died before I had time." The daughter's suicide attempt at age twenty, as much as the marriage to a father substitute ("I made a model of you ... And I said I do, I do") and the eventual symbolical exorcism ("Daddy, I have had to kill you"), are all attempts to return to the primal scene of her father's death when she was a child ("I was ten when they buried you"). Most interesting for our purposes, however, the emotional victimization that the daughter feels in her relationship to her dead father and her husband is figured as the historical victimization of Jews by their German Nazi oppressors. The daughter imagines her husband, the "model" that she makes of her dead father, as "A man in black with a Meinkampf look/ And a love of the rack and screw," extending the demonization of her father as Nazi officer:

> I have always been scared of <u>you</u>,
> With your Luftwaffe, your gobbledygoo.
> And your neat moustache
> And your Aryan eye, bright blue.
> Panzer-man, panzer-man, o You!

The daughter attempts to rid herself of the suffocating love for her father by turning love into hate, imagining him as Nazi and thus de-humanizing him. At the same time, she also casts herself in the role of Jewish victim in order to articulate her emotional oppression, musing: "I think I may well be a Jew." Overall, Plath uses the historical matrix of the Holocaust as material for the psychological drama of "a girl with an

---

[56] Cf. Nance/Jones, 125. According to Steven Axelrod, "Plath wrote 'Daddy' several months after Hughes [poet Ted Hughes, her husband] left her, on the day she learned that he had agreed to a divorce (October 12, 1962)" (52).

Electra complex" whose "father died while she thought he was God" as she explained the poem herself (quoted in Alvarez 65).

In spite of the poem's obvious biographical relevance, "Daddy" has also been read in the light of recent feminist re-interpretations of the canon as an allegory of "the woman poets' struggle with 'daddy poetry'" (Axelrod 52). And clearly, "Daddy" not only imagines a return to a highly idiosyncratic primal scene by reconfiguring it as the killing of a Nazi father, but similarly re-enacts poetic sexual politics by describing the male oppression of female voices against the background of German persecution of Jews:

> I never could talk to you.
> The tongue stuck in my jaw.
>
> It stuck in a bark wire snare.
> Ich, ich, ich, ich!
> I could hardly speak.
> I thought every German was you.
> And the language obscene
>
> An engine, an engine
> Chuffing me off like a Jew.
> A Jew to Dachau, Auschwitz, Belsen.
> I began to talk like a Jew.
> I think I may well be a Jew.

I quote this passage at length because it illustrates perfectly the confluence of an idea of "Germanness," language and sexual politics that shapes Plath's poem. Plath collapses the German language, the moral bestiality of the Nazis and patriarchal domination of the female poet. As a result, the father's German language becomes genocidal technology directed against the daughter ("an engine/Chuffing me off like a Jew"). Like Norman Mailer, for instance, and the Beat poets who imagined themselves as "White Negroes" in order to articulate their revolt against middle-America, Plath uses Jewish culture as image of radical marginalization, illustrating the plight of the female poet ("I think I may well be a Jew"). Even if one feels somewhat uncomfortable with Plath's appropriation of the Holocaust in her re-telling of the Freudian "family romance" or her allegorical description of the situation of the female poet, "Daddy," like Hawkes's The Cannibal utilizes the idea of Germanness in a self-reflexive (American) critique that seems to have an existentialist rather than a specifically historical or political thrust.[57]

Like Plath, who likens the autobiographical and literary struggle between father and daughter to the Nazi persecution of the Jews, Oates equates the the German dream of racial superiority with dominating male attitudes towards women in "Master Race" (1985). Two other stories, "Ich Bin Ein Berliner" (1982) and "Our Wall" (1982) transform the Berlin Wall into a powerful symbol of existential limitations. In every one of these stories, Oates subtly disconnects the German elements from their specific historical and cultural contexts and transforms them into tropes for the human condition in general.

In "Master Race," an unmarried female art historian, Cecilia Heath, accompanies a successful older married American historian of German descent, Philip Schoen, to Germany to interview scholars for foundation grants. Both in America and abroad, Cecilia is able to deflect Schoen's indirect advances. The relationship between the two becomes more and more strained, and to escape, Cecilia hits the bars on her own. After getting into a conversation with American soldiers in a German bar, Cecilia is raped by an American, presumably a soldier, whom she does not recognize, however. Later, on the same evening, Cecilia and Schoen attend a dinner given in his honor, which develops into an exercise in intercultural misunderstanding between the Germans and the Americans. Scheduled to fly on to Berlin on the next morning, Cecilia impulsively decides to leave Schoen and fly back to the States.

---

[57] Axelrod rather uncritically claims that "for Plath, as later for Adrienne Rich, the Holocaust and the patriarchy's silencing of women were linked outcomes of the masculinist interpretation of the world" (55). This kind of sweeping mono-causal analysis of contemporary problems seems to be as questionable as the blanket indictment of American political institutions as "fascist" by over-zealous political activists in the late 1960's, or Pynchon's critique of the presumed Western death drive as the reigning spirit in America.

   The real drama of Oates' story lies neither in its plot, nor in the anguish of the rape or in the increasing complications of Cecilia's relationship with Schoen, but rather is to be found in Cecilia's emancipation from the domination of Schoen's master race-like attitudes as a scholar and person. While Schoen is drawn to Cecilia for transparently sexual reasons, it soon becomes clear that he does not respect her as an art historian. When, once in Germany, they argue about European history, Cecilia is made acutely uneasy by Schoen's overbearing manner. The narrator reports her thoughts: "Her field of training is art history[...]; it is probably insulting to Philip for her to attempt to argue with him. Quoting statistics, referring to treaties, invasions, acts of parliament, acts of duplicity and vengeance of which Cecilia, frankly, has never heard, [...] Philip makes Cecilia appear to be something of a fool" (Oates, "Master Race" 576). The male-female power lines in this exchange and the domination of Schoen, who merely asserts preconceived notions, over Cecilia, who tries to be open to the impressions in her surroundings, Oates makes clear, parallel Cecilia's ordeal as rape victim and an earlier experience at a conference.

   The philosophical conference that is set up as structural analogue to Cecilia's victimization as woman is dominated by scientific approaches, "linguists, logicians, mathematicians, a topologist, a semiotician," while "no aesthetician participated; no specialists in metaphysics or ethics" (Oates, "Master Race" 571). Significantly enough, while the conference runs the predictable course of more or less abstract technical debates, "Cecilia drifted into a dream thinking of 'male' and 'female' as acquired habits of thinking. Acquired habits of thinking ... ?" (Oates, "Master Race" 572; author's emphasis). Clearly, while not essentially male or female, the scientific attitude of the male philosophers around Cecilia implies their role as an intellectual and academic master race dominating the (absent) humanistic approaches in the same way that Schoen's quantitative history dominates Cecilia's cultural approach and the rapist dominates her body. Little by little, Cecilia realizes that the subtle institutional abuse she has to suffer from Schoen is almost harder to bear than her sexual victimization in the rape. She also comes to recognize Schoen's male attitude of superiority both over herself and over the Germans he meets as no different from Nazi notions of racial supremacy.

On the flight to Germany, talking about his family background on their transatlantic flight, Schoen had reminisced about the supremacist attitudes in his family, who, as Germans, "proclaimed the natural superiority of the Homeland and the inevitable inferiority of other nations, races, religions." And, summing up his forbears' attitudes, Schoen remarks "the Germans really are a master race, [...] even when they -- or do I mean we? -- pretend humility" (Oates, "Master Race" 571). As the story progresses, it becomes increasingly clear that although Schoen sees even the residual supremacist beliefs in his German hosts critically, he fails to recognize his own intellectual and psychological master-race attitudes. While one could argue that Oates's portrayal of Schoen might be intended as a self-reflexive critique of the American intelligentsia, it is important that Schoen is primarily intended as an example of male rather than American attitudes. Like Plath in "Daddy," Oates thus describes sexual politics within the framework of German-American relations and history, and not vice versa as in Hollywood's engagement with foreign policy. Eventually, after the dinner party, Schoen sums up his impressions of his German hosts, Cecilia instantly realizes that unwittingly he describes himself. Schoen holds forth that "that quintessential German-ness he'd find amusing if it weren't so terrifying -- the secret gloating pride in their blood, in their race -- in sin, guilt, history, whatever they choose to call it --" (Oates, "Master Race" 589), but Cecilia interrupts him by starting to laugh, and then leaves to turn in for the night. She finally sees that she has had enough of male delusions of superiority and will finally be able to liberate herself from male domination.

In "Master Race," the (German) master race idea provides a point of articulation and symbolic focus for Oates's feminist critique of male attitudes of intellectual superiority. Reversing, as it were, the practice of displacing cultural into sexual otherness analyzed earlier in Hollywood's representation of Germany, Oates illustrates and symbolically heightens sexual difference and gender attitudes by projecting them onto cultural alterity. While Oates's story comments on endemic racist attitudes both in Germany and America, it primarily takes the German conception of the master race to characterize male domination of women generally rather than to attack any specifically American political attitudes. "Master Race" is thus an allegory of sexual politics played out in the arena of cultural and racial relations and takes one idea or metaphor of Germany to drive home a more general point.

Just as Oates uses the doctrine of the master race as a striking metaphor for the arrogance of male power in "Master Race," the Berlin Wall provides her with the poetic correlative for paradoxical and contradictory psychic needs in "Ich Bin Ein Berliner." In this story , Oates again takes part of the idea of Germany and transforms it into a more general symbol. In "Ich Bin Ein Berliner," an American first person narrator flies to Berlin to find out what has led to his older brother's bizarre death in trying to cross the Wall from West Berlin into East Germany. Although the story leaves unresolved what may have been the actual motive among many possible ones, it soon becomes clear that the dead brother probably took the isolation of West Berlin as an image of not only his own life, but of life in general. As the first person narrator soon realizes, "the wall is finitude. An absolute end" (Oates, "Berliner" 110), an image for death, but at the same time "has become all walls" (Oates, "Berliner" 109), an externalization of the manifold limitations circumscribing daily life, or even an expression of the imprisonment of the spirit in the body. Corroborating his findings, the narrator comes across a heavily marked copy of Freud's Beyond the Pleasure Principle and the phrase "the aim of all life is death" (Oates, "Berliner" 105). Consequently, he begins to understand the brother's paradoxical attempt to invert the customary direction of scaling the wall (from totalitarian East Germany into West Berlin) as a "triumph of the will over biology" (Oates, "Berliner" 103). His brother's suicide thus becomes an affirmation of the independence of the spirit over the body.

In spite of the intricate allusions to the historical and geographical specificity of the city in "Ich Bin Ein Berliner," West Berlin and the Wall function symbolically in this parable of the human desire for freedom which is a desire for transcendence of the limitations of life in death. Thus, for instance, the narrator's brother chose to cross the deadly border on a June 17, the West German republic's national holiday commemorating the anniversary of the East German uprising in 1954, thus seemingly providing a provocative political and historical commentary both on the nature of the West German equivalent of "independence day" and the tyranny of the Wall. With the title of the story, John F. Kennedy's famous proclamation on a visit to Berlin in 1963, Oates similarly seems to insert her piece into the particular cultural and historical context of German-American relations in the Cold War. But while Kennedy tried to articulate the essentially military conception of West Berlin as an extension of the U.S. and nuclear tripwire for Warsaw pact forces in Europe, the narrator's dead brother in Oates's story intends the words "I am a Berliner" as an existential pronouncement similar to the Christian "Ecce Homo," in this case expressing the claustrophobic suffering of the human mind and the hope for redemption in suicide. Or yet again, Oates's description of West Berlin's entertainment district, the Hardenbergstrasse, as a clone of an American Broadway -- "It is America. But no it is Berlin. West Berlin. Germany. But no it is America. No? Yes? America? But with such strong accents?" (Oates, "Berliner" 100), the narrator finds himself thinking -- seems to imply the existence of analogous walls in America, perhaps even inviting a reading of crazy West Berlin as part of the American unconscious. Yet, Oates, less interested in intercultural commentary than in broad existential inquiry, consistently deflects specific allusions to history and culture by recontextualizing them as general images.

Oates clearly demands her Berlin story be read as parable of the human mind by ending "Ich Bin Ein Berliner" with another short parable, the story of a medieval nobleman who devised a particularly cruel form of punishment. Guaranteeing his prisoners the integrity of their lives, he would lock them up atop a tower with only one irresistible opening, big enough for a man to force himself through -- but high above the ground so that the escape could only end in death. The moral of the parable is summed up with the remark that the perversity of human nature is such "that 'freedom' (though also Death) [always] exerted its ineluctable attraction over imprisonment (though also Life)" (Oates, "Berliner" 112) and prisoners, transfixed by the promise of the hole in the walls, would rather jump to their death than be forced to contemplate day after day the paradoxical choice presented by the opening. The deadly gap as non-wall is only a variation of the murderous Berlin Wall in the first part of the story, and both dramatize allegorically the dialectic of freedom and death.

   In parallel to the parable of tortured prisoners in the medieval tower and the American scaling the Berlin Wall from the West, all undone by their own minds, Oates again describes "the most exquisite temptations" of an all embracing Wall in "Our Wall" (239). Oates pushes the transformation of Germany into allegory and parable to the limits in this story, constructing a hallucinated existential labyrinth reminiscent of Kafka and Borges. The story provides a glimpse through the eyes of a child of a society and culture of the Wall. The Wall circumscribes the world in the same way that the Library becomes the universe in Borges' "The Library of Babel" or that the Kafkaesque Castle doubles the succession of life's endless corridors. The inhabitants of Oates's fictional world speculate about the shape of the Wall, what might lie behind it in the "Forbidden Zone," and why the Wall exists in the first place. Although the story could again be read as an engagement with the problematic of life under totalitarianism -- and the story gives no direct indication that it takes place in a futuristic East Berlin and not some other place that has taken up the idea of the Berlin Wall -- Oates's concerns are clearly more epistemological than a political or historical. "Our Wall" tries to paint the picture of the human mind at work, and not the vagaries of history.

   In Oates's Berlin stories, "the Wall offers the felicity of an object that is, yet is not, a metaphor" (Oates, "Berliner" 110), as the narrator of "Ich Bin Ein Berliner" realizes at one point. Unlike a rose, which expresses but does not cause love, the Wall is both a metaphor for death and its agent. And as metaphor only and agent of death in "Ich Bin Ein Berliner," the Wall is severed from its specific cultural and historical contexts and transformed into a symbol. Halfway through the story, the narrator contemplates the ideologically mandated and politically motivated non-existence of West Berlin on Eastern maps and in the Soviet-influenced perspective, and realizes that officially in the East, "'West Berlin' is thus a trope; a way of speaking; a fiction" (Oates, "Berliner" 105). In "Ich Bin Ein Berliner" and "Our Wall," Oates similarly transforms Germany into an idea, reduces the country to the existential trope of the life-denying and freedom-granting Wall.

The Idea of Germany: Walter Abish's How German Is It

Walter Abish's novel How German Is It (1979) is at once the most perfect illustration and the most radical limiting case of the overall thesis of this study, namely that American representations of Germany not only reflect realities abroad but also often comment on the shape of things at home. On the one hand, even the most perfunctory reading of Abish's novel makes clear that the author tries to depict an imaginary and fictional country, quite literally an American Germany that only superficially resembles the actual Germany in spite of a welter of topical allusions. On the other hand, to the same extent that How German Is It denies its readers access to the new Germany, it also defies interpretation as a commentary on America. While How German Is It in its extended portrayal of bourgeois Germany and its experimentation with political and aesthetic shock could be read as a critique of what Tom Wolfe has labelled "radical chic," the impulse of the (American) upper-middle class to embrace (political) ideas antithetical to its very existence, Abish's novel lacks the specificity of a satirical or critical depiction of American mores. Similarly, while Abish's depiction of left-wing terrorism adds an element of mystery and perverse excitement to his novel (similar to the vague political atmosphere in many of Antonioni's films, such as Blow Up but most obviously in the pseudo-revolutionary Zabriskie Point), to take these references as a direct commentary on the excesses of revolutionary fervor in post-1968 America (such as the "Weather Underground" or the "Symbionese Liberation Front") seems to read too much into the novel.[58] But while Abish may not attempt a historically

---

[58] It seems that Abish's fascination with the left-wing terrorists can mainly be explained with reference to the historical context of the novel's genesis. The late 1970's saw the apex of terrorist activity in Germany, and consequently media attention devoted to Germany tended to be dominated by reporting on political extremism. Yet, the figure of the German terrorist also seems to appeal to the popular imagination for another reason, namely because it combines the figure of the sadistic Nazi with that of the modern bugaboo, the terrorist. Thus, for instance, the terrorists who take over a Los Angeles high-rise in the film Die Hard (1988) are not of Middle-

specific commentary on contemporary America in How German Is It, his avowed aim is to call attention to (American) habitual responses to Germany and to reflect on the complexity of reality contrasting with the seductiveness of conventional explanations embedded in fiction. Abish is thus not interested in questioning particular American realities by depicting Germany, probing the very structure of reality itself in his novel. Or, to use a term often used to describe postmodern writing, his novel is a metafiction, a fictional exploration of literary representation.

The protagonist of How German Is It is named Ulrich, like the hero of Robert Musil's The Man Without Qualities. But while Musil's hero lacks a stable characterological outlines because of a confluence of talents or qualities that cancel each other out, Abish's text is held in abeyance because of conflicting and contradictory messages that cancel each other. Musil is reported to have said about his monumental novel, "I have not, I must insist, written a historical novel. I am not concerned with actual events [...] I am interested [...] in what one may call the ghostly aspect of reality" (quoted in Graff 212). Like Musil, who tried to depict the after-image, as it were, of "Kakania," the culture of the shattered Austro-Hungarian empire on the eve of the Great War, Abish attempts to describe the imprint that narrative conventions, culturally evolved ways of seeing, leave on our perception of the world. Like an anthropologist of the everyday, Abish dissects the underlying structures that channel our experience of reality, and in order to accomplish that task repeatedly has recourse to foreign topographies such as Africa (in Alphabetical Africa [1975], for instance) or Germany.

The novel begins with German writer Ulrich Hargenau's return to the town of Würtenburg after a forced stay in Paris in the wake of a terrorist trial. Ulrich, married to one of the activists in the leftist Einzieh group (modeled after the historical German Baader-Meinhof terrorist gang, prominent in international news in the late 1970's), became a witness for the prosecution and helped sentence them to long prison terms. As a payoff he and his wife go free. Ulrich's story in this first part of How German Is It is superficially concerned with several things: Ulrich's

---

Eastern nationality, as might be expected considering recent history, but rather Germans under the command of a "Nazi clone" leader.

relation to his successful brother, the psychological importance of their father, executed in 1944 as a co-conspirator of the assassination attempt on Hitler, the parallels between Ulrich and his father as members both of a political resistance (echoing Jillian Becker's thesis in Hitler's Children) and Ulrich's betrayal of the Einzieh group and his relation to political actionism (reminiscent of Sartre's Les Maines Sales).

Yet, the thematic core of this introductory section of the novel is an exploration of the relationship between the writer's biography and work. Ulrich is in the process of transforming his Paris diary, the record of an abortive love affair, into his next book, while getting romantically involved with another woman, the American Daphne, in Würtenburg. Daphne has a mysterious connection to Ulrich's wife Paula, and when she disappears to Geneva, Ulrich follows her there, but nothing comes of it. Ulrich eventually decides to join his brother Helmuth back in Germany, and consequently the book's focus shifts from Ulrich, who becomes a nearly invisible ancillary character, to Helmuth's sexual exploits. Ulrich becomes the story's focus again only towards the end, when he follows Daphne to the North Sea coast, has the opportunity to make a few more remarks on the relation between fiction and life to a fan, and is nearly killed by chance when terrorists blow up a bridge. How German Is It ends with Ulrich's visit to a hypnotist, whom he consults in order to get in touch with his personal origins and to resolve the lingering doubts about the identity of his natural father (who may have been, after all, not the executed von Hargenau but the family retainer, Franz). None of these questions are resolved and the book closes provocatively with Ulrich under hypnosis raising his right arm for the Hitler salute.

In spite of the resistance to interpretation put up by the text, the story of Ulrich -- even if not intended to be taken as such -- can be read as one kind of German engagement with the past. In Ulrich, German left-wing terrorism is explained as Freudian "family romance," as the postwar German generation's fantasy of being (politically or ideologically) orphaned and the ensuing search for and the invention of true parents. Regardless of its degree of usefulness as an explanatory concept, Abish seems to gloss this radical version of the "inability to mourn" and the curious disconnection from and repetition of the sins of the fathers as one established way to explain the new Germany. In an interview Abish has pointed out that "hardly anyone can mention Germany, or write about Germany, without feeling the necessity to [...] 'wrap up Germany.' Everything German necessitates an explanation and, of course, it is invariably the same familiar explanation" (McCaffery 16). The depiction of Ulrich seems to advance just such a "familiar explanation" of the German as extremist and unstable. Yet, as a character Ulrich is so overdetermined as to undercut successfully readerly expectations for a straightforward explanation. For instance, Ulrich is only a hanger-on in the Einzieh group, and it is never made quite clear what he thinks of their radical solutions to political problems. As a rather unconvinced terrorist sympathizer, Ulrich is thus only a sorry example of one of "Hitler's children," a generation resorting to Nazi-like political terror in their revolt against the their Nazi parents. At the same time, it is never clear whether his doubts about his father are justified or merely the product of an overheated imagination. Similarly, the significance of his Hitler salute at the end of the story is left unresolved. Does it mean that he is not his resistance father's son after all, or is it merely a radical form of Oedipal struggle? Is it evidence for his kinship with Franz, who is obsessed with Nazism and builds a match stick replica of a concentration camp? Does it express his German proclivity to political extremism, be it left or right wing? In short, the predictability of the American readerly response to Germany is undercut by the ambiguous and contradictory character of such crucial episodes.

With Ulrich's return from Geneva, attention begins to shift to the fictional German town Brumholdstein, named after the equally fictional philosopher Brumhold, whom Abish models on Martin Heidegger. The story concentrates on Ulrich's brother Helmuth and his the consecutive affairs with several of his friends' wives and mistresses, providing a kind of panoramic view of the vacuous upper-middle class landscape peopled by professionals and intellectuals (somewhat reminiscent of Woody Allen's Manhattan [1979]). Interwoven with this second narrative strand is that of Franz, the erstwhile retainer of the Hargenau family and present waiter in a fashionable hotel. Franz, with his petty bourgeois aspirations as a waiter, his veneration of power and especially the Hargenau family, and his barely submerged aggressiveness embodies another customary explanation of Germany and the appeal of fascism to the lower middle class. Franz seems the perfect illustration of the so-called passive-aggressive personality that is irresistibly drawn to and repelled by authority and domination. In his match stick model of the Durst extermination camp Franz plays out his fantasies of being at once victim and oppressor; through the model, Franz playfully appropriates for himself the absolute domination of the Nazi state, but also stages his own helplessness as outcast in a new Germany whose sensibilities he has offended by bringing up the repressed past. Not surprisingly, given the nature of the text, How German Is It again leaves open whether Franz is an inveterate Nazi sympathizer who merely yearns for the return of the good old days, or whether he is a political iconoclast who tries to undercut Brumholdstein and the new republic's historical repression by confronting it with a model of the death camp it is literally built on.

In his obsession with the past, in his veneration for and rage directed against the Hargenaus, and his uncontrollable nightly howling, Franz illustrates the displaced return of the repressed German past, which is staged in yet another form when one day a sidewalk in Brumholdstein collapses and a mass grave is discovered. While the episode again seems to confirm readerly expectations, its significance is not at all clear since the issue of the bodies' nationality is left unresolved. People speculate that they could be the bodies of camp inmates, killed shortly before the arrival of allied troops; then again, the bodies could be those of townspeople killed by rampaging liberated inmates; or yet again, the mass grave might hold the bodies of transient displaced persons and refugees who died in the aftermath of the war. Like so many other elements of How German Is It, the opened mass grave raises readerly expectations for a clear-cut explanation of Germany but never makes good on that promise.

If Franz dramatizes the painful German struggle to prevent the return of the repressed Nazi past, and shows the dark underside of the new Germany, Helmuth depicts the bright side of the new country, that of the "economic miracle." Helmuth holds forth on "the splendid history of architecture. Greece, Rome, Byzantium, a slow parade of architectural achievement, culminating in the new police station in Würtenburg" (Abish, How German 14) designed by himself. Believing that success validates itself, Helmuth chooses to ignore the obvious roots in Nazi bombast of his kind of official architecture -- police stations, post offices, libraries, museums. Helmuth also embodies the spirit of Brumholdstein (and by extension the new Germany in general), literally constructed after the war on the site of a concentration camp. Helmuth's life, the shape of German cities, and the new Germany in general all rely on deceptive surfaces to hide the old atrocities (what Abish, quoting John Ashbery, has called the "English Garden" effect in the story of the same name). In the opening pages of How German Is It, the narrator thus comments on the shape of the German city, which he sees dominated by a "wide expanse of glass on the buildings, the glass reflecting not only the sky but also acting as a mirror for the older historical sites, those clusters of carefully reconstructed buildings that are an attempt to replicate entire neighborhoods obliterated in the last war" (Abish, How German 3). Just as the German cities in How German Is It are built on old death camps and hidden mass graves and are made up false fronts and depthless surfaces, the lives of the upper-middle class people in Helmuth's circle consist of deceptive surfaces and hidden menaces. Like photographer Rita Tropf-Ulmwehrt in the novel, who inventories the lives of successful people like Helmuth and his friends Egon and Gisela for the magazine Treue, Abish's picture of the lives of the new German bourgeoisie relies on "an emphasis on the startling, on the shocking, on the erotic, on the unexpected" (Abish, How German 198) to create a sense of uneasiness and dark foreboding in contrast with the picture book surfaces of respectability.

Of course, this recourse to an aesthetics of defamiliarization -- the combination of incongruous elements in order to disrupt the surface of the familiar -- and the "instinct to combine what is essentially 'perfection' with the 'menacing'" (Abish, How German 127) is not a uniquely German upper- and upper middle-class trait, as the narrator of How German Is It claims. In practically all of Abish's short stories, the familiar is paired with the shocking in order to disrupt the automatism of perception; the unexpected, the vaguely threatening is introduced to defamiliarize and reinvigorate the familiar world. Thus, for instance, in the story "In So Many Words," a successful female professional with a perfect loft, perfect taste and perfect friends invites three leather jacketed thugs into her apartment to have sex with her in order to shield herself against the infinite tedium of the familiar. Commenting on the defamiliarizing effect of the three men, the heroine of the story muses that "their black leather jackets enhance the perfection of her possessions" (Abish, In the Future Perfect 90). The threatening, the menacing, and the incongruous are introduced into the familiar world in order to make it visible again, as it were, to give it new charm.

Like the heroine of "In So Many Words," Abish in his fiction aims for "a well balanced perfection of terror" (Abish, Future Perfect 92), in which postwar Germany, with its newly created surface perfection and the terror of the past, seems an almost inevitable setting for the disruption of readerly expectations. In one way or another, Abish explores in every one of his stories the relationship between the medium and the message. In Alphabetical Africa, a book in 52 chapters in which the words in the first chapter all begin with the letter "a," those in the second chapter with "b" and so on until, in the middle of the book, the author has the whole alphabet at his disposal before his choices narrow down again to the letter "a" in the last chapter, he investigates how the very materiality of language constricts and determines the content of communication.

The idea is taken up with variations in other experimental stories that are all structured by some formal constraint. In an attempt to highlight the "already-used" character of language and the over-determination of literary meaning, Abish has constructed literary "ready-mades," stories consisting of passages from other authors combined to form new meaning (cf. "99: The New Meaning"). But apart from these forays into conceptual art (which is often rather tedious in practice even if exciting as idea), Abish has consistently probed how habitually formed notions (what Wittgenstein called "forms of life") determine our perception of reality. A given signal elicits a predictable response, Abish would say, and his project as artist is both to call attention to the problematical character of that chain and to disrupt it. "Abish is rarely interested in re-telling events or describing reality," remarks one critic. "Rather, he seeks ways to disturb our sense of the familiar, to re-energize it, to explore the ambiguous elements that surround us, typically unexamined or unnoticed" (McCaffery 8). In his experimental fiction as well as in How German Is It, Abish explores the strategies we use to represent reality, by disrupting habitual patterns of perception. Like the arbitrary formal constraints that shape his experimental stories, Abish uses the stereotypical elements of American encounters with Germany to structure How German Is It.

In his story "The English Garden," which encapsulates the main themes of How German Is It, the pictures in a children's coloring book structure the perceptions of his American protagonist, come to Brumholdstein to interview the German writer Wilhelm Aus (WA=Walter Abish!). The simplified, two-dimensional and even colorless version of German life in the coloring book has to be read as an allegory of Abish's Germany in both "The English Garden" and How German Is It. Like the country in the coloring book, Germany in How German Is It -- as much as Africa in Alphabetical Africa -- is an abstracted space created out of the fantasies we have about it with only perfunctory and general resemblance to reality. Asked why he had chosen Africa as locale for his experimental alphabetical novel, Abish pointed out that "it is the continent to which our childhood as well as adult fantasies [...] are inextricably linked. Africa is a continent of taboos" (McCaffery 19). Germany -- as metaphor for evil -- is a similarly fantasized foreign topography, attractive for its exotic alterity, and because it gives Abish more imaginative freedom than a more familiar backdrop. As he admits himself, he prefers a foreign surface for his fiction because

> [in America] I know what is familiar, and I don't feel as free to break away from it. On the other hand, I tend to establish or reestablish the familiar in what is foreign, allowing the familiar to determine the subsequent defamiliarization. The result is a tension, a sense of unbehagen, a discomfort. (Lotringer 161)

Thus Abish picks an unfamiliar setting and by placing familiar elements in it energizes his text. In spite of all the threatening elements, the unfamiliar, in Abish's How German Is It -- things like mass graves, dead fathers, terrorist friends, sniper attacks and so forth -- the novel's fictional space is also determined by the familiarity of small town life and its institutions. By contrast with a purely surrealist account like Hawkes's

The Cannibal, Abish's novel derives its force from the combination of real and fantastical elements. The appeal of Africa's or Germany's alterity to which Abish refers in the interview is the freedom that results from the aura of the foreign, the strange. Yet, that sense of alterity results mostly from the confrontation between the familiar and the unfamiliar, the juxtaposition of reassuring and threatening elements.

Defamiliarization as aesthetic effect points beyond itself and the confines of the work of art and has the potential for a critique of culture and reality. The confrontation between the familiar and the unfamiliar, the tension resulting from the collision of American and German cultural spaces in How German Is It, results in a reevaluation of American spaces, of what is taken for granted. The description of Germany is a reevaluation or even a critique of -- America. As Sylvère Lotringer puts it, Abish is "not writing about Germany in order to 'understand' another culture; [he is] using the signs of a foreign culture to establish another attitude toward our own" (163).

And here, finally, we see that How German Is It not only constitutes a limiting case of self-reflexive American representations of Germany, but also most perfectly describes the dynamics of such self-reflexive accounts in a metafictional way. Abish's novel refuses to provide clear-cut and unambiguous commentaries either on Germany or the U.S., exploring instead the way in which the subject matter, Germany, predetermines American responses. How German Is It thus is a perfect example of America's Germany -- with a twist, providing an American meta-representation of Germany in commenting on the customary way in which cultural otherness is approached. In an interview Abish has pointed out how he turns to Germany both to explore the message already predetermined in the subject matter and to call attention to it:

> Everything German necessitates an explanation and, of course, it is invariably the same familiar explanation. I suspect that one brings up the subject of Germany only in order to arrive at the explanation. To me the literary challenge was to see to what degree it would be possible to write about Germany without fulfilling those obligations. (McCaffery 16)

As a consequence of this program of once to circumscribing and circumventing familiar explanations of Germany, How German Is It can be understood as the most radical attempt to probe the American self by depicting the German other because, after all, the familiar explanations that Abish is concerned with as American author are primarily American explanations. The habitual response that he portrays is an American response. "My interest in Germany is not to explain it," Abish makes clear, "but to highlight the German 'signs' that elicit a set response" (McCaffery 22).

Both the Jean Luc Godard quotation used as epigraph to the novel, "What is really at stake is one's image of oneself," and the title of the book itself both point to its crucial function as American self-exploration (if not self-critique). The title of Abish's novel also seems to be another variation on Emerson's despairing cry quoted in the first chapter, "how impossible to find Germany." The title, How German Is It, illustrates the postmodern sensibility which makes the crisis of knowledge its topic and transforms it into an artistic program: no longer despairing to find the actual Germany, Abish seems to rest content with giving an imaginary account of it and measuring it against the expectations of his audience. The title of Abish's novel may even allude to an American comedy routine (standard at Chicago's "Second City" theater until fairly recently, as I am told) that consists in feeding back American stereotypes about Germany and the Germans to the audience for approval under the heading "How German is it?" Abish, however, drops the question mark in the title of his novel, and although the question is not a question any more, and the aim is no longer to gauge how accurately the stereotypes have been rendered, Abish still deals in stereotypes, but to different ends, for a different effect.

Interviewed about his work in progress, the writer Ulrich in How German Is It describes what can be taken as an indication of the significance of Germany in Abish's novel:

> What is the title of your forthcoming book?
> The Idea of Switzerland.
> The idea of Switzerland?

> Well, it's based on something I read about Paganini. Apparently Berlioz loved the idea of Paganini but was revolted by his music. [...] I am, of course, thinking of <u>the image</u> Switzerland <u>evokes in people</u>. A kind of controlled neutrality, a somewhat antiseptic tranquility that even I find soothing. (Abish, <u>How German</u> 52; my emphasis)

In the same way, something that can be called the idea of Germany would be the common contemporary response that country evokes in people, the common response Abish also toys with in his novel: fascism, and left wing terrorism. Moreover, like his protagonist's fascination and concern with the idea, but not the reality of, Switzerland, Abish as author is interested in the cultural construct, the (contemporary) American image of Germany. Abish not only has the protagonist of <u>How German Is It</u> spell out Germany's relevance as background of the novel, he also comments on the essentially American character of the novel's Germany in an interview saying that "the Germany in one's head is frequently more valuable as a source than the Germany one may visit. [...] As for our vision of America -- for that one may have to turn to the mail-order catalogs, <u>National Geographic</u>, movies, novels, the <u>New York Times</u>" (McCaffery 11).[59] With Emerson Abish seems to be saying that the genius of Germany "is in one's head," and that the imaginary Germany is much more interesting and inspiring than the actual country.

Even if the novel seems to lack a specific American self-critique if compared with many of the cultural productions analyzed throughout this study, thus constituting a limiting case, <u>How German Is It</u>, finally, also most perfectly bears out the main point of my argument, illustrating Germany's catalytic function as a point of articulation for American self-evaluations in the post-World War II era. Abish's novel meta-fictionally thematizes that very process of looking to the cultural other in order to

---

[59] On the genesis of the Germany in his novel, Abish remarked: "I kept looking at the maps of towns and small cities in old Baedekers and Michelin guides of Germany, trying to piece together a map of Brumholdstein and all the other places I had invented" (McCaffery 20). Abish only came to Germany for the first time two years after publication of <u>How German Is It</u>, in 1982 (cf. McCaffery 20).

perceive the cultural self. How German Is It highlights what we have seen throughout this study, that Germany is not defined by what it is, but by what it is not: America. And finally, with Daphne, the American woman in the novel who has come to Würtenburg as a student, Americans turning to Germany in order to find their own country have consistently found that the foreign topography allowed them to see themselves more clearly, because the alterity of Germany did not conjure up "an entire panorama of familiar associations that blunted the preciseness needed in order to bring her philosophical investigation to a satisfactory conclusion. Could this be the reason why she had come to Germany? To think in German, to question herself in a foreign language?" (Abish, How German 38).

References

A. Works Cited

Abish, Walter, <u>How German Is It</u>. London: Faber and Faber. 1983.
  -- , <u>In the Future Perfect</u>. London: Faber and Faber. 1984.
Adams, Henry, <u>The Education of Henry Adams</u>. Boston: Houghton Mifflin. 1974.
Alvarez, A., "Sylvia Plath." Charles Newman (ed.), <u>The Art of Sylvia Plath</u>. Bloomington: Indiana University Press. 1970. 56-68.
Ambrose, Stephen, <u>Eisenhower</u>. Vol. 2, "The President." New York: Simon and Schuster. 1984.
Ambruster, Howard Watson, <u>Treason's Peace. German Dyes and American Dupes</u>. New York: Beechhurst Press. 1947.
Arnold, Thurman, <u>The Folklore of Capitalism</u>. New Haven: Yale University Press. 1937.
Axelrod, Steven Gould, <u>Sylvia Plath</u>. Baltimore: Johns Hopkins University Press. 1990.
Bach, Julian, <u>America's Germany. An Account of the Occupation</u>. New York: Random House. 1946.
Badger, Anthony J., <u>The New Deal. The Depression Years, 1933-40</u>. Noonday Press. New York: Farrar, Straus and Giroux. 1989.
Baker, William J., <u>Jesse Owens. An American Life</u>. New York: Free Press. 1986.
Berger, Thomas, <u>Crazy in Berlin</u>. New York: Delta. 1982.
Bernstein, Barton J., "The New Deal: The Conservative Achievements of Liberal Reform." In <u>Towards a New Past. Dissenting Essays in American History</u>. New York: Vintage. 1968. 263-88.
Berry, Lelah and Ann Stringer, "An Army Wife Lives Very Soft -- in Germany." <u>Saturday Evening Post</u>. 15 Feb. 1947. 24/25, 119-22.
Beymer, William G., <u>Middle of Midnight</u>. New York: McGraw. 1947.
<u>The Big Lift</u>. Dir. George Seaton. With Montgomery Clift and Paul Douglas. Twentieth Century-Fox. 1950.

Bleicher, Thomas, "Elemente einer komparatistischen Imagologie." Komparatistische Hefte, 2 (1980). 12-24.

Blum, John Morton, Roosevelt and Morgenthau. A Revision and Condensation of From the Morgenthau Diaries. Boston: Houghton Mifflin. 1970.

-- , V was for Victory. San Diego: Harcourt Brace Jovanovich. 1976.

Botting, Douglas, From the Ruins of the Reich. Germany 1945-1949. New York: Crown. 1985.

Bourke-White, Margaret, "Dear Fatherland Rest Quietly." A Report on the Collapse of Hitler's "Thousand Years." New York: Simon and Schuster. 1946.

Boyle, Kay, The Smoking Mountain [1951]. With a foreword by William L. Shirer. New York: Alfred A. Knopf. 1968.

Brandeis, Louis D., The Curse of Bigness. Miscellaneous Papers. New York: Viking. 1934.

Brown, Charles Brockden, Wieland. Bicentennial Edition. Kent: Kent State University Press. 1977.

Brown, Earl, "American Negroes and the War." Harper's Magazine. Vol. 184 No. 1103 (April 1942). 545-52.

Buchanan, A. Russel, Black Americans in World War II. Santa Barbara: Clio. 1977.

Buxton, David, From the Avengers to Miami Vice. New York: St. Martin's Press. 1990.

Carpenter, Richard C., "State of Mind: The California Setting of The Crying of Lot 49." In Charles L. Crow (ed.), Itinerary: Criticism. Essays on California Writers. Bowling Green, OH: Bowling Green University Press. 1978. 105-13.

Carr, Victoria Spencer, Dos Passos. A Life. Garden City: Doubleday. 1984.

Carter, Dale, The Final Frontier. The Rise and Fall of the American Rocket State. London: Verso. 1988.

Carter, J.F., The New Dealers. New York: Literary Guild. 1934.

Chandler, Alfred A., "The United States: Seedbed of Managerial Capitalism." In Alfred A. Chandler and Herman Daems (eds.), Managerial Hierarchies. Cambridge: Harvard University Press. 1980. 9-40.

Christadler, Martin, "German and American Romanticism." Christoph

Wecker (ed.), American-German Literary Interrelations in the Nineteenth Century. American Studies Vol. 55. München: Wilhelm Fink. 1983. 9-26.

Cooper, James Fenimore, The Pioneers. Albany: State University of New York Press. 1980.

Davis, Mike, City of Quartz. London: Verso. 1990.

Dick, Philip K., The Man in the High Castle. New York: Ace Books. 1988.

Dos Passos, John, Tour of Duty. Boston: Houghton and Mifflin. 1946.

Dr. Strangelove. Dir. Stanley Kubrick. With Peter Sellers and George C. Scott. Columbia. 1964.

Edel, Leon (ed.), The Henry James Letters (1843-1875). Cambridge: Harvard University Press. 1974.

Emerson, Ralph Waldo, The Journals and Miscellaneous Notebooks of Ralph Waldo Emerson. Ed. William Gilman et. al. Vol 11. Cambridge: Belknap. 1975.

Fiedler, Leslie, Love and Death in the American Novel. New York: Dell. 1966.

A Foreign Affair. Dir. Billy Wilder. With Jean Arthur and Marlene Dietrich. Paramount. 1948.

Fräulein. Dir. Henry Koster. With Dana Wynter and Mel Ferrer. Twentieth Century-Fox. 1958.

Frederiksen, Oliver J., The American Military Occupation of Germany 1945-1953. N.p.: Historical Division, Headquarters, United States Army, Europe. 1953.

Freese, Peter, "Exercises in Boundary Making: The German as the 'Other' in American Literature." Germany and German Thought in American Literature and Cultural Criticism. Essen: Verlag Die Blaue Eule. 1990. 93-132.

Friedländer, Saul, Reflections of Nazism. New York: Harper Row. 1984.

Friedman, Alan and Puetz, Manfred, "Science as Metaphor: Thomas Pynchon and Gravity's Rainbow." In Richard Pearce, Critical Essays on Thomas Pynchon. Boston: Hall. 1981. 69-81.

Gaddis, John Lewis, "The Emerging Post-Revisionist Synthesis on the Origins of the Cold War." Diplomatic History Vol. 7 No. 3 (Summer 1983). 171-90.

"Germany Meets the Negro Soldier." Ebony, Vol. 2 No. 10 (Oct. 1946).

5-9.

Gimbel, John, Science, Technology, and Reparations. Exploitation and Plunder in Postwar Germany. Stanford: Stanford University Press. 1990.

Glaser, Daniel, "The Sentiments of American Soldiers Abroad Toward Europeans." American Journal of Sociology, Vol. 51 No. 5 (Mar. 46). 433- 38.

Graff, Gerald, Literature Against Itself. Chicago: University of Chicago Press. 1979.

Gramsci, Antonio, Selections from Cultural Writings. Ed. by D. Forgacs and G. Nowell-Smith. Transl. by W. Boelhower. Cambridge: Harvard University Press. 1985.

Graves, Robert, The White Goddess. A Historical Grammar of Poetic Myth. Amended and enlarged ed. New York: Farar , Straus and Giroux. 1966.

Greene, Graham, The Third Man. Modern Film Scripts. London: Lorrimer. 1969.

Hauser, Ernest O., "The Germans Resist 'Liberation.'" Saturday Evening Post 10 Aug. 1946. 17, 121-22.

Hawkes, John, The Cannibal. Introduction by Albert J. Guerard. 2nd ed. New York: New Directions. 1962.

-- , Humors of Blood and Skin. A John Hawkes Reader. With autobiographical notes by the author. New York: New Directions. 1984.

-- , Interview. Allan Burns and Charles Sugnet, The Imagination on Trial. British and American Writers Discuss Their Working Methods. London: Allison and Busby. 1981. 66-82.

-- , "Life and Art: An Interview with John Hawkes." (By Patrick O'Donnell.) Review of Contemporary Fiction. Vol. 3 (Fall 1983). 107-26.

Hawley, Ellis W., The New Deal and the Problem of Monopoly. Princeton: Princeton University Press. 1966.

Hawthorne, Nathaniel, "The Celestial Railroad." Mosses from an Old Manse. Centenary Edition Vol. X. Columbus: Ohio State University Press. 1974. 186-206.

-- , The Marble Faun. Centenary Edition Vol. IV. Columbus: Ohio State

University Press. 1968.

-- , The Scarlet Letter. Centenary Edition Vol. I. Columbus: Ohio State University Press. 1962.

-- , "Young Goodman Brown." Mosses from an Old Manse. Centenary Edition Vol. X. Columbus: Ohio State University Press. 1974. 74-90.

Hess, Gary R., "After the Tumult: The Wisconsin School's Tribute to William Appleman Williams." Diplomatic History Vol. 12 No. 3 (Fall 1988). 483-99.

Hodges, LeRoy S., Portrait of an Expatriate. William Gardner Smith, Writer. Contributions in Afro-American and African Studies, Number 91. Westport: Greenwood. 1985.

Hofstadter, Richard, et. al., The American Republic. Vol. 2. Englewood Cliffs: Prentice Hall. 1970.

Howells, William Dean, The Rise of Silas Lapham. Riverside Literature Series. New York: Houghton and Mifflin. 1937.

Hughes, Emmet John, "A European Year of Destiny." Life 10 May 1954. 167-84.

Hunt, Michael H., Ideology and U.S. Foreign Policy. New Haven: Yale University Press. 1987.

Irving, John, The Mare's Nest. Boston: Little, Brown. 1964.

JanMohamed, Abdul R., "The Economy of Manichean Allegory: The Function of Radical Difference in Colonial Literature." Critical Inquiry 12 (Autumn 1985). 59-87.

Jonas, Manfred, The United States and Germany. A Diplomatic History. Ithaca: Cornell University Press. 1984.

Kahn, Arthur D., Betrayal. Our Occupation of Germany. New York: Kahn. 1950.

Kazin, Alfred, On Native Grounds. New York: Rynal and Hitchcock. 1942.

Keil, Hartmut, "The Presentation of Germany in American Television News." In Peter Freese (ed.), Germany and German Thought in American Literature and Cultural Criticism. Essen: Verlag Die Blaue Eule. 1990. 26-50.

Klinkowitz, Jerome, "Walter Abish: An Interview." Fiction International 4/5 (1975). 93-100.

Kocka, Jürgen, "The Rise of the Modern Industrial Enterprise in Germany."

In Alfred A. Chandler and Herman Daems (ed.), <u>Managerial Hierarchies</u>. Cambridge: Harvard Universtiy Press. 1980. 77-116.

Krafft, John M., "Thomas Pynchon." In Sonyha Sayres et. al. (eds.), <u>The 60's Without Apology</u>. 283-286.

Lasby, Clarence G., <u>Project Paperclip. German Scientists and the Cold War</u>. New York: Atheneum. 1971.

Leuchtenberg, William E., <u>Franklin D. Roosevelt and the New Deal</u>. New York: Harper and Row. 1963.

Lotringer, Sylvère, "Wie Deutsch Ist Es. [Interview with Walter Abish]." <u>Semiotext(e)</u> 4 (1982). 160-78.

Luce, Henry R., "The American Century." <u>Life</u> 17 Feb. 1941. 61-65.

Mailer, Norman, <u>The Naked and the Dead</u>. New York: Holt, Rinehart and Winston. 1976.

--   , "The White Negro." F. Feldman and M. Gartenberg (eds.), <u>The Beat Generation and the Angry Young Men</u>. Secaucus, NJ: Citadel. 1984. 342-363.

Marcus, George E. and Fischer, Michael M.J., <u>Anthropology as Cultural Critique</u>. Chicago: University of Chicago Press. 1986.

Martin, James S., <u>All Honorable Men</u>. Boston: Little, Brown. 1950.

Martin, Richard, "Clio Bemused: The Uses of History in Contemporary American Fiction." <u>Sub-Stance</u> 27 (1980). 13-24.

Mason, Peter, <u>Deconstructing America. Representations of the Other</u>. New York: Routledge. 1990.

May, Ernest R. "Writing Contemporary International History." <u>Diplomatic History</u> 8 (Spring 84). 103-13.

McCaffery, Larry and Gregory, Sinda, "An Interview with Walter Abish." In <u>Alive and Writing</u>. Urbana: University of Illinois Press. 1987. 7-25.

McCormick, Thomas J., <u>America's Half-Century. United States Foreign Policy in the Cold War</u>. Baltimore: Johns Hopkins University Press. 1989.

McCraw, Thomas K., <u>Prophets of Regulation</u>. Cambridge: Harvard University Press. 1984.

Mead, Chris, <u>Champion. Joe Louis, Black Hero in White America</u>. New York: Scribner's. 1985.

Melville Herman, Moby Dick. Harmondsworth: Penguin. 1972.

Morgenthau, Henry, Germany is our problem. New York: Harper. 1945.

Nance, Guinevara A. and Jones, Judith P., "Doing Away with Daddy: Exorcism and Sympathetic Magic in Plath's Poetry." Linda Wagner (ed.), Critical Essays on Sylvia Plath. Boston: G.K. Hall. 1984. 124-30.

Niebuhr, Reinhold, "The Fight for Germany." Life 11 Nov. 1946. 65-72.

Norris, Frank, McTeague. Garden City: Doubleday. 1928.

-- , The Octopus. In Novels and Essays. Ed. Donald Pizer. Library of America. New York: Literary Classics of the United States. 1986.

Oates, Joyce Carol, "Ich Bin Ein Berliner." In Last Days. New York: Dutton. 1986. 97-112.

-- , "Master Race." Partisan Review. Fiftieth Anniversary Issue, Vol. 51/5-52/1 (1984/85). 566-590

-- , "Our Wall." "Ich Bin Ein Berliner." In Last Days. New York: Dutton. 1986. 233-241.

One, Two, Three. Dir. Billy Wilder. With James Cagney, Horst Buchholz and Lilo Pulver. United Artists. 1961.

Padover, Saul K., "Why Americans Like German Women." American Mercury Vol. 63, No. 273 (Sep. 1946). 354-57.

"Patterns of Force." Star Trek episode No. 52. Dir. Vincent McEveety. With William Shatner and Leonard Nimoy. Paramount Pictures. First aired 16 February 1968.

Paul, Barbara Dotts, The Germans after World War II. An English-Language Bibliography. Boston: G.K. Hall. 1990.

Plath, Sylvia, "Daddy." Encounter Vol. 21 No. 4 (October 1963). 52.

Pocket Guide to Germany. Prep. by Army Information Branch, Army Services Forces, United States Army. U.S. Government Printing Office: n.p. 1944.

Poe, Edgar Allan, "Preface [to Tales of the Grotesque and Arabesque]." Poetry and Tales. Library of America. New York: Literary Classics of the United States. 1984. 129-30.

Puzo, Mario, The Dark Arena. New York: Random House. 1955.

Pynchon, Thomas, The Crying of Lot 49. New York: Harper & Row. 1986.

-- , Gravity's Rainbow. New York: Viking, 1973.

--   , "Is It O.K. to Be a Luddite?" <u>New York Times Book Review</u>. 28
          October 1984. 1,40-41.
--   , <u>V.</u>. New York: Harper & Row. 1986.
Reynolds, Grant, "What the Negro Soldier Thinks About This War." <u>The
          Crisis</u>. Sep. 1944. 289-91, 299.
Said, Edward, <u>Orientalism</u>. New York: Pantheon. 1978.
Sanders, Scott, "Pynchon's Paranoid History." <u>Twentieth Century
          Literature</u>. Vol. 21, No. 2 (May 1975). 177-92.
Sasuly, Richard, <u>IG Farben</u>. New York: Boni and Gaer. 1947.
Scholes, Robert, "A Talk with Kurt Vonnegut, Jr." Interview. Jerome
          Klinkowitz and John Somer (eds.), <u>The Vonnegut Statement</u>.
          n.p.: Delacorte. 1973. 90-118.
Schultz, Arthur R., <u>German-American Relations and German Culture in
          America: A Subject Bibliography, 1941-1980</u>. Vol. 1.
          Millwood, N.Y.: Kraus International. 1984.
Seed, David, <u>The Fictional Labyrinths of Thomas Pynchon</u>. Iowa City:
          University of Iowa Press. 1988.
Shaw, Irwin, <u>The Young Lions</u>. New York: Random House. 1948.
Slatoff, Walter J., "GI Morals in Germany." <u>The New Republic</u> May 1946.
          686-87.
Smith, Michael L., "Selling the Moon." In Richard Wightman Fox and T.J.
          Jackson Lears (eds.), <u>The Culture of Consumption</u>. New York:
          Pantheon, 1983. 175-209.
Smith, Robert Freeman, "Republican Policy and the Pax Americana 1921-
          1932." In William Appleman Williams (ed.), <u>From Colony to
          Empire</u>. New York: John Wiley and Sons. 1972. 253-92.
Smith, William Gardner, <u>Last of the Conquerors</u>. New York: Farar, Straus.
          1948.
"Song of Girls and GI's." <u>Ebony</u>, Vol. 2 No. 10 (Oct. 1946). 10-11.
Sontag, Susan, "Fascinating Fascism." <u>Under the Sign of Saturn</u>. New
          York: Farar, Straus, Giroux. 1980. 71-105.
Takaki, Ronald T., <u>Iron Cages. Race and Culture in Nineteenth-Century
          America</u>. New York: Alfred A. Knopf. 1979.
Taylor, Graham D., "The Rise and Fall of Antitrust in Occupied Germany,
          1945-48." <u>Prologue</u>. Vol. 11 (1979). 23-39.
Tölölyan, Khachig, "War as Background in <u>Gravity's Rainbow</u>." In Charles

Clerc (ed.), <u>Approaches to Gravity's Rainbow</u>. Columbus: Ohio State University Press. 1983. 31-67.

Twain, Mark, <u>A Tramp Abroad</u>. Vol. 1. New York: Harper. 1907.

Varg, Paul A., <u>America, from Client State to World Power</u>. Norman: University of Oklahoma Press. 1990.

Vonnegut, Kurt, <u>Slaughterhouse-Five</u>. New York: Dell. 1985.

Weber, Max, <u>The Protestant Ethic and the Spirit of Capitalism</u>. Trans. Talcott Parsons. New York: Scribner's. 1958.

Weisenburger, Steven, <u>A Gravity's Rainbow Companion</u>. Athens: University of Georgia Press. 1988.

White, Walter, <u>A Rising Wind</u>. Reprint. Westport: Negro Universities Press. 1971.

Willett, Ralph, "Billy Wilder's 'A Foreign Affair' (1945-1948): 'the trials and tribulations of Berlin.'" <u>Historical Journal of Film, Radio and Television</u> Vol. 7 No. 1 (1987). 3-14.

Williams, Raymond, <u>The Sociology of Culture</u>. New York: Schocken. 1981.

Williams, William Appleman, <u>Empire as a Way of Life</u>. New York: Oxford University Press. 1980.

Wolfe, Tom, <u>The Right Stuff</u>. New York: Bantam. 1980.

Yergin, Daniel, <u>The Prize. The Epic Quest for Oil, Money and Power</u>. New York: Simon and Schuster. 1991.

-- , <u>Shattered Peace. The Origins of the Cold War</u>. Revised and updated edition. Harmondsworth: Penguin. 1990.

Young, Hugo et. al., <u>Journey to Tranquility</u>. Garden City, NY: Doubleday. 1970.

Zavarzadeh, Mas'ud, <u>Seeing Films Politically</u>. Albany: State University of New York Press. 1991.

B. Works Consulted

i. Books, Periodicals, Films and Reviews

Abish, Walter, <u>How German Is It</u>. London: Faber and Faber. 1983.

--   <u>Alphabetical Africa</u>. New York: New Directions. 1974.

--   In the Future Perfect. London: Faber and Faber. 1984.

--   Ninety-Nine: The New Meaning. Providence, RI: Burning Deck. 1990.

--   "Self Portrait." In Alan Sondheim (ed.), Individuals: Post-Movement Art in America. New York: Dutton. 1977. 1-25.

--   "The Writer-to-Be: An Impression of Living." Sub-Stance 27 (1980). 104-114.

Adams, Henry, The Education of Henry Adams. Boston: Houghton Mifflin. 1974.

Adams, Willi Paul and Krakau, Knud (eds.), Deutschland und Amerika. Perzeption und Historische Realität. Berlin: Colloquium. 1985.

Adorno, Theodor W. and Horkheimer, Max, Dialektik der Auflärung. Frankfurt/M.: Suhrkamp. 1972.

Alperovitz, Gar, Atomic Diplomacy. Harmondsworth: Penguin. 1985.

--   Cold War Essays. Garden City, NJ: Doubleday. 1970.

Alvarez, A., "Sylvia Plath." Charles Newman (ed.), The Art of Sylvia Plath. Bloomington: Indiana University Press. 1970. 56-68.

Ambrose, Stephen, Eisenhower. Vol. 2 ("The President"). New York: Simon and Schuster. 1984.

Ambruster, Howard Watson, Treason's Peace. German Dyes and American Dupes. New York: Beechhurst Press. 1947.

Anger, Kenneth, Hollywood Babylon. New York: Simon and Schuster. 1975.

Arendt, Hannah, "The Aftermath of Nazi Rule." Commentary Vol. 10 No. 4 (Oct. 1950). 342-53.

Arnold, Thurman, The Folklore of Capitalism. New Haven: Yale University Press. 1937.

Asherman, Alan, The Star Trek Compendium. New York: Pocket Books. 1989.

Axelrod, Alan, Charles Brockden Brown. An American Tale. Austin: University of Texas Press. 1983.

Axelrod, Steven Gould, Sylvia Plath. Baltimore: Johns Hopkins University Press. 1990.

Ayçoberry, Pierre, The Nazi Question. An Essay on the Interpretation of National Socialism (1922-1975). New York: Pantheon. 1981.

Bach, Julian, America's Germany. An Account of the Occupation. New

York: Random House. 1946.

Badger, Anthony J., The New Deal. The Depression Years,k1933-40. New York: Farrar, Straus and Giroux. 1989.

Baker, William J., Jesse Owens. An American Life. New York: Free Press. 1986.

Balitas, Vincent D., "Charismatic Figures in Gravity's Rainbow." Pynchon Notes 9. 38-53.

Banta, Martha, "About America's 'White Terror': James, Poe, Pyncheon [sic], and others." Luanne Frank (ed.) Literature and the Occult. Arlington: University of Texas Arlington. 1977. 31-53.

Baughman, James L., Henry R. Luce and the Rise of the American News Media. Boston: Twayne. 1987.

Becker, Howard, "Das Deutschlandbild in Amerika." Politische Studien. Vol. 10 No. 115 (November 1959). 737-47.

Becker, Jillian, Hitler's Children. The Story of the Baader-Meinhof Terrorist Gang. Philadelphia: Lippincott. 1977.

Berger, Thomas, Crazy in Berlin. New York: Delta. 1982.

Bernstein, Barton J., "The New Deal: The Conservative Achievements of Liberal Reform." In Towards a New Past. Dissenting Essays in American History. New York: Vintage. 1968. 263-88.

"BeWildered in Berlin" [Review of One, Two, Three]. Time 8 December 1961. 96.

Beymer, William G., Middle of Midnight. New York: McGraw. 1947.

The Big Lift. Dir. George Seaton. With Montgomery Clift and Paul Douglas. Twentieth Century-Fox. 1950.

"The Big Lift" [Review]. Newsweek 1 May 1950. 75.

"The Big Lift" [Review]. Time 8 May 1950. 90-92.

Black, Joel D., " Probing a Post-Romantic Paleontology: Thomas Pynchon's Gravity's Rainbow." Boundary 2 Vol. 8 (Winter 1980). 229-54.

--   "Pynchons Eve of De-struction." Pynchon Notes 14 (Feb. 1984). 23-38.

Bleicher, Thomas, "Elemente einer komparatistischen Imagologie." Komparatistische Hefte, 2 (1980). 12-24.

Bloom, Harold (ed.), Thomas Pynchon's Gravity's Rainbow. New York:

Chelsea House. 1986.

Blum, John Morton, Roosevelt and Morgenthau. A Revision and Condensation of From the Morgenthau Diaries. Boston: Houghton Mifflin. 1970.

-- V was for Victory. San Diego: Harcourt Brace Jovanovich. 1976.

Bocock, Robert, Hegemony. London: Tavistock Publications. 1986.

Botting, Douglas, From the Ruins of the Reich. Germany 1945-1949. New York: Crown. 1985.

Bourke-White, Margaret, "Dear Fatherland Rest Quietly." A Report on the Collapse of Hitler's "Thousand Years." New York: Simon and Schuster. 1946.

Boyle, Kay, The Smoking Mountain [1951]. With a foreword by William L. Shirer. New York: Alfred A. Knopf. 1968.

Brandeis, Louis D., The Curse of Bigness. Miscellaneous Papers. New York: Viking. 1934.

Breitenstein, Rolf, Der häßliche Deutsche? Wir im Spiegel der Welt. München: Desch. 1968.

Bright, Arthur, The Electric-Lamp Industry. Technological Change and Economic Development from 1800 to 1947. New York: Macmillan. 1949.

Brown, Charles Brockden, Wieland. Bicentennial Edition. Kent: Kent State University Press. 1977.

Brown, Norman O., Life Against Death. The Psychoanalytical Meaning of History. Middletown, CT: Wesleyan University Press. 1959.

Buchanan, A. Russel, Black Americans in World War II. Santa Barbara: Clio. 1977.

Buxton, David, From the Avengers to Miami Vice. New York: St. Martin's Press. 1990.

Campbell, Edwina S., "Dilemma's of an Atlantic Dialogue." In Gale A. Mattox and John H. Vaughn (eds.), "Germany Through American Eyes. Foreign Policy and Domestic Issues. Boulder: Westview. 1989. 3-15.

Capra, Frank, Dir., Why We Fight. 1942.

Carpenter, Richard C., "State of Mind: The California Setting of The Crying of Lot 49." In Charles L. Crow (ed.), Itinerary: Criticism. Essays on California Writers. Bowling Green, OH: Bowling

Green University Press. 1978. 105-13.

Carr, Victoria Spencer, Dos Passos. A Life. Garden City: Doubleday. 1984.

Carter, Dale, The Final Frontier. The Rise and Fall of the American Rocket State. London: Verso. 1988.

Carter, J.F., The New Dealers. New York: Literary Guild. 1934.

Chandler, Alfred A., "The United States: Seedbed of Managerial Capitalism." In Alfred A. Chandler and Herman Daems (eds.), Managerial Hierarchies. Cambridge: Harvard University Press. 1980. 9-40.

Christadler, Martin, "German and American Romanticism." Christoph Wecker (ed.), American-German Literary Interrelations in the Nineteenth Century. American Studies Vol. 55. München: Wilhelm Fink. 1983. 9-26.

Clay, Lucius D., Decision in Germany. Garden City: Doubleday. 1950.

Clerc, Charles (ed.) Thomas Pynchon and Gravity's Rainbow. Columbus: Ohio State University Press. 1983.

Coates, Paul, "Unfinished Business: Thomas Pynchon and the Revolution." New Left Review 160 (November/December 1986). 122-28.

"Cola Chaser" [Review of One, Two, Three]. Newsweek 25 December 1961. 72-73.

Collier, Basil, The Battle of the V-Weapons. New York: William Morrow. 1965.

Cooney, James A. et. al. (eds.), The Federal Republic of Germany and the United States. Changing Political, Social and Economic Relations. Boulder: Westview. 1984.

Cooper, James Fenimore, The Pioneers. Albany: State University of New York Press. 1980.

Cowart, David, "Germany and German Culture in the Works of Thomas Pynchon." In Peter Freese (ed.), Germany and German Thought... Essen: Verlag die blaue Eule. 1990. 305-18.

-- Thomas Pynchon: The Art of Allusion. Carbondale: Southern Illinois University Press. 1980.

Crowther, Bosley, "Realistic Romance" [Review Big Lift]. New York Times 30 April 1950. 2:1.

Davis, Mike, City of Quartz. London: Verso. 1990.

Daw, Laurence, "Banishing the Pesky Demon." Pynchon Notes 22-23

(1988). 99-101.

Dawers, William, "That Other Sentimental Surrealist: Walter Benjamin."
Pynchon Notes 20/21 (Spring/Fall 1987). 46-47.

Deyer, Ronald, The Mind of Official Imperialism. Essen: Hobbing. 1987.

Dick, Philip K., The Man in the High Castle. New York: Ace Books. 1988.

Dos Passos, John, Tour of Duty. Boston: Houghton and Mifflin. 1946.

Dörfel, Hanspeter, "Images of Germany and the Germans in Some of
Joyce Carol Oates' Short Stories." In Peter Freese (ed.)
Germany and German Thought in American Literature and
Cultural Criticism. Essen: Verlag die blaue Eule. 1990. 267-
284.

Dr. Strangelove. Dir. Stanley Kubrick. With Peter Sellers and George C.
Scott. Columbia. 1964.

Dyserinck, Hugo, Komparatistik. 2nd ed. Bonn: Bouvier. 1981.

--   "Zum Problem der 'images' und 'mirages' und ihrer Untersuchung
im Rahmen der Vergleichenden Literaturwissenschaft."
Arcadia 1 (1966). 107-20.

--   and Syndram, Karl Ulrich, Europa und das nationale
Selbstverständnis. Imagologische Probleme in Literatur,
Kunst und Kultur des 19. und 20. Jahrhunderts. Bonn:
Bouvier. 1988.

Edel, Leon, Henry D. Thoreau. Minneapolis: University of Minnesota Press.
1970.

--   (ed.), The Henry James Letters (1843-1875). Cambridge:
Harvard University Press. 1974.

Edmonds, Anthony O., Joe Louis. Grand Rapids, MI: Eerdmans. 1973.

Eich, Hermann, The Unloved Germans. London: Macdonald. 1965.

Eisenhower, Dwight D., The White House Years. Waging Peace. 1956-61.
Garden City, NJ: Doubleday. 1965.

Emerson, Ralph Waldo, The Journals and Miscellaneous Notebooks of
Ralph Waldo Emerson. Ed. William Gilman et. al. Vol 11.
Cambridge: Belknap. 1975.

--   "Self Reliance." Essays and Lectures. Library of America. New
York: Literary Classics of the United States. 1983.

Epstein, Klaus, "Das Deutschlandbild der Amerikaner." In Hermann Ziock
(ed.), Sind die Deutschen wirklich so? Herrenalb:

Schriftenreihe des Instituts für Auslandsbeziehungen
Stuttgart. 1965. 181-211.

Erickson, Erik, Young Man Luther. New York: Norton. 1958.

Falkenberg, Betty, "Literary Games [on How German Is It]." New York Times Book Review 4 January 1981. 8-9.

Fetscher, Iring, Terrorismus und Reaktion. Reinbek: Rowohlt. 1977.

Fiedler, Leslie, "Italian Pilgrimage: the Discovery of America." An End to Innocence. Boston: Beacon Press. 1952. 91-108.

--   Love and Death in the American Novel. New York: Dell. 1966.

Fischer, Manfred S., "Komparatistische Imagologie." Zeitschrift für Sozialpsychologie. 10/1 (1979). 30-44.

--   "Literarische Seinsweise und politische Funktion nationalbezogener Images." Neohelicon Vol. 10 No. 2 (1983). 251-274.

A Foreign Affair. Dir. Billy Wilder. With Jean Arthur and Marlene Dietrich. Paramount. 1948.

Fowler, Douglas, A Reader's Guide to Gravity's Rainbow. Ann Arbor, MI: Ardis. 1980.

Franklin, Benjamin, The Autobiography and Other Writings. Harmondsworth: Penguin. 1986.

Fräulein. Dir. Henry Koster. With Dana Wynter and Mel Ferrer. Twentieth Century-Fox. 1958.

Frederiksen, Oliver J., The American Military Occupation of Germany 1945-1953. N.p.: Historical Division, Headquarters, United States Army, Europe. 1953.

Freese, Peter, "Exercises in Boundary Making: The German as the 'Other' in American Literature." Germany and German Thought in American Literature and Cultural Criticism. Essen: Verlag Die Blaue Eule. 1990. 93-132.

--   (ed.) Germany and German Thought in American Literature and Cultural Criticism. Essen: Verlag die blaue Eule. 1990.

Freud, Siegmund, "Das Unbehagen in der Kultur." Gesammelte Werke 14. London: Imago. 1948. 419-506.

Friedländer, Saul, Reflections of Nazism. New York: Harper Row. 1984.

Friedman, Alan and Puetz, Manfred, "Science as Metaphor: Thomas Pynchon and Gravity's Rainbow." In Richard Pearce, Critical

Essays on Thomas Pynchon. Boston: Hall. 1981. 69-81.

Friedrich, Otto, _Decline and Fall_ [demise of _Saturday Evening Post_]. New York: Harper and Row. 1970.

Fromm, Erich, _The Fear of Freedom_. London: Kegan Paul. 1942.

Gaddis, John Lewis, "The Corporatist Synthesis: A Skeptical View." _Diplomatic History_ Vol. 10 No. 4 (Fall 1986). 357-62.

-- "The Emerging Post-Revisionist Synthesis on the Origins of the Cold War." _Diplomatic History_ Vol. 7 No. 3 (Summer 1983). 171-180.

-- "New Conceptual Approaches to the Study of American Foreign Relations: Interdisciplinary Perspectives." _Diplomatic History_ Vol. 14 No. 3 (Summer 1990). 405-23.

Gammerschlag, Kurt, "Walter Abish, _How German Is It_. Vom Sinn des Unbehagens." _Anglistik und Englischunterricht_ 29-30 (1986) 199-215.

Gatzke, Hans W., _Germany and the United States. A "Special Relationship"?_ Cambridge: Harvard University Press. 1980.

Gay, Peter, _Weimar Culture_. New York: Harper Row. 1968.

Gill, Brendan, "The Current Cinema. Faster, Faster" [Review of _One, Two, Three_]. _New Yorker_ 6 January 1962. 68-72.

Gimbel, John, _Science, Technology, and Reparations. Exploitation and Plunder in Postwar Germany_. Stanford: Stanford University Press. 1990.

Gitlin, Todd, _The Sixties. Years of Hope, Days of Rage_. New York: Bantam. 1989.

Glaser, Daniel, "The Sentiments of American Soldiers Abroad Toward Europeans." _American Journal of Sociology_, Vol. 51 No. 5 (Mar. 46). 433- 38.

Goodrich-Clarke, Nicholas, _The Occult Roots of Nazsim_. Wellingborough: Aquarian Press. 1985.

Graff, Gerald, _Literature Against Itself_. Chicago: University of Chicago Press. 1979.

Gramsci, Antonio, _Selections from Cultural Writings_. Ed. by D. Forgacs and G. Nowell-Smith. Transl. by W. Boelhower. Cambridge: Harvard University Press. 1985.

Graves, Robert, _The Greek Myths_. New York: G. Braziller. 1959.

--   The White Goddess. London: Faber and Faber. 1952.

Greene, Graham, The Third Man. Modern Film Scripts. London: Lorrimer. 1969.

Greiner, Donald J., Comic Terror. The Novels of John Hawkes. N.p.: Memphis State University Press. 1978.

--   Understanding John Hawkes. N.p.: University of South Carolina. 1985.

Halley, Anne, "Der 'väterliche Deutsche': Ein Stereotyp des Ausländers im Werk amerikanischer Schriftstellerinnen. In Wolfgang Paulsen (ed.), Die USA und Deutschland. Wechselseitige Speigelungen in der Literatur der Gegenwart. Bern/München: Francke. 1976. 138-51.

Hariman, W. Averell and Abel, Elie, Special Envoy to Churchill and Stalin. New York: Random House. 1975.

Hassan, Ihab, The Dismemberment of Orpheus: Toward a Postmodern Literature. 2nd edition. Madison: University of Wisconsin Press. 1982.

Hauser, Heinrich, The German Talks Back. New York: Holt. 1945.

Hawkes, John, The Cannibal. Introduction by Albert J. Guerard. 2nd ed. New York: New Directions. 1962.

--   Humors of Blood and Skin. A John Hawkes Reader. New York: New Directions. 1984.

--   Interview. Allan Burns and Charles Sugnet, The Imagination on Trial. British and American Writers Discuss Their Working Methods. London: Allison and Busby. 1981. 66-82.

--   "Life and Art: An Interview with John Hawkes." (By Patrick O'Donnell.) Review of Contemporary Fiction. Vol. 3 (Fall 1983). 107-26.

Hawley, Ellis W., The New Deal and the Problem of Monopoly. Princeton: Princeton University Press. 1966.

Hawthorne, Nathaniel, "The Celestial Railroad." Mosses from an Old Manse. Centenary Edition Vol. X. Columbus: Ohio State University Press. 1974. 186-206.

--   The Marble Faun. Centenary Edition Vol. IV. Columbus: Ohio State University Press. 1968.

--   The Scarlet Letter. Centenary Edition Vol. I. Columbus: Ohio

State University Press. 1962.

--   "Young Goodman Brown." <u>Mosses from an Old Manse</u>. Centenary
        Edition Vol. X. Columbus: Ohio State University Press. 1974.
        74-90.

Hayes, Peter, <u>Industry and Ideology. IG Farben in the Nazi Era</u>. Cambridge:
        Cambridge University Press. 1987.

Hermand, Jost, "From Nazism to NATOism: The West German Miracle
        According to Henry Luce." F. Trommler and J. McVeigh
        (eds.), <u>America and the Germans. An Assessment of a three-
        hundred-year history</u>. Vol. 2. Philadelphia: University of
        Philadelphia Press. 74-87.

Hersch, Gisela, <u>A Bibliography of German Studies 1945-1971</u>.
        Bloomington: Indiana University Press. 1972.

Hess, Gary R., "After the Tumult: The Wisconsin School's Tribute to
        William Appleman Williams." <u>Diplomatic History</u> Vol. 12 No. 3
        (Fall 1988). 483-99.

Hexner, Ervin, <u>International Cartels</u>. Chapel Hill: University of North
        Carolina Press. 1945.

Hobbes, Thomas, <u>Leviathan</u>. Ed. Richard Tuck. Cambridge: Cambridge
        University Press. 1991.

Hodges, LeRoy S., <u>Portrait of an Expatriate. William Gardner Smith,
        Writer</u>. Contributions in Afro-American and African Studies,
        Number 91. Westport: Greenwood. 1985.

Hofstadter, Richard, et. al., <u>The American Republic</u>. Vol. 2. Englewood
        Cliffs: Prentice Hall. 1970.

Hogan, Michael J., "Corporatism: A Positive Appraisal." <u>Diplomatic History</u>
        Vol. 10 No. 4 (Fall 1986). 363-72.

Hohmann, Charles, <u>Thomas Pynchon's Gravity's Rainbow: A Study of its
        Conceptual Structure and of Rilke's Influence</u>. New York:
        Peter Lang. 1986.

Holmes, John R., "A Hand to Turn the Time: History as Film in <u>Gravity's
        Rainbow</u>." <u>Cithara</u> Vol. 23 No. 1. 5-16.

Hormann, Michael, "Letting Down Daddy [Review of <u>How German Is It</u>]."
        <u>Times Literary Supplement</u> 2 April 1982. 395.

Howells, William Dean, <u>The Rise of Silas Lapham</u>. Riverside Literature
        Series. New York: Houghton and Mifflin. 1937.

Hryciw-Wing, Carol, John Hawkes. A Research Guide. New York: Garland Publishing. 1986.

Hunt, Linda, Secret Agenda. The United States Government, Nazi Scientists, and Project Paperclip, 1945 to 1990. New York: St. Martin's Press. 1991.

--   "U.S. Coverup of Nazi Scientists." Bulletin of the Atomic Scientists April 1985. 16-24.

Hunt, Michael H., Ideology and U.S. Foreign Policy. New Haven: Yale University Press. 1987.

Huzel, Dieter K., Peenemünde to Canaveral. Englewood Cliffs, NJ: Prentice-Hall. 1962.

Ickstadt, Heinz , Ordnung und Entropie. Zum Romanwerk von Thomas Pynchon. Reinbek: Rowohlt. 1981.

269269Irving, John, The Mare's Nest. Boston: Little, Brown. 1964.

Irving, Washington, The Sketchbook of Geoffrey Crayon, Gent. Complete Works Vol. 8. Boston: Twayne. 1978.

JanMohamed, Abdul R., "The Economy of Manichean Allegory: The Function of Radical Difference in Colonial Literature." Critical Inquiry 12 (Autumn 1985). 59-87.

Johnson, James Weldon, The Autobiography of an Ex-Colored Man. In Three Negro Classics, with an introduction by John Hope Franklin. New York: Avon. 1965.

Jonas, Manfred, The United States and Germany. A Diplomatic History. Ithaca: Cornell University Press. 1984.

Jones, Robert and Marriott, Oliver, Anatomy of a Merger. A History of G.E.C., A.E.I. and English Electric. London: Jonathan Cape. 1970.

Kael, Pauline, "One, Two, Three." Film Quarterly Vol. 15 No. 3 (Spring 1962). 62-65.

Kahn, Arthur D., Betrayal. Our Occupation of Germany. New York: Kahn. 1950.

"Kay Boyle." In Lina Mainiero (ed.), American Women Writers. New York: F. Ungar. 1979. 207f.

Kazin, Alfred, On Native Grounds. New York: Rynal and Hitchcock. 1942.

Keesey, Douglas, "Facing Up To the Reading Dilemma." Pynchon Notes 22/23 (1988). 103-122.

Keil, Hartmut, "The Presentation of Germany in American Television News." In Peter Freese (ed.), Germany and German Thought in American Literature and Cultural Criticism. Essen: Verlag Die Blaue Eule. 1990. 26-50.

Kennan, George F., Memoirs 1925-1950. Boston: Little, Brown. 1967.

Klee, Ernst and Merk, Otto, The Birth of the Missile. The Secrets of Peenemünde. New York: Dutton. 1965.

Klinkowitz, Jerome, "Walter Abish: An Interview." Fiction International 4/5 (1975). 93-100.

--   "Walter Abish and the Surfaces of Life." Georgia Review Vol. 35 No. 2 (Summer 1981) 416-20.

Knapp, Manfred et. al. (eds.), Die USA und Deutschland 1918-1975. Deutsch-amerikanische Beziehungen zwischen Rivalität und Partnerschaft. München: C.H. Beck. 1978.

Knauth, Percy, "Movie of the Week: A Foreign Affair." Life 9 August 1948. 59-64.

Kocka, Jürgen, "The Rise of the Modern Industrial Enterprise in Germany." In Alfred A. Chandler and Herman Daems (ed.), Managerial Hierarchies. Cambridge: Harvard Universtiy Press. 1980. 77-116.

Koppes, Clayton R. and Black, Gregory D., Hollywood Goes to War. New York: Free Press. 1987.

Kovel, Joel, White Racism: A Psychohistory. New York: Pantheon. 1970.

Kracauer, Siegfried, From Caligari to Hitler. A Psychological History of the German Film. Princeton: Princeton University Press. 1947.

Krafft, John M., "Thomas Pynchon." In Sonyha Sayres et. al. (eds.), The 60's Without Apology. 283-286.

Krakau, Knud, "Einführende Überlegungen zur Entstehung und Wirkung von Bildern, die sich Nationen von sich und anderen machen." In Willi Paul Adams and Knud Krakau (eds.), Deutschland und Amerika. Perzeption und Historische Realität. Berlin: Colloquium. 1985. 9-18.

Krampikowski, Frank (ed.), Amerikanisches Deutschlandbild und deutsches Amerikabild in Medien und Erziehung. Baltmannsweiler: Pädagogischer Verlag Burgbücherei Schneider. 1990.

Krodel, Gerhard, "CBS-TV and the Germans." <u>American-German Review</u>. Vol. 34 No. 5 (1968). 30-35.

Kühnl, Reinhard, <u>Formen bürgerlicher Herrschaft. Liberalismus-Faschismus</u>. Reinbek: Rowohlt. 1971.

Lane, Barbara Miller, <u>Architecture and Politics in Germany, 1918-1945</u>. Cambridge: Harvard. 1968.

Lange, Victor, "An Untidy Love Affair: The American Image of Germany since 1930." F. Trommler and J. McVeigh (eds.), <u>America and the Germans. An Assessment of a three-hundred-year history</u>. Vol. 2. Philadelphia: University of Philadelphia Press. 1985. 232-42.

Lasby, Clarence G., <u>Project Paperclip. German Scientists and the Cold War</u>. New York: Atheneum. 1971.

Lasky, Melvin J., "Ulrike and Andreas." <u>New York Times Magazine</u> 11 May 1975. 14-15, 73-80.

--   "Ulrike Meinhof and the Baader-Meinhof Gang." <u>Encounter</u> Vol. 44 No. 6 (June 1975). 9-23.

Le Vot, André, "The Rocket and the Pig: Thomas Pynchon and Science Fiction." <u>Caliban</u> Vol. 12 No. 2 (1975). 111-118.

Leuchtenberg, William E., <u>Franklin D. Roosevelt and the New Deal</u>. New York: Harper and Row. 1963.

Leverenz, David, "On Trying to Read <u>Gravity's Rainbow</u>." In George Levine et. al. (eds.), <u>Mindful Pleasures. Essays on Thomas Pynchon</u>. Boston: Little and Brown. 1976. 229-49.

Levine, George et. al. (eds.), <u>Mindful Pleasures. Essays on Thomas Pynchon</u>. Boston: Little and Brown. 1976.

Ley, Willy, <u>Another Look at Atlantis</u>. Garden City, NY: Doubleday. 1969.

--   <u>The Lungfish, the Dodo, and the Unicorn. An Excursion into Romantic Zoology</u>. New York: Viking. 1948.

--   "Pseudoscience in Naziland." <u>Astounding Science Fiction</u>. Vol. 39 (1947). 90-98.

Lloyd, Ann, and Fuller, Graham, <u>The Illustrated Who's Who of the Cinema</u>. New York: Macmillan. 1983.

Locke, Richard, "Gravity's Rainbow." <u>New York Times Book Review</u> 11 March 1973. 7.1-13.

Lotringer, Sylvère, "Wie Deutsch Ist Es. [Interview with Walter Abish]."

Semiotext(e) 4 (1982). 160-78.

Ludwig, Karl Heinz, Tecchnik und Ingenieure im Dritten Reich. Düsseldorf: Droste. 1974.

Lübbe, Hermann, "Freiheit und Terror." Merkur Vol 31 No. 9 (September 1977). 819-29.

Mackey, Louis, "Thomas Pynchon and the American Dream." Pynchon Notes 14 (Feb. 1984). 7-22.

Mailer, Norman, The Naked and the Dead. New York: Holt, Rinehart and Winston. 1976.

--   The Presidential Papers. New York: Putnam's. 1963.

--   "The White Negro." F. Feldman and M. Gartenberg (eds.), The Beat Generation and the Angry Young Men. Secaucus, NJ: Citadel. 1984. 342-363.

Manthey, Jürgen, "Der Künstler ist Tyrann und Teufel. Gespräch mit dem amerikanischen Schriftsteller John Hawkes." Zeit 7. December 1990. 10.

Marcus, George E. and Fischer, Michael M.J., Anthropology as Cultural Critique. Chicago: University of Chicago Press. 1986.

Marquez, Antonio, "The Nightmare of History and Thomas Pynchon's Gravity's Rainbow." Essays in Literature. Vol. 8. No. 1 (Spring 1981). 53-62.

Marriott, David, "Gravity's Rainbow: Apocryphal History or Historical Apocrypha?" Journal of American Studies Vol. 19 No. 1 (1985). 69-80.

Martin, James S., All Honorable Men. Boston: Little, Brown. 1950.

Martin, Richard, "Clio Bemused: The Uses of History in Contemporary American Fiction." Sub-Stance 27 (1980). 13-24.

--   "Walter Abish's Fictions: Perfect Unfamiliarity, Familiar Imperfection." American Studies Vol. 17 No. 2. 229-250.

Mason, Peter, Deconstructing America. Representations of the Other. New York: Routledge. 1990.

Mattox, Gale A. and Vaughn, John H. (eds.), Germany Through American Eyes. Foreign Policy and Domestic Issues. Boulder: Westview. 1989.

May, Ernest R. "Writing Contemporary International History." Diplomatic History 8 (Spring 84). 103-13.

McCaffery, Larry and Gregory, Sinda, "An Interview with Walter Abish." In Alive and Writing. Urbana: University of Illinois Press. 1987. 7-25.

McCarron, William E. and Braley, Mark, "Slothrop, Berlin, and Pynchon's Use of Periodicals." Notes on Contemporary Literature Vol. 18 No. 5 (November 1988). 10-12.

McCormick, Thomas J., America's Half-Century. United States Foreign Policy in the Cold War. Baltimore: Johns Hopkins University Press. 1989.

--   "Something Old, Something New: John Lewis Gaddis' 'New Conceptual Approaches.'" Diplomatic History Vol. 14 No. 3 (Summer 1990). 425-32.

McCraw, Thomas K., Prophets of Regulation. Cambridge: Harvard University Press. 1984.

Mead, Chris, Champion. Joe Louis, Black Hero in White America. New York: Scribner's. 1985.

Mead, Clifford, Thomas Pynchon: A Bibliography of Primary and Secondary Materials. Elmwood Park: Dalkey Archive. 1989.

Melville, Herman, Moby Dick, or The Whale. Ed. Harrison Hayford et al. Evanston: Northwestern University Press. 1988.

Mendelson, Edward, "The Sacred, the Profane, and The Crying of Lot 49." Kenneth H. Baldwin and David K. Kirby (eds.), Individual and Community. Durham, NC: Duke University Press. 1975. 182-222.

Messer, Robert L. The End of an Alliance. Chapel Hill: Univ. of North Carolina. 1982.

Metzger, Michael M., "Deutschland und die Deutschen in den Werken Kurt Vonneguts." In Wolfgang Paulsen (ed.), Die USA und Deutschland. Wechselseitige Speigelungen in der Literatur der Gegenwart. Bern/München: Francke. 1976. 152-59.

Meyer, Henry Cord, Five Images of Germany. Half a Century of American Views on German History. Publ. No. 27. Washington: Service Center for Teachers of History. 1960.

Michaels, Walter Benn, The Gold Standard and the Logic of Naturalism. Berkeley: University of California Press. 1987.

Mirow, Kurt Rudolf and Maurer, Harry, Webs of Power. International

Cartels and the World Economy. Boston: Houghton and Mifflin. 1982.

Mitscherlich, A. and M., The Inability to Mourn. New York: Grove. 1975.

Morgan, Edmund S., "The Puritan Ethic and the American Revolution." William and Mary Quarterly Vol. 24 No. 1 (January 1967). 3-43.

Morgenthau, Henry, Germany is our problem. New York: Harper. 1945.

Muller, Gilbert H., John A. Williams. Boston: Twayne. 1984.

Musgrave, Marian E., "Deutsche und Deutschland in der schwarzen und weißen amerikanischen LIteratur des zwanzigsten Jahrhunderts." In Wolfgang Paulsen (ed.), Die USA und Deutschland. Wechselseitige Speigelungen in der Literatur der Gegenwart. Bern/München: Francke. 1976. 119-37.

Muste, John M., "Singing Back the Silence: Gravity's Rainbow and the War Novel." Modern Fiction Studies Vol. 30 No. 1 (Spring 1984). 5-23.

Mühlen, Norbert, "Deutsche, wie sie im Buche stehen. Das amerikanische Deutschalnd-Bild im Spiegel der neuesten Literatur." Der Monat Vol. 5 No. 171 (December 1962). 38-45.

Nance, Guinevara A. and Jones, Judith P., "Doing Away with Daddy: Exorcism and Sympathetic Magic in Plath's Poetry." Linda Wagner (ed.), Critical Essays on Sylvia Plath. Boston: G.K. Hall. 1984. 124-30.

Nelson, John, "Das Bild der Deutschen im amerikanischen Fernsehen." In Wolfgang Paulsen (ed.), Die USA und Deutschland. Wechselseitige Speigelungen in der Literatur der Gegenwart. Bern/München: Francke. 1976. 174-85.

Ninkovich, Frank, Germany and the United States. The Transformation of the German Question Since 1945. Boston: Twayne. 1988.

--   "Interest and Discourse in Diplomatic History." Diplomatic History Vol. 13 No. 2 (Spring 1989). 135-61.

Noakes, Jeremy and Pridham, Geoffrey, Documents on Nazism, 1919-1945. New York: Viking. 1975.

Norris, Frank, McTeague. Garden City: Doubleday. 1928.

--   The Octopus. In Novels and Essays. Ed. Donald Pizer. Library of America. New York: Literary Classics of the United States.

1986.

"Nun Liebchen [Review of How German Is It]." Der Spiegel 24 (1981).
        195-97.

O'Donnell, Patrick, John Hawkes. Boston: Twayne. 1982.

Oates, Joyce Carol, "Ich Bin Ein Berliner." In Last Days. New York: Dutton.
        1986. 97-112.

--   "Master Race." Partisan Review. Fiftieth Anniversary Issue, Vol.
        51/5-52/1 (1984/85). 566-590

--   "Our Wall." "Ich Bin Ein Berliner." In Last Days. New York:
        Dutton. 1986. 233-241.

Olin, Spencer C., "Free Markets and Corporate America." Radical History
        Review No. 50 (Spring 1991). 211-20.

One, Two, Three. Dir. Billy Wilder. With James Cagney, Horst Buchholz
        and Lilo Pulver. United Artists. 1961.

Ordway, Frederick I. and Shope, Mitchel R., The Rocket Team. New York:
        Thomas Y. Crowell. 1979.

"Paraphernalia of Intrigue" [Review of Middle of Midnight]. New York
        Times Book Review, 13 April 1947. 35.

Parry, Albert, Terrorism. From Robespierre to Arafat. New York:
        Vanguard. 1976.

"Patterns of Force." Star Trek episode No. 52. Dir. Vincent McEveety.
        With William Shatner and Leonard Nimoy. Paramount
        Pictures. First aired 16 February 1968.

Paul, Barbara Dotts, The Germans after World War II. An English-Language
        Bibliography. Boston: G.K. Hall. 1990.

Paulsen, Wolfgang (ed.), Die USA und Deutschland. Wechselseitige
        Speigelungen in der Literatur der Gegenwart. Bern/München:
        Francke. 1976.

Pächter, H., "Das Deutschlandbild der Amerikaner." Die Neue Gesellschaft.
        Vol. 14 (September/October 1967).

Pearce, Richard , Critical Essays on Thomas Pynchon. Boston: Hall. 1981.

Peavy, Charles D., Afro-American Literature and Culture Since World War
        II. Detroit: Gale. 1979.

Perret, Geoffrey, A Country Made by War. From the Revolution to
        Vietnam -- the Story of America's Rise to Power. New York:
        Random House. 1989.

Plath, Sylvia, "Daddy." Encounter Vol. 21 No. 4 (October 1963). 52.

Pochmann, H.A., German Culture in America, 1600-1900. Madison: University of Wisconsin Press. 1957.

Pocket Guide to Germany. Prep. by Army Information Branch, Army Services Forces, United States Army. U.S. Government Printing Office: n.p. 1944.

Poe, Edgar Allan, "Preface [to Tales of the Grotesque and Arabesque]." Poetry and Tales. Library of America. New York: Literary Classics of the United States. 1984. 129-30.

Polan, Dana, Power and Paranoia. History, Narrative, and the American Cinema, 1940-1950. New York: Columbia University Press. 1986.

Pusateri, Joseph C., A History of American Business. Arlington Heights, Ill.: Harlan Davidson. 1984.

Puzo, Mario, The Dark Arena. New York: Random House. 1955.

Pütz, Manfred, "Thomas Pynchon's V.: Geschichtserfahrung und narrativeer Diskurs." In Heinz Ickstadt, Ordnung und Entropie. Zum Romanwerk von Thomas Pynchon. Reinbek: Rowohlt. 1981. 75-103.

Pynchon, Thomas, The Crying of Lot 49. New York: Harper & Row. 1986.

--   Gravity's Rainbow. New York: Viking. 1973.

--   "Is It O.K. to Be a Luddite?" New York Times Book Review. 28 October 1984. 1,40-41.

--   "A Journey into the Mind of Watts." New York Times Magazine, 12 June 1966. 34-35, 78-84.

--   V.. New York: Harper&Row. 1986.

Quinlan, David, The Illustrated Guide to Film Directors. Totowa: Barnes and Noble. 1983.

Reitz, Bernhard, "'A Very German Question': Der Mitläufer als Voyeur und als Opfer in Pynchon's V. und Gravity's Rainbow. Anglistik und Englischunterricht 29/30 (1986). 173-98.

Reumann, Kurt, "Of Murder and Secret Pleasures." Encounter Vol. 49 No. 10 (October 1977) 66-70.

Rilke, Rainer Maria, Duino Elegies. Trans. David Young. New York: Norton. 1978.

Saalmann, Dieter, "Walter Abish's How German Is It: Language and the

Crisis of Human Behavior." <u>Critique</u> (Spring 1985). 105-121.

Said, Edward, <u>Orientalism</u>. New York: Pantheon. 1978.

Sanders, Scott, "Pynchon's Paranoid History." <u>Twentieth Century Literature</u>. Vol. 21 No. 2 (May 1975. 177-192.

Sasuly, Richard, <u>IG Farben</u>. New York: Boni and Gaer. 1947.

Scholes, Robert, "A Talk with Kurt Vonnegut, Jr." Interview. Jerome Klinkowitz and John Somer (eds.), <u>The Vonnegut Statement</u>. n.p.: Delacorte. 1973. 90-118.

Schuhmann, Kuno, <u>Die Erzählende Prosa Edgar Allan Poes</u>. Heidelberg: Carl Winter. 1958.

Schultz, Arthur R., <u>German-American Relations and German Culture in America: A Subject Bibliography, 1941-1980</u>. Vol. 1. Millwood, N.Y.: Kraus International. 1984.

Schwab, Gabriele, "Creative Paranoia and Frost Patterns of White Words." In Harold Bloom (ed.), <u>Thomas Pynchon's Gravity's Rainbow</u>. New York: Chelsea House. 1986. 97-111.

"The Screen in Review" [Review <u>Big Lift</u>]. <u>New York Times</u> 27 April 1950. 37.

Seed, David, <u>The Fictional Labyrinths of Thomas Pynchon</u>. Iowa City: University of Iowa Press. 1988.

Seidman, Steve, <u>The Film Career of Billy Wilder</u>. Boston: Hall. 1977.

Shaw, Irwin, <u>The Young Lions</u>. New York: Random House. 1948.

Shelley, Mary Wollstonecraft, <u>Frankenstein; or The Modern Prometheus</u>. Ed. with an introduction by M. K. Joseph. London: Oxford University Press. 1969.

Shirer, William L., <u>The Rise and Fall of the Third Reich. A History of Nazi Germany</u>. New York: Simon Schuster. 1960.

Siegle, Robert, "On the Subject of Walter Abish and Kathy Acker." <u>Literature and Psychology</u> Vol. 33 No. 3/4. 38-58.

Simmon, Scott, "A Character Index: <u>Gravity's Rainbow</u>." <u>Critique</u> Vol. 16 No. 2 (1974). 68-72.

Sinyard, Neil and Turner, Adrian, <u>Journey Down Sunset Boulevard: The Films of Billy Wilder</u>. Ryde, Isle of Wight: BCW Publishing. 1979.

Smith, Michael L., "Selling the Moon." In Richard Wightman Fox and T.J. Jackson Lears (eds.), <u>The Culture of Consumption</u>. New York:

Pantheon. 1983. 175-209.

Smith, Robert Freeman, "Republican Policy and the Pax Americana 1921-1932." In William Appleman Williams (ed.), From Colony to Empire. New York: John Wiley and Sons. 1972. 253-92.

Smith, William Gardner, Last of the Conquerors. New York: Farar, Straus. 1948.

Smith, Woodruff D., The Ideological Origins of Nazi Imperialism. Oxford: Oxford University Press. 1986.

Snell, John L., Wartime Origins of the East-West Dilemma Over Germany. New Orleans: Hauser. 1959.

Sontag, Susan, "Fascinating Fascism." Under the Sign of Saturn. New York: Farar, Straus, Giroux. 1980. 71-105.

Spanier, Sandra Whipple, Kay Boyle. Artist and Activist. Carbondale: Southern Illinois University Press. 1986.

Stark, John O., Pynchon's Fictions: Thomas Pynchon and the LIterature of Information. Athens: Ohio State University Press. 1980.

Steiner, Wendy, "Collage or Miracle: Historicism in a Deconstructed World." Sacvan Bercovitch (ed.), Reconstructing American Literary History. Cambridge, MA: Harvard University Press. 1986. 323-351.

Stocking George W., and Watkins, Myron W., Cartels in Action. New York: Twentieth Century Fund. 1947.

Sullivan, Walter, "Terrors Old and New [Review of How German Is It]." Sewanee Review 1982. 484-92.

Swanberg, W.A., Luce and his empire. New York: Scribner's. 1972.

Takaki, Ronald T., Iron Cages. Race and Culture in Nineteenth-Century America. New York: Alfred A. Knopf. 1979.

Taylor, Graham D., "The Rise and Fall of Antitrust in Occupied Germany. 1945-48." Proloque. Vol. 11 (1979). 23-39.

Taylor, Robert R., The Word in Stone. The Role of Architecture in the National Socialist Ideology. Berkeley: University of California Press. 1974.

Todorov, Tzvetan, The Conquest of America: The Question of the Other. Trans. Richard Howard. New York: Harper and Row. 1984.

Tölölyan, Khachig, "War as Background in Gravity's Rainbow." In Charles Clerc (ed.) Thomas Pynchon and Gravity's Rainbow.

Columbus: Ohio State University Press. 1983. 31-67.

Trevor-Roper, H.R., The Last Days of Hitler. New York: Macmillan. 1947.

Trommler, Frank and McVeigh, Joseph (eds.), America and the Germans. An Assessment of a three-hundred-year history. Vol. 2. Philadelphia: University of Philadelphia Press. 1985.

Twain, Mark, A Tramp Abroad. Vol. 1. New York: Harper. 1907.

Varg, Paul A., America, from Client State to World Power. Norman: University of Oklahoma Press. 1990.

Vogel, S., German Literary Influences on the American Transcendentalists. Yale University Studies Vol. 127. New Haven: Yale University Press.1955.

Vonnegut, Kurt, Slaughterhouse-Five. New York: Dell. 1985.

Weber, Max, The Protestant Ethic and the Spirit of Capitalism. Trans. Talcott Parsons. New York: Scribner's. 1958.

Wecker, Christoph (ed.), American-German Literary Interrelations in the Nineteenth Century. American Studies Vol. 55. München: Wilhelm Fink. 1983.

Weiler, A.H., "The Screen: 'Fraulein.'" New York Times 9 June 1958. 27.

Weinberg, Gerhard L., "From Confrontation to Cooperation: Germany and the United States, 1933-1949." F. Trommler and J. McVeigh (eds.), America and the Germans. An Assessment of a three-hundred-year history. Vol. 2. Philadelphia: University of Philadelphia Press. 45-58.

Weisenburger, Steven, "The End of History? Thomas Pynchon and the Uses of the Past." Twentieth Century Literature Vol. 25. No. 1 (Spring 1979). 54-72.

--   A Gravity's Rainbow Companion. Athens: University of Georgia Press. 1988.

Wellek, René, Confrontations. Princeton: Princeton University Press. 1965.

--   "The Crisis of Comparative Literature." Proceedings of the Second Congress of the ICLA Chapel Hill: Univ. of N. Carolina. 1958.

West, Nathanael, Miss Lonelyhearts and The Day of the Locust. New York: New Directions. 1962.

West, Paul, "Germany in the Aftermath of War [Review of How German Is

It]." Washington Post ("Book World") 9 November 1980. 4/9.

Weyl, Michael, "America's Image of Europe." In N.N., Deutsch Amerikanische Konferenz, Stuttgart, 1972. Tübingen: Erdmann. 1972.

White, Walter, A Rising Wind. Reprint. Westport: Negro Universities Press. 1971.

Whitfield, Stephen J., The Culture of the Cold War. Baltimore: Johns Hopkins University Press. 1991.

Willett, Ralph, The Americanization of Germany 1945-1949. London: Routledge. 1989.

--   "Billy Wilder's 'A Foreign Affair' (1945-1948): 'the trials and tribulations of Berlin.'" Historical Journal of Film, Radio and Television Vol. 7 No. 1 (1987). 3-14.

Williams, John A., Captain Blackman. A Novel. Garden City, New York: Doubleday. 1972.

Williams, William Appleman, Empire as a Way of Life. New York: Oxford University Press. 1980.

--   The Tragedy of American Diplomacy. 2nd rev. and enlgd. ed. New York: Dell. 1972.

Wippermann, Faschismustheorien. Zum Stand der gegenwärtigen Diskussion. Darmstadt: Wissentschaftliche Buchgesellschaft. 1972.

Wolfe, Tom, The Right Stuff. New York: Bantam. 1980.

Yergin, Daniel, The Prize. The Epic Quest for Oil, Money and Power. New York: Simon and Schuster. 1991.

--   Shattered Peace. The Origins of the Cold War. Revised and updated edition. Harmondsworth: Penguin. 1990.

Young, Hugo et. al., Journey to Tranquility. Garden City, NY: Doubleday. 1970.

Zapf, Hubert, "Aesthetic Experience and Ideological Critique in Joyce Carol Oates's 'Master Race.'" International Fiction Review Vol. 16 No. 1 (Winter 1989). 48-55.

Zavarzadeh, Mas'ud, Seeing Films Politically. Albany: State University of New York Press. 1991.

Ziegler, Heide, "Heidelbeereberg - Huckleberry Mountain. Mark Twains

Beziehung zum Südwesten." Radio essay. <u>Süddeutscher Rundfunk 2</u>, 30 Nov. 1985.

Ziock, Hermann (ed.), <u>Sind die Deutschen wirklich so?</u> Herrenalb: Schriftenreihe des Instituts für Auslandsbeziehungen Stuttgart. 1965.

ii. Newsmedia (Articles and Editorials)

"A New Outlook." <u>Life</u> 29 October 1945. 6.

"Airlift to Berlin." <u>National Geographic Magazine</u> Vol. 95 No. 5 (May 1949). 595-614.

"Airlift's Camel: Clarence carries German gift to children blockaded in Berlin." <u>Life</u> 8 Nov. 1948. 53f.

"American Troops find they like Germany with buttered side up." <u>Newsweek</u> 30 July 1945. 42-44.

"Arms for Europe." <u>Life</u> 8 August 1949. 26-27.

"The Babies They Left Behind Them." <u>Life</u> 23 August 1948. 41-48.

"Ban lifted" [fraternization]. <u>Time</u> 30 July 1945. 42f.

"The Bear looks South" (graphic). <u>Newsweek</u> 1 Oct. 1945. 44.

"Behind the battle of Berlin." <u>Newsweek</u> 12 Apr. 1948. 32-36.

"Berlin, the cold war's outpost, pursues its normal life of tension" (picture essay). <u>Life</u> 11 Oct. 1948. 34-35.

"Berlin: 'We will not be coerced'" (cover). <u>Newsweek</u> 2 August 1948.

"Berlin: red Nazism on the march" (cover). <u>Newsweek</u> 29 May 1950.

Berry, Lelah and Ann Stringer, "An Army Wife Lives Very Soft -- in Germany." <u>Saturday Evening Post</u>. 15 Feb. 1947. 24/25, 119-22.

Bess, Demaree, "American Viceroy in Germany." <u>Saturday Evening Post</u> 3 May 1947. 15-16,142-46; and 10 May 1947. 72-85.

"The Bitch Again." <u>Time</u> 4 October 1948. 27.

"Bremen Boys Club." <u>Life</u> 9 December 1946. 36-37.

Brown, Earl, "American Negroes and the War." <u>Harper's Magazine</u>. Vol. 184 No. 1103 (April 1942). 545-52.

Buruma, Ian, "From Hirohito to Heimat." <u>New York Review of Books</u> 26 October 1989. 31-45.

--   "The Pax Axis." <u>New York Review of Books</u> 25 April 1991. 25-

39.

"Democracy at Work" [report on boys club in Bremen]. Time 7 October 1946. 28-30.

"Distaff Invasion" [army wives in Germany]. Time 29 April 1946. 27.

"Do the Fräuleins change our Joe? Not a bit of it, he's all wised up." Newsweek 24 December 1945. 50-52.

"Dragnet" [black market and prostitution in Berlin]. Time 6 August 1945. 47.

"For What I Am" [Martin Niemöller]. Time 18 June 1945. 26-27.

"Furor Teutonicus." Life 10 May 1954. 34.

"G.I. Joe Wouldn't Play Herrenvolk" [editorial]. Saturday Evening Post 4 August 1945. 112.

Galbraith, John Kenneth, "The U.S. Policy. It seeks to neutralize but not ruin the German state." Life. 10 February 1947. 95-103.

"German Girls." Life 23 July 1945. 35-38.

"Germany Meets the Negro Soldier." Ebony, Vol. 2 No. 10 (Oct. 1946). 5-9.

"The GI in Germany: Wild Oats vs. Red Tape" (cover). Newsweek 16 June 1947.

"The GI Legacy in Germany" [fraternization]. Newsweek 16 June 1947. 48-50.

"GI Poll: Sweetkraut" [impressions]. Newsweek 4 February 1946. 58.

Gibbs, Eric, "Along the Iron Curtain." Life 7 June 1951. 133-46.

"Good enough to marry" [fraternization]. Time 30 December 1946. 15.

"The Great Airlift sustains Berlin." Life 9 August 1948. 15-19.

Hale, William Harlan, "Germany's Deformed Conscience." Harper's Vol. 192 No. 1148 (January 1946). 1-9.

Hauser, Ernest O., "The dead-end kids of Cologne." Saturday Evening Post 16 June 1945. 28-29, 84.

--   "A German Family Takes down its hair." Saturday Evening Post 27 September 1947. 15-17,114-119.

--   "Tame Germans are Headaches Too." Saturday Evening Post 2 June 1945. 18-19,79-80.

--   "The Germans Just Don't Believe Us." Saturday Evening Post 3 August 1946. 18-19,82-84.

--   "The Germans Resist 'Liberation.'" Saturday Evening Post 10

Aug. 1946. 17, 121-22.

"Hausfrau under siege" [Berlin crisis]. Newsweek 2 August 1948. 28-29.

Heiden, Konrad, "The Germans on Our Side: What Are They Like Today?" Life 7 June 1952. 104-115.

Hibbs, Ben, "Journey to a Shattered World." Saturday Evening Post 9 June 1945. 20-22,83-86.

Hughes, Emmet John, "A European Year of Destiny." Life 10 May 1954. 167-84.

"Industrial Revival" [of occupied Germany]. Life 10 February 1947. 93-94.

"Jets over Germany. Their pilots are keeping an aerial 'watch on the Rhine.'" Life 10 Oct. 1948. 101-105.

"Justice for Negroes." Life 19 November 1945. 8.

Knauth, Percy, "Anna on the Autobahn. Hitler's superhighway is a road of despair." Life 14 June 1948. 5-11.

--   "Fraternization. The word takes on a brand-new meaning in Germany." Life 2 July 1945. 26.

"Leave your helmet on" [fraternization]. Time 2 July 1945. 25.

"Letter from Germany." American Mercury. Vol. 61, No. 260 (Aug. 1945). 155-59.

Life special issue: "Germany. A Giant Awakened." 10 May 1954.

"Life spends a day with a GI occupying Germany." Life 22 October 1945. 142-45.

"Like American Jets in Britain, Anglo American diplomacy is 'rady and waiting'" (picture). Newsweek 2 August 1948. 26.

"The 'little man' turns on the reds." Life 20 Sep. 1948. 35-37.

Löwe, Rüdiger, "Besuch aus einem fernen Land. Notizen zum Deutschlandbild von Amerikaners." Süddeutsche Zeitung am Wochende. 8/9. January 1977. 73-74.

Luce, Henry R., "The American Century." Life 17 Fe 41. 61-65.

"Mass Murdress. Woman leader of Nazi guards at Belsen camp sets record for evil." Life 8 October 1945. 40.

Mead, Walter Russel, "Dark Continent. A Grand, Grim Tour of the New Europe." Harper's April 1991. 45-53.

Moseley, Ray, "Buchenwald Haunts Muses' Valley." Chicago Tribune 23 June 1991. 1/ 14.

"Nazi Brains Help U.S. German Scientists are revealed as Army Researchers." Life 9 December 1946. 49-52.

Niebuhr, Reinhold, "The Fight for Germany." Life 11 Nov. 46. 65-72.

--   "For peace, we must risk war." Life 20 Sep. 1948. 38-39.

"No Road Back?" [occupation realities]. Time 28 July 1947. 23-24.

"Now Is the Time Not to Be Silent." The Crisis January 1942.

"The occupation. It's got to work." Time 25 June 1945. 21-24.

"Occupied Germany." Life 10 February 1947. 85-93.

"On a sandy plain" [Berlin crisis]. Time 17 May 1948. 30-32.

"On Berlin time" [army wives in Berlin]. Time 13 May 1946. 26.

"Operation Vittles: Air lift for Western diplomacy." Newsweek 12 July 1948. 28.

"Our Germans." Life 11 November 1946. 34.

Padover, Saul K., "Why Americans Like German Women." American Mercury Vol. 63, No. 273 (Sep. 1946). 354-57.

"Painful Surprise/The Age of the Cigaret" (Occupation tensions). Time 13 January 1947. 28-29.

"The price for peace -- two worlds." Newsweek 16 Aug. 1948. 26-30.

"Purchase of Freedom" [on Operation "Vittles"]. Time 19 July 1948. 28.

"Pushbutton Marked 'Obliteration'" [Berlin crisis]. Newsweek 19 July 1948. 22 ff.

"Races: Face the Music." Time 12 April 1948. 21.

"Racial: Mädchen and Negro." Newsweek 16 September 1946. 29-30.

"Red rallies pushing for a showdown." Newsweek 9 Oct. 1950. 38.

Reynolds, Grant, "What the Negro Soldier Thinks About This War." The Crisis. Sep. 1944. 289-91, 299.

"Russians put the squeeze on Berlin." Life 19 Apr. 1948. 46-47.

Seaton, George, "Of Small Headaches." New York Times 16 April 1950. 2:4.

"The Siege" [Berlin crisis]. Time 12 July 1948. 17-20.

Slatoff, Walter J., "GI Morals in Germany." The New Republic May 1946. 686-87.

"Song of Girls and GI's." Ebony, Vol. 2 No. 10 (Oct. 1946). 10-11.

"Speaking of Pictures" [on VD cartoons]. Life 17 June 1946. 12-17.

"The Squeeze on the Corridors" [Berlin crisis]. Newsweek 26 July 1948. 30-32.

Stein, Gertrude, "Off we all went to see Germany." Life 6 August 1945. 54-58.

"Text of Kennedy's Inaugural Outlining Policies on World Peace and Freedom." New York Times 21 January 1961. 8.

"The Troops: Skin Game." Newsweek 2 July 1945. 45.

"The U.S. in Germany" (editorial). Life 28 January 1946. 32.

"U.S. Tests Rockets in New Mexico." Life 27 May 1946. 31-35.

"U.S. Victors and German Vanquished" [picture of fräuleins and GIs]. Time 13 August 1945. 28.

"Unterstitzen on the Bleiweis." Life 4 June 1945. 2-4.

"Walpurgisnacht is celebrated by GIs." Life 28 May 1945. 122-24.

"Will Europe erupt next winter? Ingredients of disaster are there." Newsweek 3 September 1945. 43-45.

"Willy Brandt und das Zeichen des Kain. Spiegel Report über das Deutschland Bild der Amerikaner." Der Spiegel. Vol. 24 No. 15 (6 April 1970). 132-40.

"The Witch of Buchenwald: The Good and the Horrible." Newsweek 28 July 1947. 38-39.

"Wives in Germany." Life 27 May 1946. 56-57.

"The world weighs chances of war." Life 4 Oct. 1948. 46-47.

"Wounded Knee and My Lai." Editorial. The Christian Century 20 January 1971.

"Zoot Riots Are Race Riots." The Crisis July 1943. 200-201,222.

Zuckmayer, Carl, "Germany's lost youth." Life 15 September 1947. 124-138.

Index to Names

Appendix

A. Published Articles with material from America's Germany

Schmundt-Thomas, Georg, "Grab-bagging in Gravity's Rainbow. Incidental (Further) Notes and Sources" Pynchon Notes. No. 26-27. 1990. pp. 91-95.
-- "America's Germany and the Pseudo-Origins of Manned Spaceflight in Gravity's Rainbow." In Peter Freese (ed.), Germany and German Thought in American Literature and Cultural Criticism. Verlag die blaue Eule. 1990. 337-53.
-- "Hollywood's Romance of Foreign Policy: American GIs and the Conquest of the German fräulein." Journal of Popular Film and Television. Vol. 19, No. 4. 1992. pp. 187-197.
-- "Time, Life and John Hawkes' The Cannibal." Notes on Contemporary Literature Vol. 22, No. 2. 1992. pp. 10-11.

B. Works citing America's Germany

This lists works that mention Americas's Germany. The earliest citation dates from 1992, the most recent from 2017. They come from 37 different authors mostly clustering in US and German institutions but ranging as far as South Africa and Romania. By decade, the 1990s yielded 11, the 2000s 22 and the 2010s 15 so far. By subject area, history leads with 26 (African-American with 7, and gender with 10), followed by literature with 14 (Pynchon with 4), and film at 8 (Billy Wilder with 3). The overall break-down reflects my focus, while the sub-clusters more that of the audience.

Brauerhoch, Annette, "Spurensuche: Das deutsche Fräulein in Nachkriegsfilmen". WerkstattGeschichte No. 27. 2000. pp. 29-47.

Brauerhoch, Annette, Fräuleins und GIs: Geschichte und Filmgeschichte. Stroemfeld. 2006.

Butter, Michael, The Epitome of Evil. Hitler in American Fiction 1939-2002. Palgrave. 2009.

Brownlie, Alan W., Thomas Pynchon's Narratives: Subjectivity and Problems of Knowing. Peter Lang 2000.

Cagle, Chris, "The Sentimental Drama: Nostalgia, Historical Trauma, and Spectatorship in 1940's Hollywood". Quarterly Review of Film and Video. Vol. 29, No. 5. 2012. pp. 419-431.

Chester, Robert Keith, World War II and U.S. Cinema: Race, Nation and Remembrance in Postwar Film 1945-1978. Dissertation. University of Maryland. 2011.

Cowart, David, Thomas Pynchon and the Dark Passages of History. University of Georgia Press. 2012.

Daum, Andreas W., Kennedy in Berlin. Cambridge University Press. 2008.

Davis, Robert Lawrence, History and Resistance in the Early Novels of Thomas Pynchon. Dissertation. Ohio State. 1994.

Etheredge, Brian C., "The Desert Fox. Memory, Diplomacy, and the German Question in Early Cold War America". Diplomatic History. Vol. 32, No. 2. 2008. pp. 207-238.

--   Enemies to Allies: Cold War Germany and American Memory. University Press of Kentucky. 2016.

Garson, Robert A. and Kidd, Stuart S., The Roosevelt Years: New Perspectives on American History, 1933-1945. Edinburgh University Press. 1999.

D'Haen, Theo and Bertens, Johannes (ed.), "Closing the Gap". American Postmodern Fiction in Germany, Italy, Spain, and the Netherlands. Rodopi. 1997.

Engler, Bernd, "Review of Peter Freese 'Germany and German Thought in American Literature and Cultural Criticism'". Literaturwissenschaftliches Jahrbuch. No. 33. 1992. pp. 443-446.

Gemünden, Gerd, A Foreign Affair. Billy Wilder's American Films. Berghahn. 2008.

Goedde, Petra, "From Villains to Victims: Fraternization and the
        Feminization of Germany, 1945-1947". Diplomatic History.
        Vol. 23, No. 1. 1999. pp. 1-20.
--   GIs and Germans: Culture, Gender, and Foreign Relations, 1945-
        1949. Yale University Press. 2002.
Grossmann, Atina, Jews, Germans, and Allies. Cose Encounters in
        Occupied Germany. Princeton University Press. 2007.
Grossmann, Atina, Juden, Deutsche, Alliierte. Begegnungen im besetzten
        Deutschland. Wallenstein. 2012.
Haller, Oliver, Destroying Weapons of Coal, Air and Water: A Critical
        Evaluation of the American Policy of German Industrial
        Demilitarization 1945-1952. Dissertation. Marburg. 2005.
Höhn, Maria, "Heimat in Turmoil: African-American GIs in 1950's West
        Germany". In Schissler, Hanna (ed.), The Miracle Years. A
        Cultural History of West Germany 1949-1968. Princeton
        University Press. 2001. pp. 145-163.
--   GIs and Fräuleins: The German-American Encounter in 1950s West
        Germany. University of North Carolina Press. 2002.
--   "'We Will Never Go Back to the Old Way Again': Germany in the
        African-American Debate on Civil Rights". Central European
        History. Vol. 41, No. 4. 2008. pp. 605-637.
--   "Ein Atemzug der Freiheit". In Bauerkämper, Arnd (ed.),
        Demokratiewunder: Transatlantische Mittler und die kulturelle
        Öffnung Westdeutschlands 1945-1970. Vandenhoeck &
        Rupprecht. 2011. pp. 104-128.
--   Ein Hauch von Freiheit? Afroamerikanische Soldaten, die US-
        Bürgerrechtsbewegung und Deutschland. Transcript Verlag.
        2016.
Höhn, Maria and Klimke, Martin, A breath of freedom. The civil rights
        struggle, African American GIs, and Germany. Palgrave
        MacMillan 2010.
Kassem, Hadi Shakeeb, "Denazification and Germany as Wanton Woman:
        Post-WWII German Representations in American Movies."
        Romanian Review of Political Sciences & International
        Relations. Vol. 14, Issue 2. 2017. pp. 80-95.

Kersten, Bettina, "Das Fräulein" hat es so nicht gegeben: Eine Gegenüberstellung des fiktiven Bildes und realer Lebensgeschichten deutscher Frauen der Nackkriegszeit. Dissertation. West Virginia University. 2007.

Kleinschmidt, Johannes, "Do Not Fraternize". Die schwierigen Anfänge deutsch-amerikanischer Freundschaft 1944-1949. WVT Wisschenschaftler Verlag. 1997.

Klimke, Martin, "The African American Civil Rights Struggle and Germany, 1945-1989." Bulletin of the German Historical Institute, No. 43. Fall 2008. pp. 91-106.

Krauss, Kenneth, Male Beauty: Postwar Masculinity in Theater, Film, and Physique Magazines. State University of New York Press. 2014.

Krüger, Gesine, Fräulein. Ergebnisse. 2000.

Lemke Muniz de Faria, Yara-Colette, Zwischen Fürsorge und Ausgrenzung. Afrodeutsche "Besatzungskinder" im Nachkriegsdeutschland. Metropol. 2002.

Meyer, Martin, Nachkriegsdeutschland im Spiegel amerikanischer Romane der Besatzungszeit (1945-1955). Gunter Narr Verlag. 1994.

Parker, Joshua, Tales of Berlin in American Literature up to the 21st Century. Brill Rodopi. 2016.

Parrett, Aaron, The Translunar Narrative in the Western Tradition. Ashgate. 2004.

Prutsch, Ursula and Lechner, Manfred, Das ist Österreich: Innenansichten und Aussensichten. Döcker. 1997.

Setje-Eilers, Margaret, "Ferreting Out the 'Foreign': Billy Wilder's 'A Foreign Affair' (1948) and Wolfgang Becker's 'Good Bye, Lenin!' (2003)". In Schechtman, Robert and Roberts, Suin, Finding the Foreign. Cambridge Scholars Publishing. 2007. pp. 2-12.

Sloan, Anna Cooper, Imperial Hollywood: American Cinematic Representations of Europe, 1948-1964. Dissertation. Warwick. 2013.

Schroer, Timothy L., Recasting Race after World War II: Germans and African-Americans in American-occupied Germany. University Press of Colorado. 2007.

Stanek, Jennifer, Demystifying the Notion, 'The West is Better': A German Oral History Project. LAP Lambert Academic Publishing. 2012.

Vansant, Jacqueline, "Robert Wise's 'The Sound of Music' and the 'Denazification' of Austria in American Cinema". In Good, David F. and Wodak, Ruth, From World War to Waldheim: Culture and Politics in Austria and the United States. Berghahn Books. 1999. pp. 165-185.

Weber, Undine and Williams, Alison, "The 'Golden Fifties' and the 'Tide of Immorality': Wolfgang Koeppen's 'Tauben im Gras'. Acta Academica. Vol. 41, No. 1. 2009. pp. 100-125.

Weber, Undine, Wolfgang Koeppen's Auseinandersetzung mit der Tradition. Dissertation. Rhodes University. 2014.

Weisenburger, Steven C. A Gravity Rainbow Companion. 2nd Edition. University of Georgia Press. 2006.

Wulf, Hans J., "Billy Wilder: Eine Arbeitsbibliographie". Medienwissenschaft/Hamburg: Berichte und Papiere. Vol. 141. 2012

Zacharasiewicz, Waldemar, Images of Central Europe in Travelogues and Fiction by North American Writers. Stauffenberg. 1995.

--   Das Deutschlandbild in der amerikanischen Literatur. Wissenschaftliche Buchgesellschaft. 1998.

www.ingramcontent.com/pod-product-compliance
Lightning Source LLC
Chambersburg PA
CBHW062110090426
42741CB00016B/3383